DISCARD

*Today's Threat to Religion
and Religious Freedom*

THE POLITICS

OF ✝

VULNERABILITY

HOW TO HEAL MUSLIM-CHRISTIAN RELATIONS
IN A POST-CHRISTIAN AMERICA

ASMA T. UDDIN

PEGASUS BOOKS
NEW YORK LONDON

THE POLITICS OF VULNERABILITY

Pegasus Books, Ltd.
148 West 37th Street, 13th Floor
New York, NY 10018

Copyright © 2021 by Asma T. Uddin

First Pegasus Books cloth edition March 2021

Interior design by Maria Torres

ISBN: 978-1-64313-662-2

10 9 8 7 6 5 4 3 2 1

Printed in the United States of America
Distributed by Simon & Schuster
www.pegasusbooks.com

To the black sheep in a fitting-in culture

CONTENTS

INTRODUCTION

THE BALLROOM AT THE PIERRE Hotel in New York City was glittering that night. At various times the site of the Oscars, the Emmys, and high-fashion shows, on May 7, 2015, this room was celebrating a very different type of star: Barbara Green, the owner of the Hobby Lobby chain of crafts stores.

It was the twentieth annual Canterbury Medal gala of my then law firm, the Becket Fund for Religious Liberty. Spirits were buoyant, as the firm was coming fresh off its United States Supreme Court win in favor of the crafts stores. The hundreds gathered in the room that night hailed from diverse faiths: multiple Christian denominations, Jews, Sikhs, and me, the lone Muslim.

Customary for a black-tie dinner at one of New York's exclusive venues, the dinner was extravagant—surf and turf, followed by an endless dessert buffet—and scrumptious. But unlike any other swanky dinner in the city that night, one thing was missing: alcohol. Throughout the dinner and dessert reception, wine and spirits were nowhere to be seen.

The Green family is fundamentalist Protestant. While not notably ascetic, fundamentalists consider smoking and alcohol strictly forbidden by their faith. Out of deference to the honoree that night, Becket had chosen to not serve alcohol.

It was a welcome respite for me, as my religion, too, forbids the consumption of alcohol. It hasn't always been easy growing up in a drinking culture. Nearly all of the networking events hosted by my law school, and then the corporate firm where I started out my career, revolved around alcohol. I was the odd one out, sipping my Coke while everyone was getting more than a little tipsy (and naturally then finding the events way more fun than they actually were).

But finally, here not drinking was the norm, and people were having fun despite it. The Greens were strict about their beliefs. They didn't even rent their company trucks out to people who wanted to use them to transport alcohol. If your faith forbids something, helping someone else do that exact thing is almost just as bad. The idea of complicity is part of many religions, mine included—not only can I not drink, I cannot buy or bring alcohol for others or even pour it for them.

Complicity was a big part of the Greens' case at the Supreme Court. Their religious beliefs against abortion also prevented them from complying with the part of the Affordable Care Act (ACA) that required them to pay for four drugs in their employee health insurance that the Greens considered abortion-causing drugs. Those drugs were Plan B and Ella, the so-called morning-after pill and the week-after pill, and two IUDs. Paying for these drugs would have violated the Greens' deeply held religious belief that life begins at the moment of conception, when an egg is fertilized.

But the ACA required the Greens to pay for these drugs on pain of penalty, and made the Greens choose between violating their conscience and paying more than a million dollars per day to the government. The Greens decided to instead bring suit to vindicate their religious rights. They put everything on the line—their entire billion-dollar business—for their religious convictions.

Their case also made the Greens some of the most reviled people in America. Many Americans thought the Greens were using their religion to oppress women. They said that Christians like the Greens threatened to make America a theocracy, a "Bible nation" where their religion reigned supreme over others.

SUPREME COURT'S HOBBY LOBBY DECISION IS A SLAP IN THE FACE TO WOMEN, read one prominent headline.

OF COURSE HOBBY LOBBY THINKS IT'S ABOVE THE LAW, read another.

The *New Republic* declared, "We're all living in Hobby Lobby's Bible nation."

Some critics even evoked imagery from Margaret Atwood's dystopian novel *The Handmaid's Tale*. They claimed that with the *Hobby Lobby* decision, we were "slouching toward Gilead," the totalitarian patriarchal theocracy (or "Divine Republic") in Atwood's book. One writer lamented,

> It would actually be the best-case scenario if these attacks on reproductive freedom were chiefly about punishing women for having sex, because the alternatives are that the Supreme Court of the United States is deliberately hauling us toward a straight-up theocracy . . .

The court decision, as I'll explain in the coming chapters, had little to do with theocracy or policing women's sex lives. The court actually ensured that women still had access to the full range of contraceptives covered by the ACA mandate. So, all of the foregoing depictions were factually incorrect.

But more than that, the headlines missed an essential point: the Greens, like many religious believers, are duty bound to follow what their conscience demands, and our law guards the right of every American to fulfill those duties except in the narrowest of circumstances.

Our country's founders made religious freedom a core constitutional right because they knew how deep religion runs for many people and that it inspires those people to do good for others. Though our country hasn't always protected religious freedom equally and fairly for people of all religions, it's gotten better over the years.

Well, with some religions at least. Less so with mine.

Fast-forward to another gathering of religious freedom enthusiasts, this one mostly conservative Christians and all of them on the Greens' side in *Hobby Lobby*. The man at the podium was announcing to the crowd,

We do not support sharia supremacists themselves or their enablers or their apologists.

And it pains me beyond words that this program that will be coming up after the attorney general's remarks, you have such an individual who will be presented to you, I'm afraid, as someone who is a perfect example of moderate Muslims and a perfect interlocutor for us in interfaith dialogue and bridge building and the like . . .

I hope that you will not be misled into believing this individual. I've nothing against her personally. But this individual and what she stands for—and most especially what she is doing with organizations like the Council on American-Islamic Relations (one of the most aggressive Muslim Brotherhood front organizations in the country)—must not be endorsed, even implicitly, by this organization.

I had hoped that she would not be given a platform. She is. I trust you to listen attentively, but I hope that you will not give her yourselves a platform.

That's Frank Gaffney Jr. speaking, the founder of the virulently anti-Muslim organization Center for Security Policy, right before he introduced a talk by US Attorney General William Barr at the National Religious Broadcasters' NRB 2020 Christian Media Convention in February 2020.

And that ominous figure he's describing, the "sharia supremacist" bogeyman? That's me.

For the record, I am nothing of the sort. I'm not trying to impose sharia on anyone, just like the Greens weren't trying to turn the United States into a theocracy. Gaffney wanted the audience to think that I (a woman) favor a legal regime oppressive to women—just as Barbara Green (also a woman) faced similar charges. Neither claim is true; both claims are insulting and preposterous. Even though Gaffney's religious community is smeared with falsehoods every day, that didn't stop him from doing the same to me.

I watched the whole thing on the TV screen set up in the green room, my mouth agape. *Is this actually happening?!* I thought. It was my first time at NRB and I was already feeling a bit anxious about what to expect from the crowd. My panel presentation, moderated by NRB chairman Janet Parshall, was going to take place immediately after Barr's talk.

Dread welled up in my chest as Gaffney warned the audience "to not give her yourselves a platform." Gaffney is well known as a leader of what experts have dubbed "Fear, Inc.," a 1.5-billion-dollar industry that strategically pumps out anti-Muslim messaging, organizes anti-Muslim protests and rallies across the nation, and drives efforts to strip American Muslims of legal rights.

What are they going to do to me? I wondered frantically. Was Gaffney rallying his troops, people who liked him and would follow his lead? Would they boo me offstage or empty out of the room—or worse? Engage in mockery, maybe violence?

As I sat paralyzed by the various imaginings of audience insurrection, Janet came running into the green room. "I can't believe he did that! This is so upsetting!" Then, her expression changed from anger and alarm to genuine remorse. "I am so sorry, Asma. I will fix this."

Janet came through moments later as Barr was escorted off the stage and my panel was ushered on.

"[Gaffney's comments] were ill-timed, inappropriate, and hurtful," she said, standing and looking out over the audience of several hundred. She pressed, "Do I make myself clear?" She then turned to me and apologized again. As she did, I could see several rows of attendees stand up and leave, as if in protest (I would later learn that my hunch was correct).

But most of the audience stayed put. The people in the front row even smiled up at me warmly, and several approached me after my talk to offer their thanks and support.

Janet and I were joined onstage by Steven Waldman, author of *Sacred Liberty: America's Long, Bloody and Ongoing Struggle for Religious Freedom*, and Craig Parshall, NRB's general counsel and Janet's husband. Titled "Many Faiths—One First Amendment," our presentation was about the need to protect religious liberty for *all* Americans, including Muslims. As we emphasized, the very nature of human rights, including the right to religious freedom, requires that if you protect it only for some, you cease to protect it for anyone. Because if you cede to government the power to selectively protect religions that it likes (or views as politically expedient) and not protect the ones it doesn't like, you have given it power that it can use against any religion—including your own—at any point.

I made this the central point of my 2019 book, *When Islam Is Not a Religion: Inside America's Fight for Religious Freedom*. Gaffney knew exactly why I was there and what I was going to argue. He had sought to preempt that message by insinuating that the panel, and my participation in it, was a mere front for a sinister "takeover." For him, it was critical that the audience members believe they could exclude Muslims from the American fabric even as they tried to protect their own place in it. My co-panelists and I squarely rejected that notion.

Gaffney had good reason to think his message would go unchallenged. It is not uncommon for speakers at large conservative gatherings to bash Islam and American Muslims with zero resistance from the crowd. Gaffney himself makes the rounds regularly, delivering dire warnings about Islam and Muslims at the Western Conservative Summit, Values Voter Summit, and elsewhere. In July 2019, John Andrews, founder of the Western Conservative Summit and a former Colorado Senate president, stood on the Summit stage, under a banner proclaiming the importance of religious liberty, and said, "The simplistic approach of simply granting unconditional 'freedom of religion' to a religion that doesn't believe in freedom—and never doubt me, Islam does not—that approach is civilizational suicide, friends." In 2016, Michael Flynn, who would become national security adviser for twenty-two days in 2017, said in a conference address that "Islam is a political ideology" that "hides behind the notion of it being a religion," and therefore Muslims should not be afforded rights to religious freedom. Several others, including numerous state lawmakers, made similar claims in official press releases and other public statements and continue to do so with their constituents' approval.

What made NRB different from these other conservative gatherings where Muslims are attacked with zero pushback? Consider that the string of events at the NRB convention—Gaffney's comments, Janet Parshall's rebuttal, and the opportunity for the audience to take away an important message about coherence and rights for all Americans—only happened because my presence at the convention forced it. And in so doing, I helped reveal an internal fissure among conservative Christians that might not otherwise have been apparent.

The dynamics between the Gaffney constituency and the Parshall constituency in the conservative Christian audience show that often what we perceive as black-and-white isn't necessarily so. Even if everyone in that audience was inclined to accept Gaffney's divisive message, Parshall's statement and my panel presentation disrupted that bias. And the receptiveness—indeed, the warmth—of the Parshall constituency challenged the common conception that evangelicals are unshakably anti-Muslim.

What does this moment tell us about our ideological divides and how we might go about mending them? Building from that moment, I have spent more than a year exploring it, and it forms the basis of this book. In America today, we are more polarized than we have been at any time since the Civil War. We have our in-group and our out-group, and we act against the out-group members simply because they are the out-group. Increasingly today, our political alliances do not just reflect our positions;

they *drive* our positions. But at NRB, that trend was complicated and perhaps even subverted. Why?

And was there something about the fact that we were talking about religious freedom in particular that helped bridge this seemingly unbridgeable divide?

* * * *

IN *WHEN ISLAM IS NOT A RELIGION,* I looked at current threats to Americans' religious freedom through the prism of attacks on Muslims' religious freedom. Anti-Muslim advocacy, violence, and hate crimes constitute one of the most pressing areas of discrimination in the United States right now. But by no means are these attacks a problem only for Muslims—they are a problem for all Americans.

For example, I examined the assertion (mostly coming from the political Right) that Islam is not a religion, and that therefore Muslims don't have religious freedom. While courts can determine whether beliefs match up to the legal definition of religion, this is not what anti-Muslim opponents are concerned with. They are instead driven by more emotional concerns. Yet, if courts and legislatures are empowered to say that Islam is not a religion, they can accept the same claim about every other religious group the majority may fear. If courts start to parse Islamic doctrine in order to decide which parts are acceptable or likeable and which aren't, as some prominent individuals want them to do, courts could conceivably parse the beliefs of every other religious group, too. Seen this way, it becomes clear how an attack that might seem relevant only to a very particular group actually tells us something deeper and more fundamental about American rights.

In *The Politics of Vulnerability,* I have sought to look beyond legal rights and toward political polarization. Anti-Muslim sentiment (or "Islamophobia") is not just about Muslims; it is *also* a case study of the core elements of American political polarization, which now even dictates the cars we drive and the stores we shop at. America's growing religious diversity—which encompasses people of a wide variety of faiths and people who define themselves as nonreligious—is a top driver of our political polarization. Fewer Americans ascribe to Christianity, while more Americans are religiously unaffiliated (the so-called "nones"), and there is less public confidence in organized religion. With growing secularization comes open contestation of Christianity's dominance in American politics and culture. But there is also continued, even intensified, religiosity in a different subset of American society. The religious divide explains why some of the most divisive issues in politics today are social issues like same-sex marriage and abortion. And to make it worse, the different sides are part of different political parties: in the Democratic Party, the nones outnumber Catholics, evangelical Protestants, mainline Protestants, or members of historically black Protestant traditions, whereas conservative Christians are overwhelmingly Republican.

Given these dynamics, conservatives object to liberals publicly championing Muslims' rights. As I explain in this book, for conservatives, Muslims are part of what political scientist Lilliana Mason calls the liberal "mega-identity." Our partisan affiliations have morphed into *identities*, and what's more, the identities include a host of things that have nothing to do with social policy. Now, what we eat, drive, where we live and shop, what our religion or race or sexual orientation is, are all wrapped up in our political identity. We group hybrid-driving, latte-drinking, Whole Foods-shopping Americans into the Democratic Party, and the Land Rover-driving, Cracker Barrel customer into the Republican Party.

Unfortunately, this grouping has also affected religious communities, so that Christians (mostly white and conservative) are associated with the Republican Party, and religious minorities, particularly Muslims, are associated with the Democratic Party. In this battle of ideologies, Muslims are seen by conservatives less as Muslims and more as proxies for deeper issues that represent the opposing political team or out-group. This is what Gaffney was getting at, too, when he complained about NRB giving me a platform and engaging in "interfaith dialogue and bridge building and the like." He opposed my presence not just because I am Muslim but also because in having me, NRB was accommodating liberalism. (As I explain in chapter 5, his precise choice of words—especially "interfaith"—signaled to the audience that something ominous was afoot.) In this view, anti-Muslim hostility is central to many conservative Christians' "winning" and liberals "losing." And it's not just Muslims who are used as proxies in this way; as I'll show, evangelicals (for different reasons, with different outcomes, and by different people) have also become a political piñata.

But this phenomenon is not systemic to American society. American conservatives weren't always hostile toward Muslims. During George W. Bush's presidency, many Christian conservatives considered Muslims ideological allies. Even after the 9/11 terrorist attacks, public statements by Christian leaders generally refused to vilify Islam and instead talked about an alliance of "orthodox believers." Pat Buchanan said in 2004 that "conservative Americans have more in common with devout Muslims than with liberal Democrats." Three years later, conservative writer Dinesh D'Souza extended that theory in his book *The Enemy at Home: The Cultural Left and Its Responsibility for 9/11*.

The Enemy at Home went on to become a *New York Times* bestseller. In it, D'Souza, a filmmaker, political commentator, and then scholar at the Heritage Foundation, expressed a sentiment that was and is popular among conservative Christians: the political Left is responsible for the downfall of American morality and, correspondingly, for its greatest tragedies. Of 9/11, he says Osama bin Laden attacked America not because of its foreign policy but because the American cultural and political Left "has fostered a decadent American culture that angers and repulses traditional societies"; "the cultural left and its allies in Congress, the media, Hollywood, the nonprofit sector, and the universities, are the primary cause of the volcano of anger toward America that is erupting from the Islamic world." For D'Souza, terrorism is the logical outcome of "the scandalous sexual mores that [Muslims] see in American movies and television," as well as "the sight of hundreds of homosexuals kissing one another and taking marriage vows."

As political science professor Alan Wolfe [sarcastically] described D'Souza's message: "America is fighting two wars simultaneously . . . a war against terror abroad and a culture war at home. We should be using the former, less important, one to fight the latter, really crucial, one. The way to do so is to encourage a split between 'radical' Muslims like bin Laden, who engage in jihad, and 'traditional' Muslims who are conservative in their political views and deeply devout in their religious practices." (D'Souza's premise is of course false: many religiously devout Muslims, like many devout Christians, are liberal in their political views.)

D'Souza was arguing this in 2007, but the message preceded 9/11 and endured in its direct aftermath. Two days after the attack, on September 13, 2001, white evangelical leader Jerry Falwell Sr. stated on national television, "I really believe that the pagans, and the abortionists, and the feminists, and the gays, and the lesbians who are actively trying to make that an alternative lifestyle, the ACLU, People for the American Way . . . I point the finger in their face and say, 'You helped this happen.'" He said this on *The 700 Club*, a show hosted by televangelist Pat Robertson, and Robertson agreed: "Jerry, that's my feeling," and "Well, I totally concur." Granted, these same commentators blame liberals for every other tragedy, too—natural disasters included—but the relevant point here is that they chose to blame the Left for 9/11 while trying to find common cause with American Muslims.

So, conservatives in the era of "Islamophilia" admired Islam's traditional sexual mores and thought of Muslims as allies against the threatening forces of the "libertine" left. And for a while, the love appeared to be reciprocal. In 1992, American Muslims voted two to one for George H. W. Bush, and even though they supported Bill Clinton in 1996, in 2000, more than 70 percent of Muslims voted for George W. Bush on the premise that Republicans were "natural allies" on matters of faith and morality.

But then, driven by foreign policy concerns like the Iraq War and the Abu Ghraib prisoner abuse scandal, most Muslims switched teams: More than 90 percent of Muslim-Americans voted for John Kerry in 2004, 89 percent voted for Barack Obama in 2008, and 85 percent voted for him in 2014. In 2016, 75.9 percent of Muslims voted for Hillary Clinton and in 2020, 69 percent voted for Joe Biden. Even though American Muslims' positions on social issues still lean conservative, they're now more likely to prioritize civil rights and public policy above symbolic debates over private morality. Democrats, for their part, have welcomed Muslims into their ranks and have defended Muslims' rights vigorously.

And as this is happening, so is the widening divide between religious and secular Americans, with the latter associated with Democrats. Taken together, this means that the Muslims now allied with Democrats cannot benefit from the efforts of the Christian Right to defend religious liberty, because conservatives identify religious values as Christian values.

I didn't understand the full implication of this finding until recently. And that is: whether you believe that Muslims have fundamental human rights (like religious freedom) depends on your political tribe. This startling realization prompted me to dig deeper.

****

MY GOAL WITH this book is not just to diagnose the problem that arises in denying Muslims fundamental human rights—I also propose a possible solution. I seek to show how constitutional law and the public discourse of religious freedom are central to that solution.

But the messenger also matters. Even Gaffney acknowledged this when he warned the audience about me: "[A]n individual who will be presented to you, I'm afraid, as someone who is a perfect example of moderate

Muslims and a perfect interlocutor for us in interfaith dialogue and bridge building and the like."

Why am I the "perfect interlocutor"? Because I see the divide between conservative Christians and Muslims as bridgeable. I see at least a particular subset of the opponents as persuadable. Those are people who are driven by fundamentally human concerns, and it is on the basis of this shared humanity that I work with them.

This understanding stems from my professional and personal experiences. I am a lawyer specializing in religious freedom on behalf of people of all religions: A to Z, Amish to Zoroastrian. I learned a tremendous amount through my efforts, not just about theology or the law but what our constitutional rights are fundamentally about. I came to understand that religious liberty is central to our autonomy because it helps us stay true to our quests for purpose and meaning in our lives.

That philosophical basis of religious freedom, the view that centers on the person who is trying to live according to his or her deepest beliefs, really comes in handy when things get political—as, unfortunately, they have become with religious freedom. Many Americans are worried not just about the narrower conflicts over abortion, contraception, and same-sex marriage but also the bigger battles between majority white Christian interests and the interests of a diverse array of marginalized minorities.

Because I advocate for parties across the spectrum, I have supported Christian cases that many Americans think involve hateful religious liberty claims: the Greens in their *Hobby Lobby* case and other Christian for-profit and nonprofit entities that object to paying for some or all contraceptive drugs; Christian marital counselors and adoption agencies who do not counsel LGBTQ couples or allow them to adopt, and so on. That I advocate for these claims doesn't necessarily mean I agree with them; I simply recognize that our law creates space for a wide variety of beliefs and practices. What makes my position unique is that even as I support these legal claims, I belong to a marginalized religious minority group that is routinely attacked through word and action by Christian conservatives and others on the political Right. In sum, I exist at the intersection of law, majority interests, and minority experiences.

My cross-sectional vantage point means that on the one hand, I see a torrent of media coverage painting Christian conservatives as bigots and their religion as nothing but a pretext for hate, and on the other hand, I see many of those same Christians genuinely worried, even scared, about the world that they are living in. I understand that they bring their religious claims to court as a way of carving out a space for themselves in a fast-changing world.

Recall from my opening story that my NRB panel was preceded by a talk by US Attorney General William Barr. His presentation perfectly reflected these precise concerns. He bemoaned the "current intensity and pervasiveness of politics in our lives," including in religion. Barr attributed the political polarization to "a conflict between two fundamentally different visions of the individual and his relationship to the state." One vision limits the power of the government and preferences personal liberty. The other vision supports a type of "totalitarian democracy" where individual needs are secondary to a "collectivist agenda" developed by elitists who think they know what is best for America.

Religion, according to Barr, is a key difference between these two conceptions. "Totalitarian democracy is almost always secular and materialistic, and its adherents tend to treat politics as a substitute for religion." To protect against "majoritarian tyranny," Barr said, we need to protect religion, because religion "allows us to limit the role of the government by cultivating internal moral values in the people that are powerful enough to restrain individual rapacity without resorting to the state's coercive power." Liberal democracy, as such, is a religious idea of government—and in Barr's view, a specifically "Christian outlook": "The wellsprings of this system are found in Augustinian Christianity."

Ironically—and unfortunately—just a few months after this address, Barr himself would be accused of "totalitarian" tactics when he authorized the teargassing of peaceful protestors after the killing of George Floyd. It would be one decision among many that earned Barr heavy criticism. But in that moment at NRB, I understood his comments in a different context. I understood that Barr and his Christian conservative audience were worried about an America that no longer reflects their traditional religious mores. There's a sense of being under siege from forces that insist they give up their way of life and abide by the status quo.

The conflict often shows up in the legal arena. When Christian practices clash with civil rights—as they often do when it comes to sexual freedom—Christians are sued or bring suits. So, I see the battles they are fighting, and I think their sense of persecution or vulnerability is at least partly based on something real. Separately (but relatedly), I also agree that the place of religion in American society needs to be defended vigorously.

But I also bristled at Barr's allusion to the United States as a Christian nation, because it echoed group dynamics that place Christians in the in-group and non-Christians in the out-group. I know to distinguish Barr from those who make insidious use of the "Christian nation" narrative (more about that in chapter 1), but his language still reminded me of the other, egregious ways Christian vulnerability results in hostility against Muslims (and a host of others). Many conservative Christians are ambivalent about, even dismissive of, anti-Muslim discrimination. For some, hate crimes against Muslims are "fake news" and don't actually happen, and discourse about Islamophobia is mere political correctness—purportedly, a liberal attempt to shut down critical discourse. They prop up and often repeat the claims of extreme anti-Muslim actors (Exhibit A: Gaffney's platform at NRB), and sometimes explicitly advocate for restrictions on Muslims' legal rights. As we'll see in chapter 5, some Christian groups are also mega-funders of initiatives that spread anti-Muslim hate; a 2019 investigation found that they donated $48.1 million to such efforts.

These actions could drive me to vilify conservative Christians. But, because I understand the vulnerabilities on both sides, I try to build peace across that divide by focusing on commonalities instead of differences. Several conflict resolution experts working to reduce polarization in the United States have said the first steps are to "be curious and listen to understand" and "show respect and suspend judgment." Vulnerability expert Brené Brown says we need to stay "zoomed in" to the people we're forming opinions about instead of relying on the news or politicians.

Experts advise us to be authentic and welcome others to do the same; to share what's important to us and to speak from our experience. I use that approach when I describe how conservative Christian vulnerability too often manifests in actions against American Muslims and other minorities. And I realize that effectively challenging Christians' attacks on Muslims requires acknowledging Christians' vulnerability; as Ezra Klein explains in *Why We're Polarized*, "To the extent that it's true that a loss of privilege *feels* like oppression, that feeling needs to be taken seriously, both because it's real, and because, left to fester, it can be weaponized by demagogues and reactionaries."

My goal, in the words of interfaith civic leader Eboo Patel, is to "speak of marginalization without exacerbating polarization" and "speak of polarization without papering over marginalization." Or, to take a phrase from Brené Brown, to be civil even as I "speak truth to bullshit."

* * * *

RELIGIOUS FREEDOM AND political polarization are two of the most intellectually complex and emotionally reactive issues of our day. To help structure this book, I have divided the narrative into four parts.

Part 1 explores why some conservative white evangelicals are more open-minded than others. It also offers a quick primer on how group identity works, particularly when a group feels vulnerable or under threat.

Part 2, which includes chapters 2 and 3, looks at two of the major threats conservative white evangelicals are worried about—demographic and cultural shifts, and religious liberty concerns. Together, these chapters explain why and how religion and religious liberty have become politically polarized.

Part 3 looks at what happens when a polarized religious liberty gets turned against Muslims as the out-group. I refer to this phenomenon as the "weaponization of vulnerability" because Christians' sense of victimization helps drive attacks on Muslims.

Part 4 offers concrete solutions grounded in both social science and successful interventions by Christians and Muslims across the political spectrum (from the most conservative to left-leaning). To overcome conflict, Muslim-Christian relations must be about honest and substantive engagement instead of politicized groupthink.

Throughout the book, I use "American Muslim" to refer to Americans of Muslim faith. I use interchangeably "the Right," "the political right," "Republicans," and "conservatives"; and "the Left," "the political left," "Democrats," "progressives," and "liberals." I generally avoid "Islamophobia" (for reasons that will become clear in chapter 4), but the sources I quote sometimes use this term. While conservative white evangelicals are the focus of the book, I sometimes use "conservative Christians" because conservative white evangelicals' interests—and their tactics—sometimes align with this broader group.

I also use "religious freedom" and "religious liberty" interchangeably. When I use these terms, I am referring to Americans' legal right to engage in religious practice free from government interference. In my discussion, this legal right is not limitless, but it's pretty broad.

In talking about anti-Muslim hostility as a facet of political polarization, I do not mean to overlook other drivers of this hostility. I recognize it's a complex matter, with elements of racialization and securitization. Racialization is the stereotyping by white Americans of Muslims as homogeneously "brown" and "Arab" instead of the ethnically diverse group that they are. The racialization of Muslims often begets racism because of the perceived negative attributes of this brownness. Securitization refers to the impact of the 9/11 attacks on perceptions of Muslims as both internal and external security threats.

And, as evidenced by the comments section on nearly every opinion-editorial I have ever written on Muslims' rights, conservatives also worry about the treatment of Christians in some majority-Muslim states; a common refrain is, "Why should the United States protect Muslims if they don't protect us in their lands?" These dynamics are all critical, and many of them have been parsed in incredible detail in other studies, including my previous book.

Finally, I also recognize that American political discourse too often focuses on immigrant Muslims (and Arab and South Asian ones in particular). This is problematic for many reasons, not least because experiences of subsets of American Muslims are importantly different; for example, black Muslims, white Muslims, and immigrant Muslims face unique challenges. I do not account for those differences here for a couple of reasons: First, the tribal dynamics I explore in this book do not make those distinctions; and second, much of my focus is on Muslims not as Muslims but as proxies in an ideological battle between conservatives and liberals.

PART I

❧

WHICH CHRISTIANS?

CHAPTER 1

Christian Nationalists ≠ Conservative White Evangelicals

"THERE ARE STILL HUGE SWATHS of American [Christians] who have never met a Muslim, as a common pattern. . . . The movement from 'moral majority' to 'persecuted minority' [has become] a norm or a pattern that is at play especially among evangelical Christians and others who have previously been hegemonically privileged and majority," Josh Good said to me. He looked at me quizzically as I considered his statement.

"What is your best piece of practical advice for those who are working at this from a position of authentic religious faith, crossing over, not retreating to tribe, and deepening in their own tradition?"

It was a complex question. I took a deep breath. "As an American Muslim, belonging to an especially despised minority in the United States, my approach has always been to use logic—that is, use the language of religious freedom because you have to be able to connect to people's self-interest . . . but white Protestants, while no longer a majority, are still very dominant as compared to other religious groups. So, it seems the approach there must be compassion . . . and creating spaces for conversation and actual personal bonding."

Our other conversation partner, Daniel Harrell, spoke up, his eyes alight with excitement. "I'm thinking of a thing that happened recently in our church where we sponsored a Syrian refugee family, a devout Muslim family. [This is] to your point, Asma, of having people in our homes where we can get to know one another and find that in so many ways there are commonalities we share, like being humans who believe in God and whose faith shapes our life. [For us] just to take those small steps as individuals can go far, I think, in dispelling so much of the myth and mischaracterization that comes with how we understand other religions."

The conversation was part of a podcast for Faith Angle Forum, a project that "aims to strengthen reporting and commentary on how religious believers, religious convictions, and religiously grounded moral arguments affect American politics and public life." Harrell and Good are both conservative white evangelical Christians. Good works with pastors, evangelical seminaries, and Christian colleges, and directs a program at the conservative Ethics & Public Policy Center. Harrell has been an evangelical pastor for most of his life, and in January 2020 he became the editor in chief of *Christianity Today*, the largest and most prominent evangelical magazine in the world.

They seem worlds apart from some of their coreligionists. In 2010, Dr. Robert Jeffress, head pastor at the nationally influential First Baptist Dallas, with a congregation thirteen thousand strong, declared that the truth about Islam [is that it] is a religion of oppression . . . Islam is an oppressive treater of women . . . and here is the deep, dark, dirty secret of Islam: it is a religion that promotes pedophilia . . . sex with children. It is an EVIL religion, it is an OPPRESSIVE religion, it is a VIOLENT religion, that has incited attacks around the world and attacks against our country, and for Christians, the worst thing about Islam is that it is a false religion that leads people away from God to spend an eternity in Hell.

(Jeffress's voice reaches a crescendo, as if to signal to his audience that a great proclamation is coming)

And I believe *as Christians* and *conservatives*, it's time to take off the gloves and stand up and tell the truth about this EVIL, EVIL religion!"

(The audience rises to its feet, offering Jeffress a standing ovation)

The hundreds of Christians filling Jeffress's church that day appeared thoroughly excited by Jeffress's passion and certainty that the 1.8 billion people around the world who are Muslim ascribe to an unequivocally evil religion. In 2015, Pastor Jeffress again gave them what they wanted: a Sunday sermon on how "Islam is a false religion and it is inspired by Satan himself."

The following year, Jeffress became a mainstay of the Trump presidential campaign. He appeared at Trump's rallies and declared that Christians who didn't vote for Trump were "fools" motivated by pride rather than principle. Throughout Trump's presidency, Jeffress called him a "Christian warrior," and Trump rewarded Jeffress by naming him a member of his Evangelical Advisory Board and White House Faith and Opportunity Initiative. After the 2020 election, exit polls showed that 75% of white evangelicals voted for Trump.

For many Americans, Jeffress represents the 81 percent of white evangelicals who secured Trump's election (nonwhite evangelicals lean Democratic). During Trump's first term, his approval ratings among white evangelicals were twenty-five points higher than the national average. Jeffress's statements are taken to reflect the sentiment of all of these voting evangelicals and American white evangelicalism broadly. But that sort of conflation overlooks the many white evangelicals who think and feel differently about their Muslim compatriots—for example, Daniel Harrell and Josh Good. Why and how are they different from white evangelicals like Jeffress?

One benefit of increased scrutiny is increased precision. As researchers and pollsters have scrutinized Trump's evangelical base, some have insisted that it isn't white evangelicalism but Christian nationalism that leads to divisive behavior. The researchers even distinguish between Americans with stronger and lesser degrees of affinity for Christian nationalism, and the unique role of religious commitment in tempering nationalist leanings.

I parse those differences below in order to understand the attitudes and experiences that separate the Jeffresses from the Harrells and Goods. I look at what makes some conservative white evangelicals warmer toward Muslims and other minorities, and what makes people gravitate toward one or the other attitude. And how does political group identity (which I sometimes call "political tribalism") hinder potential for openness?

* * * *

IMMEDIATELY AFTER THE 2016 US presidential election, a study on the role of religion in US populism found that, across all religious groups, white evangelicals scored highest for "conservative populism." They asserted their populism as a way of defending their "ethnic identity" and exhibited "anti-immigrant sentiment, nativism, 'white power' ideologies, and Islamophobia."

As President Trump continued to focus on Muslims as one of the primary targets of his vitriol, pollsters zeroed in on the Islamophobia part of this populism. One set of polls measured Americans' approval of Trump's Executive Order 13769, which temporarily blocked individuals from seven majority-Muslim countries from entering the United States. Pew Research found that 76 percent of white evangelicals supported the ban, and the Public Religion Research Institute (PRRI) revealed that white evangelicals, in supporting the ban, stood apart from all other religious groups, Catholics, mainline Protestants, and religious minorities included. The numbers of white evangelicals supporting the ban had increased from when candidate Trump first announced the ban on the campaign trail: 55 percent supported it during the election, and 61 percent supported it when it was actually implemented. For every other religious group, the trend was in the opposite direction.

Pieces like *Christian Science Monitor*'s WHY EVANGELICALS ARE TRUMP'S STRONGEST TRAVEL-BAN SUPPORTERS and *Christianity Today*'s MOST WHITE EVANGELICALS DON'T BELIEVE MUSLIMS BELONG IN AMERICA noted that white evangelicals don't just think Muslim immigrants are the problem— they also think American Muslims, and Islam generally, pose a threat to America's Christian identity. A 2017 Pew poll found that two thirds of white evangelicals believe Islam is not part of mainstream American society and that it encourages violence more than other faiths. Seventy-two percent of white evangelicals—compared to 44 percent of Americans overall—saw a natural conflict between Islam and democracy. According to a 2017 Baylor University survey, 52 percent of white evangelicals said that Muslims want to limit their freedom.

In 2018, the Institute for Social Policy and Understanding (ISPU) Islamophobia Index found that while the majority of Americans (66 percent) agree that "the negative things politicians say regarding Muslims is harmful to our country," white evangelicals were the group least likely to agree with this statement. In 2019, ISPU found that "white Evangelicals score the highest on the Islamophobia Index with as many as 44 percent holding unfavorable opinions about Muslims, which is twice as many as those who hold favorable opinions (20 percent)."

Empirical findings about white evangelicals are supported by anecdotal evidence—well beyond even Jeffress and his national pulpit. Kevin Singer and Chris Stackaruk founded Neighborly Faith while students at Wheaton College in Illinois, a standard-bearing institution for American evangelicalism. Chris told me that when they first started on the project, most people responded by talking "about Muslims with words like *dark*, *liars*, *trapped*, or *conniving*." One person even told him he was stockpiling guns for the day that Muslims "come running up my lawn."

Amassing ammunition is not as rare as it may sound; professor Michal Meulenberg, who teaches at several evangelical schools, told me stories of students and young people confiding in her that their dads had either joined a militia or started buying more guns out of fear of Muslims. One of them had said to his child that he was watching a mosque, preparing to attack if the mosque did "anything." These students are in great anguish over this, and some, with a lot of conversation and sharing stories about their friendships with Muslims, have seen their relatives change in their attitude and behavior. For others, it has led to splits in family relationships.

The general posture toward Muslims is one of "aggression and antagonism," writes Matthew Kaemingk, a professor at the evangelical Fuller Theological Seminary and author of *Christian Hospitality and Muslim Immigration in an Age of Fear*. Conservative religious liberty lawyer Luke Goodrich devotes an entire chapter to answering the question, Will Muslims Take Over? in *Free to Believe*, his 2019 book for an evangelical readership. Pastor Bob Roberts of the three-thousand-member Northwood Church, brings together evangelical and Muslim clergy to counteract evangelical animosity toward Muslims. In his YouTube video *Why Evangelicals Hate Muslims: An Evangelical Minister's Perspective*, he says 57 percent of evangelicals have negative views of Muslims and "the only group that has a worse view is evangelical pastors." In a March 2019 *Foreign Policy* piece, "America's Islamophobia Is Forged at the Pulpit," Chrissy Stroop said that her pastor told his congregation, "'A good Muslim . . . *should* want to kill Christians and Jews.' He insisted that this was the only conclusion possible from a serious reading of the Quran."

Clearly, there is a widespread problem of anti-Muslim hostility among white evangelicals. But researchers Andrew L. Whitehead and Samuel L. Perry insist that pollsters and activists are wrong in focusing on evangelicalism as the culprit.

* * * *

ROBERT JEFFRESS: Our whole foundation as a society is freedom of expression and if I could just turn this . . .

LOU DOBBS: Sure.

JEFFRESS: I'd like to turn to this whole religious liberty idea and what the president is doing on that front. You know, a year ago he made a commitment at our religious freedom rally in Washington, D.C., and he said that he believed religious liberty is not a gift from government, it's a gift from God. And now we see after a year, he is acting on that belief—you see what he is doing in helping Pastor Brunson in Turkey, and you see today the State Department issued its own Potomac Declaration calling for religious liberty around the world. And this is why evangelicals support this president . . . they care about this pro-religious liberty, pro-freedom platform of this great president.

In his book *Twilight's Last Gleaming: How America's Last Days Can Be Your Best Days*, Jeffress gives us a clue as to who he thinks American religious liberty is for. First, he states God's position: "God apparently has no appreciation for the merits of religious diversity." Jeffress then goes on to argue that protecting religious liberty for non-Christians constitutes idolatry:

> I realize that suggesting God will curse the nation that sanctions the worship of other gods is anathema in today's culture of diversity. We have been indoctrinated to believe that religious pluralism . . . is the great strength of our nation . . . But what we celebrate as diversity, God condemns as idolatry . . .

And it's all tied to the United States as a nation that serves, through law and policy, [the Christian] God's will:

> Here is the bottom-line question: Has God changed His mind about idolatry? Has God concluded that the First Amendment should usurp the First Commandment? . . . If God is unchanging, then His attitude toward any nation that rejects Him and His Word is also unchanging, which makes America's coming night inevitable.

Jeffress encapsulates what Whitehead and Perry have found to be the real problem in American religious polarization: Christian nationalism. The two sociology professors draw on national survey data and in-depth interviews to answer the questions, Why do many Americans advocate so vehemently for xenophobic policies, such as a ban on Muslims entering the United States? And why do many Americans seem so unwilling to acknowledge the injustices that ethnic and racial minorities experience in the United States? Their answer, again, is Christian nationalism.

"Christian nationalism is a cultural framework—a collection of myths, traditions, symbols, narratives, and value systems—that idealizes and advocates a fusion of Christianity with American civic life," the researchers write. The "Christianity" of Christian nationalism is not just about religion; it also "includes assumptions of nativism, white supremacy, patriarchy, and heteronormativity, along with divine sanction for authoritarian control and militarism." It is centered on America as a Christian nation and seeks to preserve that Christian character through self-identity, interpretations of US history, "sacred symbols, cherished values, and public policies."

Importantly, Christian nationalism is not the same thing as racism. Whitehead and Perry say that it is false to claim that "Christian nationalism is 'really just about racism when you get down to it.'" They found that a member of a racial minority who holds certain Christian nationalist beliefs will have a stronger racial justice orientation than a white American with Christian nationalist beliefs. What matters is the "*intersection* of race and Christian nationalism."

Christian nationalism is also distinct from the theological tradition known as evangelicalism, which requires a belief in biblical inerrancy and the importance of evangelism, or sharing the Christian faith with others. According to Whitehead and Perry, while "[r]oughly half of evangelicals . . . embrace Christian nationalism to some degree," Christian nationalism "should not be thought of as synonymous with 'evangelicalism' or even 'white evangelicalism'": "Stated simply: being an evangelical, or even a white evangelical as pollsters often define that category, tells us almost nothing about a person's social attitudes or behavior once Christian nationalism has been considered."

Researchers Allyson F. Shortle and Ronald Keith Gaddie agree that white evangelicalism and Christian nationalism are not one and the same, but they do intersect. Studies on religion in political behavior often start with the three Bs: religious belonging, belief, and behavior. Belonging is about religious affiliation; belief is about your religious worldview; and behavior is about religious practice. Shortle and Gaddie's study found that "evangelical belonging plays a secondary role in shaping out-group attitudes, while the belief that America is a divinely inspired nation lends a superior explanation of prejudicial attitudes in America."

They explain the distinction this way: Even though religion plays a big role in the lives of both evangelicals and Christian nationalists, when it comes to the question of which Americans are offered rights and liberties and which ones aren't, what matters is how one defines "nationhood" or "American identity." Shortle and Gaddie measured the level to which individuals conflated their religious and national identities by having them respond to prompts like "America holds a special place in God's plan"; "God has chosen this nation to lead the world"; "the United States was founded as a Christian nation"; and "it is important to preserve the nation's religious heritage." The people they classified as Christians nationalists were those who defined America as a divinely inspired nation specifically meant to be a home for Christians.

Shortle and Gaddie then tested for how responses to the four prompts related to attitudes about Muslims. They found that Christian nationalism was positively and significantly related to anti-Muslim sentiment. It was as clear as Jeffress's text: "God will curse the nation that sanctions the worship of other gods."

Christian nationalism, as a fusion of faith and patriotism, conflates American identity and religious identity so that Muslims are not true citizens deserving of protection. Most Americans like to think of America as rooted in civic, not ethnic, identity, but Christian nationalists promote a vision of America as a nation closely tied to a white Anglo-Saxon Protestant culture and history. In this paradigm, Muslims not only have a different religion but because they are conflated with terrorists and widely perceived as ethnically nonwhite they are, as sociologist Ruth Braunstein explains, simultaneously "*non-American* (outsiders), *anti-American* (enemies), and *un-American* (others)."

This explains why Trump's 2016 campaign rhetoric was so effective on white evangelicals like Jeffress. Trump reflected back to them their idea of Islam as the antithesis of Christian and American identities. As Yale sociologist Philip Gorski points out, there were evangelicals who supported

Trump only after he won the nomination, but there were others, like Jeffress, who supported Trump even before he won the primaries: "They could have voted for an orthodox evangelical. But Donald Trump was their first choice. Why? . . . because they are also white Christian nationalists and Trumpism is inter alia a reactionary version of white Christian nationalism." (In a *Washington Post* interview leading up to the 2020 election, Jeffress underscored Gorski's point: "I was one of the earliest . . . I said, 'Mr. Trump, I believe you're going to be the next president of the United States, and if that happens, it's because God has a great plan for you and for our country'. . . Daniel 2 says God is the one who installs kings and establishes kings and removes kings.")

Trump identifies Muslims as threatening and polluting by saying, "Islam hates us" and "there's a tremendous hatred." Then he offers solutions: "a complete and total shutdown of Muslims entering the United States until our country's representatives can figure out what the hell is going on" and the creation of a "special registry" for Muslims already in the country. The logic, Gorski says, is "to expel the infectious agents and seal off the body politic."

This is how Christian nationalism works—to sow hate of the Muslim "other." But it is not enough to know about these theoretical connections; we also have to figure out how to use this information to mend the divide. I explore that next.

* * * *

WHITEHEAD AND PERRY found that roughly half of evangelicals embrace Christian nationalist beliefs. Shortle and Gaddie said that "[e]vangelicals primarily, but not exclusively, subscribe to this religiously conflated version of national identity." That not all white evangelicals are Christian nationalists can be explained in part by pointing to the "evangelical left"—people like Jim Wallis, founder of the social-justice-committed group Sojourners, or the progressive former US president Jimmy Carter. But politically *conservative* white evangelicals are also not synonymous with Christian nationalists. Some, like Harrell and Good, are quite open to dialogue.

Kevin Singer of Neighborly Faith often reminds his audiences that "many, many [evangelicals] are not okay with the direction our society is moving politically . . . there are a lot of evangelicals who are deeply compassionate and deeply concerned about the way our tradition is coming off today." Singer himself has gathered prominent evangelical leaders together with Muslim religious and civic leaders to discuss everything from modest fashion, to spirituality in the time of COVID-19, to whether states could shut down houses of worship during a global pandemic (on that last topic, I engaged Johnnie Moore Jr., president of the Congress of Christian Leaders, in a lively conversation). At a March 2020 Neighborly Faith event, J. D. Greear, president of the Southern Baptist Convention, and the Muslim leader Omar Suleiman addressed a live audience of over a thousand college students. Greear dove into how young evangelicals could change their "posture of fear" by talking about his own personal relationships with Muslims. His message on behalf of evangelicals to Muslims: "We love you. We think you belong in this society, and we want to stand beside you to be your friends."

The Christian speakers and audiences at these events are largely conservative white evangelicals. They come with open hearts and minds and leave with an even bigger sense of openness. Singer sometimes polls his audience and, in each case, finds that the Christians' attitudes toward Muslims improved. After the Greear event, for example, 76 percent of Christian respondents said their attitude toward Islam was more positive than before, and 83 percent said they were more interested in friendships with Muslims.

So there are real possibilities for fruitful dialogue. I am a part of it, I see it, but I think there is space for so much more. For those who want to keep expanding the opportunities for engagement, how do we know which evangelical Christians might be willing?

Or more precisely: What is it about certain conservative white evangeli-cals that makes them lean away from Christian nationalism? Age might be part of it: Pew found in 2017 that millennials are more likely than older adults to take liberal positions on a host of issues. Ed Stetzer, the executive director of the Billy Graham Center at Wheaton College in Illinois, says younger evangelicals are pushing back against the "God and country idea" and "don't want those things inappropriately mixed." Russell Moore of the Southern Baptist Convention puts it this way: Young evangelicals "never expected a nominally Christian culture in which being a church member would be the equivalent of being a good American." Singer works with Gen Z evangelicals and says many of them invest "emotional capital" in their relationships with Muslims.

But Singer and others also warn that official surveys mask an entrenched tribalism among young evangelicals. "People can show up to the Neigh-borly Faith events and say these are people Jesus wants us to reach out to, but they often also step out and return to their tribe and continue to pos-ture as good members of the tribe." Pastor Bob Roberts says he's observed a similar phenomenon and encourages young evangelicals to have "one conversation"—that is, be consistent—when they are with and without their tribe. Political scientist Andrew Lewis, too, says shifting opinions don't always translate to a desire for policy change, and that survey results reflect "expressive" rather than "mobilizing" attitudes: "This softening doesn't seem to be changing their partisanship, which is driven by more salient commitments and socialization."

To help map some of this attitudinal complexity among Christians old and young as well as non-Christian Americans, Whitehead and Perry have created a scale of greater and lesser degrees of Christian nationalism. Based on where Americans fall on this scale, they belong to one of four categories: Rejecters, Resisters, Accommodators, and Ambassadors.

Rejecters do not think of America as a Christian nation and believe that Christianity should not play a role in American politics. Some of them are evangelical. While Rejecters "wholly oppose" Christian nationalism, Resisters "merely resist it." Resisters distinguish between Christian nationalists and Christian conservatives and have warmer views toward the latter. They think that Christianity is important to American history and culture and that Americans should acknowledge Christianity's important contributions to, for example, the fight for social justice. Compared to Rejecters, they "signal a bit more indecision" about whether the United States is a Christian nation; while they oppose prayers in public schools, they are open to the display of religious symbols in public. Demographically, there are clear similarities between Rejecters and Resisters in age, gender, and education, but they differ significantly in their degree of religiosity. Much more religious than Rejecters, 80 percent of Resisters believe in God, two thirds are Christian, 18 percent are evangelicals, and 17 percent are political conservatives.

Accommodators are a "mirror image of Resisters." Resisters are a little indecisive but generally oppose Christian nationalism, whereas Accommodators are also indecisive but lean the other way. They think their version of traditional Christian values is a positive guide for society, but they also believe these values are shared by other world religions. A third of Accommodators are evangelicals, and 44 percent are political conservatives.

As for Ambassadors—those are the Robert Jeffresses of the world. They believe unequivocally that the United States was founded as a Christian nation and that Christianity should guide American policy. Despite copious scholarship arguing otherwise, their view is that most of America's founders were Christian, that they intended to establish the nation based on Christian principles, and, according to one ambassador Whitehead and Perry interviewed, "'most of the laws were founded off of Christian principles. Just about every law in every state, and most of the federal government's initial laws were founded off of Christian principles.'" America, according to Ambassadors, has a special relationship with God, and its prosperity is commensurate to Americans' obedience to God, as defined by Christian Scriptures. Ambassadors are 70 percent white, 55 percent evangelical, and 69 percent political conservatives.

The more inclined an American is toward Christian nationalism, the more clearly he or she wants to privilege Christianity in the United States. Whereas Rejecters are focused on making space for atheists and religious minorities, Ambassadors believe that America should favor Christianity over all other religions because, as expressed by one Ambassador, "non-Christian minorities are deceived by Satan, and thus Christians have no obligation to treat their perspective as equally legitimate."

The flip side of privileging Christianity is the disempowerment of the threatening, non-Christian outsider. And Christian nationalists see Muslims as the most threatening group of all. To fight the Muslim "threat," they use more than words—they also oppose Muslims' political freedoms and civil liberties, including religious freedom. As the classic nationalist Ambassador Robert Jeffress captured so well in his book, when Christian nationalists talk about religious freedom, they are talking about protecting Christian interests only.

Whitehead and Perry also offer other insights that can help pinpoint the set of conservative Christians who would be open to transcending the Muslim-Christian divide.

First, regardless of which category of nationalism a person belongs to, religious commitment (defined by how frequently one attends religious services, prays, and reads their sacred scriptures) makes them more open to dialogue. Higher commitment has an independent relationship with more openness. In an interview with *Salon*, Whitehead notes, "Christian nationalism encourages people generally to think and believe one way," but "once we take that level of Christian nationalism into account, individual Americans who are more religious will actually be moving in the opposite direction."

This applies to anti-Muslim sentiment, too: "The way I explain it is that if you could take a carbon copy of me and the only thing you change—increase or decrease—is my Christian nationalism, then I will be more fearful of Muslims as you increase that. But if you took a carbon copy of me, and my level of Christian nationalism stayed the same level, and all you increased or decreased was my religious practice—as you increase my religious practice, I would actually feel less threatened by Muslims. So, these things aren't one and the same." (Other studies, like a 2009 analysis conducted by three political scientists at University of Maryland, have also documented the "positive effect of worship attendance" on perceptions of Muslims.)

Second, Christian nationalists and non-Christian nationalists might appear to hold some of the same beliefs, but these groups are fundamentally different from each other because they have different goals in mind. Religious commitment is more about the personal and less about social order and hierarchy than Christian nationalism is; it is about devotion to God, one's religious community, and a system of moral beliefs, rather than to particular political ideas. For Christian nationalists, "[r]eligious interests rank second, if they rank at all" because Christian nationalism is "rooted in claims about who 'we' are as a people and, more importantly, whose preferences should be reflected in 'our' cultural symbols and implemented in 'our' public policies." Christian nationalism even influences political attitudes in a way that is "often diametrically opposed to Christian ethics" and uninterested in "instituting explicitly 'Christ-like' policies." Jeffress even said he preferred Donald Trump over someone who "expresses the values of Jesus."

Even appeals to a "Christian nation" are fundamentally different depending on whether the appeal is to a Christian nation as a *religious* goal versus a *political* goal. The first set of people wants to mobilize religious action and influence American society with its pious Christian example. The second set wants to define the parameters of what America is and who true Americans are. That's Jeffress: "God will curse the nation that sanctions . . . [a] culture of diversity."

The distinction between political and religious goals also applies to beliefs about gender roles, divorce, same-sex marriage, and accommodations for transgender people. In a section of their book titled "When Christian Nationalism Looks Like Religious Commitment," Whitehead and Perry explain that there's a correlation between higher levels of religious commitment and traditional beliefs, and there's also a correlation between Christian nationalism and traditional beliefs. But the purpose of the beliefs in each case are different, which is why you can find traditional beliefs in any of the four categories of Americans.

Consider Brian, a conservative Christian who is also a Resister: "I'm working from the basis that homosexuals seeking marriage are not Christians . . . As a Christian I desire for every person to come to faith in Christ, and that certainly extends to the homosexual community. However, I also try not to allow my desire for them to become Christians to lead me to a place where I think mandates and laws should strip [their] American liberties away." Similarly, Blake, a "weak" Accommodator, thinks that homosexuality is a sin, but he also believes that society should accommodate gays and lesbians. In contrast, Christian nationalists want to see their beliefs reflected in American public policy. In their view, "[n]ations that enforce 'wicked laws' are not only violating what is 'wholesome and necessary for public good,' they are inviting God's judgment."

The difference between white evangelicals who are more or less nationalistic can also be seen as the difference between an offensive and defensive posture. Ambassadors are on the offensive; they actively seek to exclude others because they imagine America to be theirs only. Religion, for them, is merely a tool to secure these political ends. On the other hand, more open-minded people like Brian and Blake aren't trying to exclude anyone from American belonging, but they and others like them need America to accommodate their positions, too. (We'll see in chapter 3 how this sentiment plays out in legal cases.) Andrew Lewis agrees: "These more pluralistic types see that religious life is threatened and want to see religion protected," he told me. "They are more open to pluralism, because protection, not domination, is the main goal."

Whitehead echoed the idea: "Rejecters and Resisters may feel besieged . . . For these groups, they may have actually experienced inequalities and been shut out of equal access to power." Yale sociologist Philip Gorski said the same: "religious conservatives" worry about "a slippery slope that would eventually strip them of their First Amendment right to religious freedom." Speaking from the trenches, Johnnie Moore Jr. said he also agrees with the distinction: "The data has to be carefully curated to distinguish between politically active evangelicals," who advocate for religious liberty among other things, "and those who seek a theocracy."

So, taking all this together, we see that higher levels of religiosity make a conservative white evangelical more open to Muslims but also more likely to hold traditional religious beliefs about sexuality. Why does religious commitment work this way? According to the famed social psychologist Gordon Allport, "while nativism or racism may be completely foreign to a certain faith system originally, one's religious identity . . . becomes co-opted to reinforce ethnic, racial, or national boundaries such that to be one of 'us' in a religious sense is also to be one of 'us' in an ethnic or national sense." Christian nationalism is this sort of co-optation of Christianity. But unlike these ethnic or national issues, beliefs about marriage, family, and sexuality are "*elemental* to religion." "Thus, to be more committed to religion personally is to be more committed to a certain 'traditional' model of family life, sexual behavior, or gender, regardless of one's views on Christian nationalism."

That religious commitment works this way is pretty essential to understand. Often, when conservative Christians talk about sexuality from a traditional, religious perspective, many Americans group them with Christian nationalists and dismiss and deride them as "bigots" or "misogynists." Even though the research shows that religiosity correlates with open-mindedness toward Muslims, nonwhites, and immigrants, the language of "bigotry," "hate," and "misogyny" pervades the conversation about conservative Christians who decline to celebrate gay weddings or facilitate abortion. The disconnect suggests that perhaps "bigotry" and "misogyny" aren't the best way to describe these Christians' motivations. As I discuss in chapter 3, religious claims about abortion and same-sex marriage are the subject of several legal cases, and the Christians involved in those cases are often deeply religious. For these people, the focus is not on nationalist domination; instead, as Lewis, Whitehead, and Gorski point out, these white evangelicals are more concerned about their own ability to live out their faith.

To make matters even more complex, we have what social scientists call the "false enforcement of unpopular norms." People who are open-minded express a close-minded position because of perceived social pressure to conform. In turn, they end up further—and falsely—enforcing something they privately disapprove of. So, at least some of the conservatives expressing nationalist positions are likely not themselves nationalists.

The nonprofit More in Common distinguished between "traditional conservatives" and "devoted conservatives" in a way that tracks the differences between conservatives who privilege religion and politics in different ways. In its 2018 report, "Hidden Tribes: A Study of America's Polarized Landscape," More in Common grouped Americans into seven "tribes" based on their political attitudes. Traditional conservatives are Americans who tend to be "religious, patriotic, and moralistic"; devoted conservatives are "deeply engaged with politics and hold strident, uncompromising views. They feel that America is embattled, and they perceive themselves as the last defenders of traditional values under threat." Between the two, traditional conservatives are more religious and more open to dialogue (unlike Christian nationalists), even as they exhibit some of the same reluctance about liberal norms that devoted conservatives do.

And that last bit—the shared opposition to liberal norms—is the other important piece of this.

* * * *

TO RECAP THE chapter so far, evangelical hostility toward Muslims is a real problem, with many evangelicals taking a posture of aggression against Muslims. Studies show, however, that this hatred is exacerbated by Christian nationalist beliefs—the more nationalist an evangelical is, the more he or she hates the religious, racial, ethnic "other," including Muslims. Meanwhile, religious commitment has the opposite effect and helps make evangelicals more open-minded.

So, Muslims as non-Christians are a religious out-group. And in our current polarized climate, where—as *Politico* puts it—we're experiencing the "ferocious politicization of everything," Muslims are also a political out-group.

I once asked a roundtable of people who work on religious engagement programs and religious freedom advocacy whether political tribalism drives anti-Muslim hostility among white evangelicals. They responded, "Definitely. Everything is tribal nowadays. Muslims are part of a different religious tribe and inasmuch as they align with progressives, a different political tribe also," and "Yes. [Conservative white evangelicals] believe Democrats are trying to encourage Muslim immigration because it will help them de-Christianize America."

To understand this dynamic, let's start with a general overview of what Ezra Klein calls "your brain on groups." Much of our understanding of group dynamics is based on a series of experiments conducted by social psychologist Henri Tajfel in the 1970s. Tajfel was a Polish Jew who immigrated to France in the 1930s and enlisted in the French army during World War II. He was captured by the Germans in 1940 and spent five years in the German prisoner-of-war camps, where he escaped death only because the Nazis thought he was a French, not Polish, Jew. Reflecting on the fact that the only thing that kept him from being killed was his perceived social category (French Jew), regardless of his personal characteristics or his relationships with the German guards, Tajfel understood there was something powerful about group identity. As Klein explains, Tajfel "theorized that the instinct to view our own with favor and outsiders with hostility is so deeply learned that it operates independent of any reason to treat social relations as a competition." You can turn against people outside your identity group even if you don't fear them. And you can oppose them even if you don't stand to gain anything material from that opposition.

Tajfel tested this in a series of experiments. In his first study, he took sixty-four boys from the same school; the boys all knew each other and already had a sense of community among them. First, the researchers told the boys they wanted to test visual judgment. The boys were shown clusters of dots and had to estimate how many dots they saw. After the researchers tallied (or pretended to tally) the results, the researchers told the boys they were dividing them into groups: one group included boys who had guessed a high number of dots on the visual judgment test and one included those who had guessed low. In reality, the researchers divided the group randomly; their purpose was only to test what happened next.

The researchers then gave the two groups some money and asked them to distribute it to other boys in the study. The boys couldn't keep any money for themselves; they had to give it to the others, but they chose how they would allocate the money, and they knew if it went to members of their own group or the out-group. What Tajfel learned from the study shocked him about the power of group identity, despite even his own tragic history: most of the boys in each group gave money to their own group members instead of to the out-group. The boys had been divided on the basis of completely meaningless criteria, but they still chose their own group over the other one. There was no substantive benefit to choosing their own group, but they still did it because of the powerful pull of group identity.

In a second study, Tajfel changed the setup so he could test whether the boys prioritized making money for their own group or making sure the out-group lost in a big way. When the boys were allocating money, they had to choose between, on the one hand, maximizing the amount everyone received, and on the other hand, maximizing their group's amount relative to the out-group, even if that meant their group ended up with less money. The boys chose the latter. The boys were okay with giving their own group less as long as they had significantly more money than the out-group.

Tajfel went on to test this in a series of other studies, which themselves were replicated by other researchers in a variety of different conditions with different sets of participants. The results were always the same: people exhibit discriminatory intergroup behavior in a way that creates the biggest gap between their group and the out-group. By far, money is not the prime motivator; winning is.

Group loyalty helps people avoid the strong psychological and physical effects of rejection. Studies have shown that we don't experience social isolation or stigma only psychologically; they also trigger a physical assault on our body. What this means in practice is that humans are programmed, even evolutionarily, to signal their allegiance to their tribe as a way of avoiding the loneliness and stress that come with being cast out.

Our allegiance to our political tribes is no different. Elections are pure team rivalry. Similar to Tajfel's findings, other studies have found that in the election context, winning is what's most important and Americans are driven by what they oppose rather than what they support. For example, a 2016 Pew study found that a "deeper affection" for the Republican Party increased voting much less than "very unfavorable views" of the Democratic Party. Among Americans who are highly engaged in politics, this disparity became even starker—the more they hated the other side, the more likely they were to donate money to their own party. This is why politicians focus so much of their messaging on generating fear and hatred of the other party.

In our present political climate, these group rivalries pose ever more serious implications because of what Lilliana Mason in *Uncivil Agreement:*

How Politics Became Our Identity calls the emergence of "mega-identities": "A single vote can now indicate a person's partisan preference *as well as* his or her religion, race, ethnicity, gender, neighborhood, and favorite grocery store. This is no longer a single social identity. Partisanship can now be thought of as a mega-identity, with all the psychological and behavioral magnifications that implies." So, "if you told someone on the phone whom you had never met before that you are white, that single fact would not tell them much more about you. But if you told them that you are a Republican, they could reasonably assume that you are not black, lesbian, gay, transgender or bisexual, nonreligious or Jewish."

Klein explains it as the difference between sorting and polarizing. The first is issue-based—we cluster together based on our policy opinions. The second is identity-based—we cluster together based on political identities. "[O]ur political identities are polarizing our other identities, too," and issue conflicts are just one of many expressions of that hostility.

In this ever-widening circle—the "ferocious politicization of everything"—almost nothing is apolitical anymore. Consider a 2004 ad by the Club for Growth, a conservative group that advocates for lower taxes and deregulation, against then presidential candidate Howard Dean. The ad features someone asking an older white couple what they think of Dean's plan, and the man responds, "I think Howard Dean should take his tax-hiking, government-expanding, latte-drinking, sushi-eating, Volvo-driving, *New York Times*-reading—." His wife cuts in, "Body-piercing, Hollywood-loving, left-wing freak show back to Vermont, where it belongs." Each of these traits reinforces a particular mega-identity, and when you activate one, you activate them all.

I think something like this is at work when it comes to Muslims and liberals. Eboo Patel begins to get at this in *Out of Many Faiths: Religious Diversity and the American Promise*, where he notes that Muslims are given platforms by outlets like the *New York Times*, NPR, CNN, the *New Yorker*—outlets that are:

associated with urban, multicultural, progressive Whole Foods America; not so much white, rural, conservative Cracker Barrel America. One gets the sense that if Trump's America insists on casting Muslims as villains . . . then Barack Obama's America will respond by promoting Muslims whom they consider heroes . . . Muslims, in other words, have become a totem in the current chapter of the American culture wars, a symbol that signals, above all, a tribal belonging (Trump/red/rural/evangelical/Cracker Barrel versus Obama/blue/urban/secular/Whole Foods), with each tribe doing its best to foist on the category "Muslim" its preferred set of characteristics.

In other words, embracing Muslims—and especially liberal advocacy on behalf of Muslims—is a trait of the liberal mega-identity, while opposing Muslims is a trait of the conservative mega-identity. Nothing captures this political football better than variations of Obama's "Hope" poster with a woman in a hijab. The poster is used to protest Trump and was, for example, ubiquitous in the January 2017 Women's March on Washington. More generally, liberals have championed the hijab for years and featured women who wear headscarves in numerous prominent outlets. The phenomenon might seem peculiar, since the hijab—one feature of a modest (or restrictive) dress code for women—is not ordinarily something that liberals would champion. But Muslims and hijab are part of the Left's mega-identity, and the Right—which isn't normally associated with feminism—makes feminist arguments against the hijab. In the Club for Growth ad, protecting the hijab and Muslims comes right alongside "tax-hiking, government-expanding, latte-drinking, sushi-eating, Volvo-driving, *New York Times*-reading, body-piercing, Hollywood-loving, left-wing freak show."

This amalgamation of traits tells us that conservatives see liberals as people who are elitist and out of touch (lattes, sushi, *New York Times*), who restrict personal liberty (government-expanding); support freeloaders (tax-hiking);

thumb their noses at cultural norms and values (body-piercing, Holly-wood); and privilege foreign workers over American workers (Volvo). And while the Club for Growth ad doesn't reference religion explicitly, we can extrapolate from the other traits that conservatives see liberals as spurning religious traditionalism and America's Christian character specifically. (In contrast, liberals see themselves as compassionate toward the less fortunate, open to diverse cultures and new experiences, and resistant to undue restrictions—including religious restrictions—on personal autonomy.)

What happens when American Muslims get lumped into a liberal mega-identity that is defined by conservatives as anti-Christian and anti-America? Muslims take on those traits, too.

The psychological implications are very dangerous, Mason says. When our racial, religious, and other identities are wrapped up with our political party, if our party loses an election or some other partisan battle, the impact on us psychologically is a lot worse. It's as if we lost to other racial and religious groups, too. It makes us feel threatened, and when we feel threatened, we lash out against the out-group.

This is particularly the case now, when many white Christian conservatives are feeling under siege. Studies show that in-group favoritism doesn't always result in bias against an out-group. You can extend trust, cooperation, and empathy to your in-group but not the out-group, and while this is a form of discrimination, it doesn't involve any sort of aggression or hostility toward the out-group. For example, both political scientist Ashley Jardina and Klein note that white tribalism exists without attendant out-group hostility; whites can rally around their racial identity without also attacking nonwhites. Tellingly, after the May 2020 killing of George Floyd by Minneapolis police, ensuing nationwide protests, and the toppling of Confederate-era statues, David Brooks wrote in the *New York Times*:

> People have been waiting for a white backlash since the riots, or since the statues started toppling. There isn't much if any evidence

of a backlash. There's evidence of a fore-lash . . . We're seeing incredible shifts in attitudes toward race. Roughly 60 percent of Americans now believe that African Americans face a great deal or a lot of discrimination.

Similarly, political scientist Michael Tesler found that the percentage of Americans who agree that "there's a lot of discrimination against African-Americans" went up from 19 percent in 2013 to 50 percent in 2020, driven mostly by changes in white voters' attitudes.

So, tribalism in the racial context does not generally lead to out-group hostility (though there are certainly discrete incidents of white backlash). But tribalism *has* resulted in out-group hostility in the religious context—and there's evidence that Muslims, more than any other religious out-group, are the targets of this hostility. Perceptions of threat are part of the reason why. Oxford political scientists Miles Hewstone, Mark Rubin, and Hazel Willis write, "The constraints normally in place, which limit intergroup bias to in-group favoritism, are lifted when out-groups are associated with stronger emotions." Stronger emotions include things like feeling the out-group is moving against you: "an out-group seen as threatening may elicit fear and hostile actions." Whereas "high status" groups (groups that are a numerical majority and have power) don't feel threatened by minorities when the status gap is very wide, they are more likely to feel threatened when the status gap is closing.

There are several theories for why threat leads to bias. One is Tajfel's social identity theory. When a high-status group protects its members, the members feel greater self-esteem. When that status is challenged, members feel depressed and lash out at the threatening out-group. Social dominance theory says something similar. People with high social dominance orientation (SDO) want their group to dominate the out-group. Feelings of threat make this tendency worse.

Scholars have tested the connection between SDO and support for Trump. Professors Rogers M. Smith and Desmond King write that a "wide variety of studies, including experimental research, public opinion surveys, analyses of voting statistics, and panel studies show that [Trump's] victim narrative connected powerfully with those with strong attachments to traditionally dominant identities." Political scientist Diana C. Mutz found these trends even among people who in past elections might not have voted for Trump. People who felt their status was threatened experienced an increase in SDO—that is, a desire to dominate the out-group—which in turn led them to "defect to Trump."

Mutz tested this specifically with respect to attitudes toward Muslims. Respondents were asked to what extent Muslims and Christians (among others) were discriminated against in America. She found that people who voted for Trump perceived Christians as experiencing greater discrimination than Muslims. Other studies have also documented the partisan divide when it comes to attitudes about anti-Muslim discrimination. In 2020, the University of Chicago Divinity School and the Associated Press-NORC Center for Public Affairs Research (AP-NORC) found that while half of Americans believe that American Muslims' religious freedom is threatened at least somewhat, only about three in ten white evangelicals said the same. In 2019, Pew found that Democrats and those who lean Democratic "are more likely than Republicans and Republican leaners to say Muslims face at least some discrimination in the United States (92 percent vs. 69 percent) . . . At the same time, Republicans are much more likely than Democrats to say evangelicals face discrimination (70 percent vs. 32 percent)."

In 2017, Rasmussen Reports found that "[f]ifty-six percent (56%) of Democrats . . . believe most Muslims in this country are mistreated, a view shared by only 22 percent of Republicans." That same year, PRRI found that Democrats were four times as likely to believe that Muslims faced greater discrimination than Christians. Republicans thought the two groups suffered roughly equally, but among white evangelicals specifically, PRRI found that 57 percent said that anti-Christian discrimination is widespread in the United States, while only 44 percent said the same thing about anti-Muslim discrimination.

Similar to Mutz's findings, there appeared to be a correlation between the political climate and perceptions of status threat. Polls from several years or even a year before the 2016 presidential election found that fewer white evangelicals thought they faced more discrimination than Muslims. A 2013 PRRI survey found that 59 percent of white evangelicals thought Muslims faced more discrimination than evangelicals did; 56 percent responded that way to an October 2016 poll. By February 2017, that number had dropped twelve percentage points.

****

EVANGELICALS' FEELINGS OF threat, aggravated by partisan politics, are important to probe if we are to understand the nature of anti-Muslim sentiment in America today. It is vital to parse the differences between Christian nationalism and conservative white evangelicalism. We also know that Christian nationalism is not synonymous with racism, and that Americans can fall along a spectrum of greater or lesser nationalism. I examined the impact of religiosity and political tribalism on conservative white evangelicals' perceptions of Muslims. Then I looked at the interaction between group identity and psychological factors like SDO.

In the next few chapters, I examine how this in-group favoritism/out-group hostility works in the Christian-Muslim context. At times, I will refer to this hostility as the "weaponization of vulnerability"—ultimately, much of conservative Christian hostility against Muslims is rooted in feelings of victimization at the hands of people who themselves are not Muslims. It's as if Muslims are collateral damage in America's widening polarization.

In the process of telling this story, I consider the perspectives of various conservative white evangelicals and conservative Christians generally. Ultimately, this book is about healing the divide between these Christians and Muslims, and I cannot heal if I lash out at the very people I seek to make peace with. Indeed, studies on intergroup bias have found that empathy helps prevent out-group hostility because it reduces the in-group's feelings of threat. In driving toward empathy as a solution, I am careful to not just offer an argument *about* empathy; I also am (or seek to be) empathetic in *how* I present my argument.

❦

PART II

THE IN-GROUP THREAT

CHAPTER 2

The End of White Christian America

Asma,

I purchased a copy of your book yesterday and I have not been able to put it down.

I want to work with those of my ilk to better understand our liberty and what is necessary to protect and expand them. I agree that religious protection is our first freedom. I am concerned about the balkanization of our country. Our hostilities are choking the opportunities for dialogue. And dialogue is how we will make progress as diverse people to move forward peacefully.

I very much want to strengthen our First Amendment by expanding it where it does not exist, but I won't be heard over the objections of "what about conservatives' ability to speak?" without support from people like you. We will be pulling the same cart in different directions. There is a very real crackdown against conservatives' free speech. Every conservative knows it and feels it. Christians feel this . . . they get this.

You wrote "Once Islam is cast as a threatening political ideology, rather than a religion, it becomes easier to deny American Muslims all safeguards and protections that are part of religious freedom." My counterpoint is: Once conservatives can be cast as "racists" or "white supremacists" or "bigots," then the need to have political dialogue is diminished, because who wants to engage in discussion with a disgusting and vile human?

If you don't agree with [the Left], you aren't just wrong, you aren't allowed to speak, you shouldn't be allowed to operate a business . . . What I am saying is that conservatives, for no other reason than our "philosophy," are targeted for ridicule, censure, and even violence by entertainment, higher ed, and pop culture. Additionally, the Left maligns our motives and attacks our traditions.

I hope you take these statements in the way I mean them . . . as a way of fostering better understanding of each other's uniqueness and vulnerability. My eyes have been opened by you. I, too, hope that through reasonable dialogue I can shed some light on how conservatives are also under attack from an establishment.

Best,
Matthew

This is Matthew, a conservative Christian in his midfifties. He emailed me after the release of *When Islam Is Not a Religion* as his small part in helping mend America's political and religious polarization. In a series of other emails, he was open about where he agreed and disagreed with my arguments, but mostly he wanted to point out that Muslims and conservatives are facing some of the same challenges in the United States today (though he was careful not to equate the two and agreed that Muslims face a more urgent and serious threat).

In his view, the common threat is how beliefs are maligned and the people who hold them are demonized, even criminalized. The Right attacks Islam in this way, and in Matthew's view, the Left attacks conservatives in this way, too, with the aim of silencing them. Because if "conservatives can be cast as 'racists' or 'white supremacists' or 'bigots,'" then there's no need to take their views seriously. "[W]ho wants to engage in discussion with a disgusting and vile human?"

Matthew's perspective may, to some, appear overly dramatic, but he was authentic and open in sharing his views. He took the opportunity to be vulnerable, and as the conflict transformation experts all say, to mend the tribal divide, it's important to listen to his views openly and without judgment. For example, a February 2019 *New York Times* article, "They Have Worked on Conflicts Overseas. Now These Americans See 'Red Flags' at Home," tells the story of a group of conflict resolution experts who spent their careers working on conflicts abroad and are now turning their focus on the United States. They see "warning signs" here, "flashes of social distress" that look familiar to what they had seen in conflict zones abroad. As one expert explained, "People are making up stories about 'the other' — Muslims, Trump voters, whoever 'the other' is . . . 'They don't have the values that we have. They don't behave like we do. They are not nice. They are evil' . . . That's dehumanization. And when it spreads, it can be very hard to correct."

The experts decided to start tackling the problem by running dialogue sessions where a small group of people came together "not to change minds, but to broaden them." No one was persuading the other to accept their political views; instead the idea was to get the "participants to see one another as people." When the groups met, the conflict experts started by applying a basic rule of psychology: first help people feel heard and acknowledge their dignity, *then* take on harder topics like politics. The "group was able to talk about hard things because of what came before: the feeling that the other side had heard them and that they had become, in a fundamental way, equals." As one facilitator explained, they all expected it to be harder than it actually was. "I really learned that no matter how differently we think or vote, if we take a moment to see the other person for who they are, as somebody with a family and a story, that made the hard stuff easier." She characterized the process as "having a hard conversation in a soft place."

Similarly, Brené Brown says that the people who overcome polarization are those who "lean into vulnerability" by staying "*zoomed in*." They commit "to assessing their lives and forming their opinions of people based on their actual, in-person experiences." "Zooming in" means questioning what we hear on the news and from the mouths of politicians. Because when we see people close-up, it is a lot harder to hate them—a lot harder to recede into our "go-to emotions"—"pain and fear, anger and hate."

Importantly, leaning into vulnerability does not mean we have to stop fighting for what we believe in. "[N]ot everyone will be able to do both, simply because some people will continue to believe that fighting for what they need means denying the humanity of others. That makes connecting outside our bunkers impossible." However, Brown's data tell her that "most of us *can* build connection across difference and fight for our beliefs" if we're willing to "intentionally be with people who are different from us" and "learn how to listen, have hard conversations, look for joy, share pain, and be more curious than defensive, all while seeking moments of togetherness." When we stand "alone in a hypercritical environment" or stand "together in the midst of differences," we are "braving the wilderness" and even "becoming the wilderness."

This is what I hope to do in this and the following chapter: brave the wilderness so that the divides can start to heal. And to do that, again, I have to start by listening to Matthew and others like him on their own terms. Like some of the other friendly characters we've met earlier in this book, Matthew has a genuine desire to overcome tribal divides with American Muslims, but there are plenty in his community who are less willing. To build bridges with them, I have to take the experiences I have had, like the one with Matthew, and "zoom in" on who they are and what they are feeling.

And what they are feeling is, overwhelmingly, a rejection by American culture and media. This is happening alongside significant demographic shifts; white Protestants are, for the first time in American history, a minority in the United States, and the conservative evangelicals among them are an even smaller minority. These factors, together, guide their actions and color their worldview of everything associated with out-groups.

Ezra Klein gets at how big a deal this is when he describes "what happens in moments like this one, moments when a majority feels its dominance beginning to fail."

> The answer, attested to in mountains of studies and visible everywhere in our politics, is this: change of this magnitude acts on us psychologically, not just electorally. It is the crucial context uniting the core political conflicts of this era: Obama's and Trump's presidencies, the rise of reactionary new social movements and thinkers, the wars over political correctness on campuses and representation in Hollywood, the power of #MeToo and Black Lives Matter, the fights over immigration. There is nothing that makes us identify with our groups so strongly as the feeling that the power we took for granted may soon be lost or the injustices we've long borne may soon be rectified.

Klein leaves out religious polarization from his list of "core political conflicts," but that divide is mapped onto the ones he does list: Muslims as immigrants and as minorities whose rights, like the women and blacks of

#MeToo and Black Lives Matter, are championed by the political Left. Hollywood representation is also part of it—as Matthew told me, "One thing Muslims don't have happen to them is being ridiculed by every late-night show on television (other than Bill Maher's HBO show). Conservatives get this EVERY single night."

In this chapter, I will provide an overview of the so-called "evangelical persecution complex," the feelings of threat that drive Christians' hostility toward Muslims as the religious and political out-group. I will summarize how the Trump administration adroitly seized on these vulnerabilities, while the Left minimizes and often disparages them. My purpose is not to interrogate each factor in detail but simply to identify how our national discourse exacerbates perceptions of threat and contributes to the weaponization of that vulnerability.

****

TO "ZOOM IN" on conservative white evangelicals' perception of siege, it's important to understand the monumental demographic and cultural shifts in America that have fundamentally altered the historical vision and experience of America for evangelicals.

First, and for the first time in US history, white racial dominance is on the decline. In 1965, white Americans constituted 84 percent of the US population. Since then there has been an influx of immigrants, with nearly 59 million arriving in the last fifty years alone. Between 1965 and 2015, the American Asian population went from 1.3 million to 18 million, and the Hispanic population went from 8 million to almost 57 million. America's complexion is "browning," and in several states—including America's most populous ones, Texas and California—whites are already a minority. National Public Radio reported in 2016 that nonwhite babies now outnumber non-Hispanic white babies. The majority of Americans under the age of sixteen are nonwhite (and have been since the middle of 2020). Pew says whites generally will be a minority by 2055; the US Census says it'll happen even sooner, in 2044.

Second, and also for the first time in US history, white Protestant Christians are a minority in America. A 2017 PRRI study found that white Protestant Christians constitute only 43 percent of the US population. The "end of white Christian America," is what Robert Jones, the founder of PRRI, calls it. To understand the gravity of the shift, consider that in 1976, eight in ten Americans were white Christians, and 55 percent of Americans were white Protestants. In 1996, white Christians still made up two thirds of the population. Today, they don't even constitute a majority. Among these white Protestants, white evangelicals have also seen a precipitous drop. In the 1990s, white evangelicals constituted 27 percent of the US population; today it's somewhere between 17 percent and 13 percent.

Third, the demise of white Protestant America has brought with it an end to "the cultural and institutional world built primarily by white Protestants that dominated American culture until the last decade." Not only is Christianity declining but so is religion overall. More and more Americans are religiously unaffiliated (the so-called nones), and in 2019 the percentage of nones became roughly the same as the percentage of evangelicals or Catholics. (By 2016, the nones already constituted the nation's largest religious voting bloc.) The massive shift signaled growing discontent with organized religion generally. Altogether, Jones says, this has precipitated an "internal identity crisis" that has generated tremendous anger, insecurity, and anxiety. In this world, this white Christian America,

> questions like "And where do you go to church" felt appropriate in casual social interactions or even business exchanges. White Christian America was a place where few gave a second thought to saying "Merry Christmas!" to strangers on the street . . . For most of the nation's life, White Christian America was big enough, cohesive enough, and influential enough to pull off the illusion

that it was the cultural pivot around which the country turned—
at least for those living safely within its expansive confines.

White Christian America had a type of golden age in the 1950s, after the
hardships and victories of World War II and under the stewardship of evangelical leaders like Reverend Billy Graham. In the aftermath of the war, millions of Americans distraught by nearly a century of fighting and economic
devastation were drawn to Graham's message of igniting a "Holy Ghost
revival" of repentance and redemption. As he preached in cross-national
tours, he successfully brought a variety of conservative white Protestants
into the "capacious revival tent" he called "evangelicals."

Graham's message was about repudiating secularism and embracing
conservative Christian mores. But his movement wasn't about reclusion—
it was about engagement, and he preached by example: throughout his
life, he advised numerous presidents and foreign leaders and advocated for
legislation that upheld conservative values. The motivation (and reward)
for his spiritual, cultural, and political action was to earn God's blessings
the way America had earned them during the Great Awakenings, a series
of Christian revivals in the 17th and 18th centuries.

In recent years, nothing encapsulates the end of this revival more than
changes at the Supreme Court, which has had an entirely non-Protestant
composition since 2010. For conservative Christians generally, the biggest blow has been the Court's decision in *Obergefell v. Hodges*, estab-
lishing a constitutional right to same-sex marriage. *Obergefell* raised
a series of challenges for conservatives who worried about violating
their religious convictions if they facilitated gay weddings. In so doing,
it accelerated conservatives' self-perception as vulnerable minorities in
need of protection from the broader culture. It used to be that Christian conservatives tried to promote traditional morality for everyone
because the acceptance of "secular morality" would remove God's divine
favor from America. But *Obergefell* was the unequivocal assertion that

Graham-inspired evangelicalism wasn't going to win over the culture, that white Christian America was done.

The shift away from traditional sexual mores has ignited fierce debates about how to protect Christianity's role in American society. Conservative Christians of diverse sects have partaken in the discussion. Consider the Sohrab Ahmari and David French spat from May 2019. The Catholic Ahmari, an editor at the *New York Post*, had just come to learn of Drag Queen Story Hour, a public event series where drag queens read storybooks to children and lead singalongs. The news left him shaken; to Ahmari, Drag Queen Story Hour represented an American society that had completely lost its Christian moral order. "This is demonic," he tweeted. In a piece for the religious journal *First Things*, Ahmari said conservatives should not try to coexist with the political Left but should instead "fight the culture war with the aim of defeating the enemy and enjoying the spoils in the form of a public square reordered to the common good and ultimately the Highest Good."

On Twitter, he took specific aim at conservative evangelical writer and lawyer David French for his tendency to humanize his opponents, whether in the courts of law or courts of public opinion:

> If you can't see why children belong nowhere near drag, with its currents of transvestic fetishism, we have nothing to say to each other. We are irreconcilably opposed. There's no polite, David French-ian third way around the cultural civil war. The only way is through.

French, in turn, responded with a piece in the *National Review*: "We live in a strange time when fighting for fundamental liberties while treating other human beings respectfully is seen as a sign of weakness. . . . We must vindicate our core values without violating our core values, and I don't want any part in any 'conservative' movement that holds otherwise." By "vindicate," French meant using the courts of law and free speech and religious freedom protections to carve out space for conservative Christian voices. In the months to come, Ahmari and French would represent two sides in an intra-conservative culture war. The Ahmari side used militaristic language like "fight the war," "aim of defeating," and "enjoying the spoils," nostalgic of Christendom when Christianity and world power were united. French, on the other hand, pointed out that the practice of Christian faith was nominal in Christendom, and the abuse of power rampant—in contrast, America's liberal order is far more conducive to robust religious practice.

When Ahmari and French debated in person at the Catholic University of America, "pseudo-hysteric energy" permeated the crowded room. Attendees came riled up with their own emotions to watch the two men duke it out in what the *American Conservative* called "an ideological brawl." In many ways, "it was all a circus," not a real political disagreement but a display of two different ways conservatives cope with the Left's "militancy" and "debauchery."

Other Christian thinkers have suggested that for conservative Christians to live their faith today, they must do as the Benedictine monks do and "embrace exile from mainstream culture." The Eastern Orthodox Rod Dreher, in his *New York Times* bestselling book *The Benedict Option: A Strategy for Christians in a Post-Christian Nation*, argues that Christians should retreat to "intentional communities" to develop a "resilient counterculture."

> Recognizing the toxins of modern secularism, as well as the fragmentation caused by relativism, Benedict Option Christians look to Scripture and to Benedict's Rule for ways to cultivate practices and communities. Rather than panicking or remaining complacent, they recognize that the new order is not a problem to be solved but a reality to be lived with . . .

Whether going into the culture war guns ablaze, using constitutional law to vindicate rights, or withdrawing from the battle to restrategize, the responses reflect Christian conservatives' profound inner turmoil about morality in modern American culture. In response to a perceived threat to their survival, conservative Christians are literally choosing between fight or flight.

"Our days as a formidable force in American national politics are over," Dreher says. In June 2020, when the Supreme Court in *Bostock v. Clayton County* expanded LGBTQ rights, Dreher's lament became even more desperate: "Today's ruling could only have been possible in post-Christian America." That two conservative justices voted with the majority, and the prized Trump-appointee Justice Neil Gorsuch wrote the opinion, only multiplied the despair. Conservatism has been forced into retreat, and many conservatives are fearful they won't be able to live out their vision of faithful Christianity.

The plight of Christians in many places outside the United States exacerbates their hopelessness. *Christianity Today*'s 25 MOST-READ STORIES ON THE PERSECUTED CHURCH in 2017 included headlines like CHINA TELLS CHRISTIANS TO REPLACE IMAGES OF JESUS WITH COMMUNIST PRESIDENT and KIDNAPPED SAMARITAN'S PURSE WORKERS FREED AMID SOUTH SUDAN FAMINE. They tell stories of genocide, terrorism, and the criminalization of Christian conversion and evangelism, leading "Christians with a global perspective on their faith" to "identify themselves as part of a persecuted people in the 21st century." In addition to mistreatment in some majority-Muslim states, a particularly acute concern in the Christian-Muslim context is Muslim population growth in Europe at a time when Christianity is fast declining in religious observance. It's not uncommon to hear conservative Christians fretting that the United States will repeat the European trend.

Add to this the fact that evangelical theology itself reinforces feelings of persecution; many evangelicals believe that it is "an essential part of the faith . . . that every Christian will be persecuted by the world: True believers will lose jobs, face exile, and suffer from violence." The fear is real, and given the national and international climate, it is at least partly warranted. But our current tribalized culture has turned this very human impulse into a subject of tremendous scorn. Trump carefully manipulated white evangelical vulnerability, conservative media outlets fetishize it by running sensationalist stories of discrimination, and Trump's opponents ridiculed it. In our current politicization of everything, Christian vulnerability has become another—very powerful—wedge issue.

* * * *

DONALD TRUMP'S RISE to the presidency divided the country in an unprecedented way. His platform in 2016, built on many of the unheard concerns of blue-collar, rural, middle-class, white evangelical Americans, promoted a fear of the liberal agenda and an America where "progressives" are the majority. But Trump's most detailed calls for protection were on behalf of Christians. Throughout both of his campaigns and during his tenure, Trump has deliberately played to Christians' anxieties, fanned them, and weaponized them. Consider the following examples.

In September 2016, Trump told Christian groups that "Christian faith is not the past but the present and the future. Make it stronger." He went on to say, "Our media culture often mocks and demeans people of faith" and "our politicians have really abandoned" Christians, but in "[a] Trump administration, our Christian heritage will be cherished, protected, defended, like you've never seen before." He drove the message home after his win, stating forcefully in a January 2016 speech delivered to a packed auditorium at the evangelical Liberty University, "We're going to protect Christianity."

Throughout his term, President Trump routinely employed rhetoric about protecting Christianity and fighting the Democrats, who wage a "war on values." At the October 2019 Value Voters Summit, Trump linked patriotism and citizenry with Christianity, painting America as a "home for proud people of faith" and emphasizing the "power of prayer and the eternal glory of God." He went on to accuse the "ultra Left" of waging war on these "true" Americans. The "radical Left," he said, is "trying to hound you from the workplace, expel you from the public square, and weaken the American family, and indoctrinate our children. They resent and disdain faithful Americans who hold fast to our nation's historic values. And, if given the chance, they would use every instrument of government power . . . to try to shut you down." The message was indisputable: if the Democrats have their way, America will lose its familial and historical values. Or as *Politico* put it, "The president "paint[ed] the Democratic Party as standing against everything [conservative Christians] are for."

Trump revisited these themes a few months later at a Miami megachurch. Red MAGA hats filled the church, seven thousand people swaying to the sounds of Christian rock. It was Trump's first public appearance after the controversial US drone strike that killed Maj. Gen. Qassim Suleimani of Iran, and Trump's message to his evangelical supporters was that God is "on our side." He also took the opportunity to address a recent *Christianity Today* editorial that had called for his removal from the White House. He criticized it indirectly by calling on stage Cissie Graham Lynch, a granddaughter of Billy Graham, the founder of *Christianity Today*. With her by his side, Trump reminded his audience that it would be perilous for them to abandon him: "Evangelical Christians of every denomination and believers of every faith have never had a greater champion, not even close, in the White House, than you have right now. . . . We've done things that nobody thought was possible. Together we're not only defending our constitutional rights. We're also defending religion itself, which is under siege."

Moments later, faith leaders stood near him, grasping the sleeves and shoulders of his dark suit. Those who couldn't reach stretched their hands toward him, along with the masses of faithful supporters, palms upturned and yearning. Trump went on with his speech, toggling between mocking Democrats as antireligious and touting his policy focus on religion and family. On the latter, he foreshadowed his forthcoming religious liberty guidelines, which would "safeguard students and teachers' First Amendment rights to pray in our schools." (Trump oversold himself; the guidelines were merely restatements of those issued by the Bush and Clinton administrations.)

On January 16, 2020—Religious Freedom Day—he issued the guidelines in the Oval Office, noting, "Tragically, there is a growing totalitarian impulse on the far left that seeks to punish, restrict, and even prohibit religious expression." A few weeks later, at the National Prayer Breakfast in Washington, D.C., he again warned that "religion in this country and religion all over the world—certain religions in particular—are under siege. We won't let that happen. We are going to protect our religions. We are going to protect Christianity. We are going to protect our great ministers and pastors and rabbis and all of the people that we so cherish and that we so respect." Over and over again, the message was that Trump is the answer, the defender of religious freedom amid the "cultural war" with the progressive Left.

In March and April 2020, Trump and others in his orbit used the COVID-19 shutdown to prove Trump's credentials as a defender of religion. In the early weeks, Trump repeatedly said we'd have the country open in time for Easter, when he'd love to see "packed churches." In the months to follow, he seized the opportunity, threatening to overrule states that refused to open houses of worship (despite his lacking the authority to do so). The *New York Times* described it well: "President Trump may not consider church essential to his personal life, but it may be to his political future." He was speaking directly to the core of his voter base, emphasizing the need for "more prayer, not less" and the essentialness of religion to Americans' lives.

In June 2020, in the midst of nationwide protests and vandalism after the killing of George Floyd, Trump did not hesitate to wield religion as a political tool. After speaking in the Rose Garden about using law and order to quell the riots, he walked across the street to St. John's Episcopal Church. Police used tear gas and force to clear Trump's path. Once in front of the church, Trump stood awkwardly holding up a Bible. Critics assailed it as an ill-conceived "photo-op" and a perversion of the very religion he sought to represent. But to many of Trump's more conservative supporters, "the pandering wasn't an act of inauthenticity; it was a sign of allegiance" to Christian beliefs that "yes, God hates racism," but "God also hates lawlessness." Even though PRRI found a 15 percent drop in favorability among white evangelicals between the beginning of the COVID-19 shutdown in March and the protests in late May, prominent evangelicals did not reflect that disapproval. David Brody, a news anchor at the Christian Broadcasting Network, wrote, "I don't know about you but I'll take a president with a Bible in his hand in front of a church over far left violent radicals setting a church on fire any day of the week." In contrast, the Episcopal bishop of Washington, the Right Reverend Mariann Budde, said, "The president just used a Bible . . . as a backdrop for a message antithetical to the teachings of Jesus," while James Martin, a Jesuit priest, tweeted, "Let me be clear. This is revolting. The Bible is not a prop. A church is not a photo op. Religion is not a political tool. God is not your plaything."

Religion was again on full display at the August 2020 Republican National Convention. Trump set up a stark contrast between Democrats, who see America as a "wicked nation that must be punished for its sins," and Republicans, who see it as "the greatest and most exceptional nation in the history of the world!" The election was nothing less than a battle for the soul of America: "In America, we don't turn to government to restore our souls. We put our faith in almighty God." He claimed that his opponent, Joe Biden, "supports deadly sanctuary cities" and wanted to end the travel bans from "jihadist nations"; noted that during the Democratic National Convention, the words *under God* were omitted from the Pledge of Allegiance, "not once, but twice. We will never do that"; and as he neared the end of his speech, he said America's story began with our "ancestors" arriving on these shores with their Bibles handy: "They loved their families, they loved their country, and they loved their God! When opportunity beckoned, they picked up their Bibles, packed up their belongings, climbed into covered wagons, and set out west for the next adventure."

Others on Trump's team have also emphasized the theme of religion under threat. At the convention, Donald Trump Jr. took the lead: "People of faith are under attack. You're not allowed to go to church, but mass chaos in the streets gets a pass. It's almost like this election is shaping up to be church, work, and school versus rioting, looting, and vandalism." Pence went so far as to quote scripture but swapped out biblical language for political buzzwords. He paraphrased Hebrews 12 ("And let us run with perseverance the race marked out for us, fixing our eyes on Jesus, the pioneer and perfecter of faith") as "So let's run the race marked out for us. Let's fix our eyes on Old Glory and all she represents. Let's fix our eyes on this land of heroes and let their courage inspire." The paraphrase, in essence, conflated salvation with nation. Some Christians were shocked and called it "idolatry," but still others said they were grateful for Pence's "artful" incorporation of biblical references.

A few weeks after the convention, Trump again had an opportunity to give his conservative religious base exactly what it wanted. When former Supreme Court Justice Ruth Bader Ginsburg died on September 18, 2020, Trump moved quickly to fill the vacancy. With the guidance of evangelical leaders, he chose Amy Coney Barrett, whose faith had become a major talking point ever since Democratic senators chided her for being too religious. In 2017, when Senator Dianne Feinstein told Barrett "the dogma lives loudly within you, and that's a concern," Republican groups printed the line on T-shirts and framed Barrett as a hero.

Others in the Trump administration have also helped solidify its reputation as the preeminent defender of traditional Christian faith. US attorney general William Barr in an October 2019 speech at Notre Dame University accused "secularists" and "progressives" of intentionally utilizing "mass communications, popular culture, the entertainment industry, and academia" to destroy traditional religious values. In his view, the secularist project has led to mental illness, the breakdown of families, and violence: "Among these militant secularists are many so-called 'progressives.' But where is the progress?" The solution, Barr said, is a return to faith and a "Judeo-Christian moral system."

That same month, Secretary of State Mike Pompeo gave a talk titled "Being a Christian Leader" at an American Association of Christian Counselors conference. "I know some people in the media will break out the pitchforks when they hear that I ask God for direction in my work," he said, before going on to talk about how his focus "is not just on being a leader . . . I want to talk today about being a Christian leader." The talk was later featured on the homepage of the US Department of State and can still be found on the agency's website.

In June 2018, Barr's predecessor, then Attorney General Jeff Sessions, used Romans 13, a Bible passage, to justify the Trump administration's separation of families at the United States-Mexico border. He told Americans "to obey the laws of the government because God has ordained them for the purpose of order," for "orderly and lawful processes are good in themselves and protect the weak and lawful." The next month, Sessions announced the formation of the US Department of Justice's new religious liberty task force and said it was set up in part to combat the forces of secularism: "A dangerous movement, undetected by many, is now challenging and eroding our great tradition of religious freedom. There can be no doubt. This is no little matter. It must be confronted and defeated." He went on to warn, "We have gotten to the point where courts held that morality cannot be a basis for law."

Several times throughout his talk, Sessions lamented the culture where the greeting "Merry Christmas" was under attack: "President Trump heard this concern. I believe this unease is one reason that he was elected. In substance, he said he respected people of faith and he promised to protect them in the free exercise of their faith. He declared we would say 'Merry Christmas' again." Recall that in Jones's account of white Christian America, it was a place "where few gave a second thought to saying 'Merry Christmas!'" Sessions's talk was clearly aimed at a particular, nostalgic audience.

Sessions also wove into his talk three references to Jack Phillips, a Christian baker who had declined to bake a wedding cake for a gay couple. "We've all seen the ordeal faced so bravely by Jack Phillips," he said, going on to add that the Justice Department had, under Sessions's guidance, "proud[ly]" filed a brief in support of Phillips. Phillips's "ordeal" represented the "changing cultural climate for the future of religious liberty in this country."

The Trump administration time and again seized on this changing cultural climate to set up a culture war between evangelicals and liberals. This language sometimes appeals to political goals, other times to religious goals. Recall that Whitehead and Perry said non-nationalist evangelicals are thinking about a particular system of moral beliefs (religious goals), whereas Christian nationalists' interests are about who Americans are as a people and whose preferences should be reflected in public policy (political goals). Sessions's citation of Romans 13 is a classic example of the latter.

The language is also uniformly dramatic, warning of a dire threat that only Trump can forestall. As Peter Wehner notes in *The Atlantic*, Trump has succeeded in making "many white evangelical Christians . . . deeply fearful of what a Trump loss would mean for America, American culture, and American Christianity. If a Democrat is elected president, they believe, it might all come crashing down around us."

> If you listen to Trump supporters who are evangelical . . . you
> will hear adjectives applied to those on the left that could easily

be used to describe a Stalinist regime . . . During the 2016 election, for example, the influential evangelical author and radio talk-show host Eric Metaxas said, "In all of our years, we faced all kinds of struggles. The only time we faced an existential struggle like this was in the Civil War and in the Revolution when the nation began . . . We are on the verge of losing it as we could have lost it in the Civil War."

Conservative media further harden this echo chamber. "Sometimes the hosts are repeating the president's signature phrases. Sometimes the president appears to take his cues from television pundits," the *New York Times* explained in a piece on how conservative media manipulate listeners' feelings of being under "siege." Focusing on Trump rhetoric about immigration, the article noted that use of terms like "invaders" and "invasion" has surged during the Trump presidency, "appearing on more than three hundred Fox News broadcasts. The vast majority of those were spoken by Fox News hosts and guests, but some included clips of Mr. Trump using that language at rallies and other public appearances."

This language is alarming. It defines American national identity as white and Anglo-Protestant and brands diverse religions and ethnicities as un-American, even anti-American. Trump uses the language to appeal to the Christian nationalists in his base, but his critics do not differentiate between Christian nationalists and evangelicals generally, and falsely assume that Trump is appealing to all evangelicals. When critics respond to Trump, they criticize not just the media personalities and the Trump administration but also the conservative white evangelicals who voted for him. And that's where Trump's political manipulation worked doubly to his advantage.

Trump centered his remarks on conservative white evangelicals, leading his opponents to center their attacks on them, too. In the process, conservative white evangelicals and their substantive needs and concerns are excoriated as fundamentally evil. Matthew, my email buddy, told me the same thing: "The best thing for Trump is for white, Christian suburban swing voters to watch MSNBC. Those voters will be belittled, mocked, and chastised repeatedly." For example, as I'll describe in chapter 3, the religious liberty issue related to same-sex marriage typically gets scorned as an open-and-shut case of bigotry.

So, yes, Trump played on anxieties and stereotypes about evangelicals—but liberals did nothing to reduce that sense of anxiety. Conservative white evangelicals are routinely conflated with Christian nationalists and with racists. We learned earlier that nationalists actively seek power and control, whereas non-nationalists take a more defensive posture. But most popular commentary does not make this distinction. *USA Today* columnist Kirsten Powers wrote, "Conservative white evangelicals who are supporting Trump do so because they are mad that they can't impose their worldview on the rest of the country, whether it relates to gays and lesbians, transgender people and nonwhites. They . . . should stop portraying their thirst for influence as some Christian mission and be honest about their motivations in supporting Trump. This is not about God. It's about power."

In his book *Believe Me* and elsewhere, scholar John Fea called evangelical Trump voters "court evangelicals": "Courtiers have one goal: to gain access to and win the favor of the monarch. Such access brings privilege and power and an opportunity to influence the king on important matters." And in THE RACIAL DEMONS THAT HELP EXPLAIN EVANGELICAL SUPPORT FOR TRUMP, *Vox* writer Nancy Wadsworth argued that Christian commentators who think Trump's evangelical supporters are not "personally prejudiced" have it completely wrong: "Trump's racism and misogyny might actually resonate with the evangelical base . . . In fact, racism and intolerance are more woven into the fabric of evangelicalism than these Christian critics care to accept."

Still others have said these people are a "cult." In a 2018 commentary, Reza Aslan said that the "most important" fact about white evangelicals in America is that Trump turned them into a "cult." "Donald Trump has turned a large swath of white evangelical Christianity into a cult, into a religious cult, a dangerous religious cult. All the signs are there." White evangelicals almost worship Trump, and when their ideas begin to butt up "against the reality of a failed leadership," they will "double down." Aslan didn't explain what he meant by "double down" but warned it'll be "catastrophic." And in April 2020, during the first months of the coronavirus outbreak, he had his chance to elaborate. In an interview on MSNBC, he pointed to the white evangelicals who gathered in churches in defiance of stay-at-home orders. Evangelicals had long anticipated a siege, and now that it was real, they were going to fight it. That, Aslan said, was classic cultlike behavior, except this time they were "no longer a cult of personality" but "a doomsday cult": "This is the kind of behavior, this cultlike behavior, that can lead to the deaths of thousands of people."

Author Katherine Stewart took up a similar line of argument in her *New York Times* piece originally titled THE ROAD TO CORONAVIRUS HELL WAS PAVED BY EVANGELICALS. After significant online backlash, the *Times* changed the title. But the original wording captured the conflation of white evangelicals with, in Stewart's words, "a movement that denies science, bashes government and prioritize[s] loyalty over professional expertise." As one commentator noted in the *Christian Post*, "If Stewart had focused her article on the cavalier attitudes of some Christian leaders, I would [have] added my hearty Amen, having written and spoken similar things as well. But the current article paints a false picture, recklessly scapegoating evangelical Christians in the process."

The tenor of the commentary reflects the concerns Matthew expressed in his emails to me: White evangelicals are not just wrong but evil. Conservative white evangelicals are talked about as power-hungry, racist, cultlike, anti-science, dismissive of human security and public health, and blindly obedient to President Trump. The commentators might not intend to refer to all conservative white evangelicals, but the distinctions are usually lost—not just between white evangelicals and Christian nationalists but also between religious and nominal evangelicals, and even Protestants and Catholics. In popular discourse, "white evangelicals" includes Fox News consumers, nominally religious Christians who lean Republican, and even non-Protestants like "evangelical Catholics" (Vice President Mike Pence used the term on the 2016 campaign trail; he grew up Catholic but is now evangelical). While white evangelicalism in the United States has always had racial and political dimensions, the popular narrative today depicts it as primarily (or entirely) a cultural and political affiliation instead of a theological position.

The generalization makes it possible to overlook the good work being done by those who take their religion seriously. As two experts on evangelicalism wrote in the *Dallas Morning News*, "Even amid the COVID-19 pandemic, bad news about Christians (especially white evangelicals) continues. . . . Much of this criticism is, unfortunately, well-deserved. But COVID-19 has also demonstrated how profoundly America and the world depend upon the quiet work of ministries and congregations in times of crisis." They go on to describe the work many evangelicals were doing in their communities—things like providing shelters, distributing food, and offering benevolence funds for those in financial need.

The generalization also makes it possible to speak of conservative white evangelicals as a monolith with uniform motivations for supporting Trump. But as law professor John Inazu explains in *Christianity Today*, pro-Trump evangelicals can be divided into "Trump lovers" and "Pragmatists." Pragmatists didn't like Trump as a person but saw him as the only viable option "against a Democratic Party that they view as opposed to their values." Or as one of my roundtable participants told me, "Many conservative Christians don't like Trump." Their attitude is that "I'll vote for him because the Democrats hate everything I hold dear. The other party absolutely hates my guts, doesn't even want to coexist with me, and wants me punished by the law and labeled a bigot."

In a series of tweets about the 2020 election, evangelical leader Andrew Walker put it this way: "Given current rhetoric, there seems to be no operative, justificatory principle that allows one to vote as a citizen of this nation without some degree of compromise." The "rhetoric" he refers to is partly about policy. For example, most conservative white evangelicals prioritize the pro-life cause. In 2009, a number of national leaders drafted the Manhattan Declaration and placed the protection of human life— including the unborn life—as a top voting issue for religious conservatives. Despite this, across both the 2016 and 2020 presidential elections, only one Democratic nominee showed sympathy for their position. As we'll see in chapter 3, Democrats also oppose compromise measures on LGBTQ rights and religious freedom.

Walker's "rhetoric" concern is also about how conservatives and their interests are talked about. On abortion, the Democratic Party paints conservative evangelicals as sexists upholding patriarchy and misogyny in the name of religion. On religious liberty, they're portrayed as hateful bigots. On their anxious grappling with a fast-changing America, it's even worse.

We saw earlier that there's a negative correlation between religious commitment and exclusionary attitudes. On the flip side, feelings of persecution make nationalist attitudes more fervent. So, treating the range of conservative white evangelicals as uniformly racist and bigoted might make it easier to dismiss their concerns as illegitimate, but it ultimately exacerbates the problem and tribalizes the siege mentality.

It also contributes to its weaponization.

* * * *

IN *POLITICAL TRIBES*: *Group Instinct and the Fate of Nations*, Yale law professor Amy Chua shares the story of one her students, Giovanni. He "came from the humblest origins," having grown up in an old taco truck with his Mexican American family and later moving up to an eighteen-hundred-dollar motor home. A retired white couple from rural Louisiana, Walter and Lee Ann Jones, lived in the same Texas trailer park and were always kind to Giovanni's family. The Joneses helped set up the taco truck and would bring sweets for Giovanni's family from the local food pantry, where they volunteered. During Thanksgiving, they made sure Giovanni's family had a turkey and sides. Walter also loved guns and told the family that he would always protect them. "'There's a lot of bad people here, but I dare them to try and mess with you. They will regret it.'"

Ten years later, though, in the 2016 presidential election, the Joneses voted for Trump. Giovanni also learned from their social media posts that the Joneses held racist attitudes. But Giovanni saw a distinction. He acknowledged their "racist attitudes toward 'faceless brown people generally,'" but he also emphasized that the Joneses had "'treat[ed] my family with nothing but love and respect, despite our Mexican descent and immigrant status. In fact, the Joneses even consider[ed] my sister and me to be their adoptive-grandkids. Furthermore, the food pantry where Walter volunteered primarily served the black community. On multiple occasions, I observed firsthand the joy it brought Walter to help these communities.'"

According to Chua, Giovanni's view exemplifies "a critical paradox that progressives often overlook or dismiss, to their own detriment." First, he talks about racism in a way that most progressives reject. Among progressives, once you deem someone a racist, you shouldn't engage with them or compromise in any way. As Matthew put it in his email to me: if someone "can be cast as 'racists' or 'white supremacists' or 'bigots,'" then there's no need to take their views seriously. *[W]ho wants to engage in discussion with a disgusting and vile human?*" But Giovanni rejected this approach and was not only willing to engage the Joneses but also see them as decent people.

Importantly, the Joneses didn't see themselves as racist, and when liberals called them bigots, the Joneses felt unjustly attacked, which in turn created a "chasm of anger." While the Joneses likely hold unconscious or unintentional biases (defined as "social stereotypes about certain groups of people that individuals form outside their own conscious awareness"), what's relevant here is how others' rejection of them makes them feel spurned and threatened. When attacked, people retreat into their tribes. As one person shared in the *American Conservative*: "I'm a white guy. I'm a well-educated intellectual who enjoys small arthouse movies, coffeehouses and classic blues. If you didn't know any better, you'd probably mistake me for a lefty urban hipster. And yet I find some of the alt-right stuff exerts a pull even on me [because] I am constantly bombarded with messages telling me that I'm a cancer, I'm a problem, everything is my fault."

White evangelicals are pushed and pulled in the same way. Nationally influential pastor Dr. Timothy Keller, of Redeemer Presbyterian Church in New York City, thinks it's because they are "a very significant voting bloc" in America: "You have both conservative operatives doing everything they can to alienate evangelicals from the liberals, and liberal operatives doing everything they can to alienate the rest of the country from the evangelicals. We're constantly being pummeled over certain things." Keller says this is also a reason American evangelicals are so much more politically aligned than evangelicals outside the United States.

None of this is to say evangelicals aren't responsible for their choices. In chapters 6 and 7, I explore a variety of strategies for overcoming toxic tribalism, including basic mindfulness about how partisan leaders and demagogues manipulate our vulnerability to suit their political ends. If we understand how politicians use us, we won't be so quick to fall for their tactics.

Maybe we can even break the vicious cycle. Conservative white evangelicals are experiencing actual demographic shifts that would leave any previously dominant group feeling overwhelmed and vulnerable. Protestant beliefs and practices informed American social norms for nearly two and a half centuries, and the disruption of those norms acts on conservative white evangelicals psychologically. And when the so-called elite culture mocks and scorns those very real feelings of threat, they create an opening for demagogues and reactionaries, pundits and politicians, to weaponize the vulnerability: Trump "owned the libs," and conservatives loved it. Chua quotes one Trump voter as saying, "'Maybe I'm just so sick of being called a bigot that my anger at the authoritarian left has pushed me to support this seriously flawed man.'"

This phenomenon is not unique to American conservatives. In fact, it is emblematic of conservatives throughout Europe and is at the root of populism in those countries. From Marine Le Pen's National Rally in France, to Matteo Salvini's Five Star Movement in Italy, to Viktor Orbán's Fidesz in Hungary, populist leaders and their parties are becoming increasingly prominent, and scholars say political and cultural vulnerabilities are a big reason why.

The popular conception of populism on the political Left is that it is driven by some combination of factors such as racism, short-lived backlash to immigrants, "the system," and economic scarcity. But politics professor Matthew Goodwin says that although these factors play a role, their influence in the debate is "wholly disproportionate to their significance, and they distract from dealing with the actual grievances that are fueling populism." In a piece for the *Guardian* titled NATIONAL POPULISM IS UNSTOPPABLE—AND THE LEFT STILL DOESN'T UNDERSTAND IT, Goodwin writes, "Today's thinkers, writers and groups on the left have subscribed to a number of theories [about populism], all of which are incorrect." One of them is the mistaken belief that we can blame it all on racism, "and perhaps even latent public support for fascism." Racism is an important piece of the problem, but outsized focus on it takes attention away from the issues that need to be addressed to bring about real change and healing. That's what Giovanni did right: he didn't dismiss the Joneses as unworthy of engagement because they held racist attitudes.

In his book with Roger Eatwell, *National Populism: The Revolt Against Liberal Democracy*, Goodwin says what we really need to look at are "four deep-rooted societal shifts: the 'four Ds'"—high levels of political distrust;

deep-seated fears about the perceived destruction of national values and cultures amid unprecedented ethnic change and rapid rates of immigration; anxiety about deprivation and the loss of jobs and income; and de-alignment, or the breakdown of bonds between voters and traditional parties.

That second D, the perceived destruction of national values and cultures, is connected to concerns about political correctness. Such "restrictive communicative norms" make people feel like they can't vocalize their concerns, Goodwin says. What these people want is "cohesive, inclusive communities that share a core skeleton of values." They "aren't looking for a cultural straitjacket," but they do want some core similarities like language and values that are shared by all people. These similarities foster social in-group trust—they give people the self-esteem they crave from a cohesive social group—and in many parts of the world, that cohesion is lacking or perceived to be lacking.

Goodwin also points to the pace of change. He says it's not true that populists don't want diversity. Instead, the problem for them is that diversity has grown exponentially in a short amount of time and white conservatives are struggling to adapt. The debate isn't about "open versus closed"; it's more useful to think of it as a debate between people who are comfortable with fast versus slow change. "The research since 2016 shows that one of the key drivers of populism is rapid demographic change in areas that were historically predominantly white and suddenly experienced an injection of diversity." Míriam Juan-Torres González from More in Common put it this way: "Below a certain threshold, an influx of immigrants does not seem to strengthen a particular notion of the in-group. It is when immigration is perceived as posing a challenge to the 'normative order' that the need to retreat to a narrower definition of that 'us' seems to develop."

The *New York Times* podcast *The Daily* found similarly in its five-part series, "The Battle for Europe." The series examines the rise of populism in France, Italy, Poland, and Germany. In each episode, the reporters identify feelings "of being left behind, and of being ignored." In Poland, for example, the populist is "the Polish person who feels that their Catholic values are being sort of fundamentally threatened." In each country examined, the populists reject "the tenets of liberal democracy—capitalism, globalization, the protection of minorities—because in a way, each of these tenets feels like a rejection of them."

This research gives us a new way to interpret American dynamics, too. Ezra Klein says the US political correctness wars "are proxy wars for bigger, more fundamental concerns over the direction of the culture." Conservative white evangelicals in the United States—the ones who aren't necessarily inclined toward Christian nationalism but who are genuinely worried about their place in America—are similarly focused on culture. Influential evangelical leaders understand these fears and are working to help their followers overcome them. Dr. Russell Moore, president of the Ethics and Religious Liberty Commission of the Southern Baptist Convention (SBC), tells evangelicals to stop "seeing the culture as something [they] 'had' and are now 'losing.'" Instead, they need to become a "prophetic minority," or "those who have been sent into this culture in order to reach it."

Moore is careful to say that being a prophetic minority "does not mean victim status . . . The loss of a majority mind-set is hastened by cultural and political trends, and we should welcome this loss. It started with good intentions . . . to normalize Christianity by finding a goal that the church and the culture could agree on." But seeing themselves as a dominant majority also "leads to a siege mentality that seeks to catalog offenses of what's going wrong in the culture, in order to shock the faithful into action."

It's no surprise then that Moore has little patience for the evangelicals who fell for Trump's tribal rhetoric. After Trump proposed in December 2015 to ban all Muslims from entering the United States, Moore challenged his followers to "denounce this reckless, demagogic rhetoric" if they care "an iota about religious liberty." He also later filed a legal brief in support of a mosque in New Jersey—and faced tremendous backlash from the SBC.

Other leaders are also challenging the status quo. Dr. Richard Mouw, former president of the evangelical Fuller Theological Seminary, writes in his book *Restless Faith* that while it's okay to hold onto the "evangelical" label despite its politicization, believers have to assess the *way* they hold these beliefs. He preaches "a kind of evangelicalism that is both convicted yet humble, robust and generous, open-hearted and curious, faithful to the past's legacy but always restless and willing to be self-critical." Mouw openly engages with Muslims, and his protégé, Matthew Kaemingk, is at the forefront of building evangelical-Muslim relationships.

Moore, Mouw, Kaemingk, and others are working within evangelicalism to make change, but non-evangelicals who want to help bridge the gulf also have to grapple with conservatives' concerns and struggles. This is especially the case for people seeking to mend the evangelical-Muslim divide. Writing about European populism, Shadi Hamid of the Brookings Institution says its defining features are anti-Muslim and anti-Islam sentiment: attitudes toward Muslims are a "powerful proxy for a long list of primarily cultural issues and grievances, including . . . the decline of Christianity, race, and demographic concerns." French writer Renaud Camus describes the core concern as "the great replacement"; about Muslims specifically, he "warns grotesquely of a 'genocide by substitution,' the replacement of white French and European order by Muslim hordes in a plot orchestrated by cosmopolitan elite." Though the American and European situations are importantly distinct, this idea of Muslims as proxies for bigger issues is true of America, too—as evidenced by, among other things, the centrality of anti-Muslim measures to Trump's 2016 campaign.

To resolve anti-Muslim hostility and heal the Christian-Muslim divide, we have to understand both the mechanics of polarization (how group identity and intergroup bias works) and the people who are polarized.

When Klein was asked why his book, *Why We're Polarized*, doesn't have any villains, he said, "So there are obviously people I think of as villains in the sense that I find their values toxic. But, what I try to do with the book is tell you how a machine works . . . a model of how to understand politics. . . . What I want to tell you is how the thing is working." On mechanics, it's important to understand that religious tribalism in times of threat results in out-group hostility, not just in the form of prejudice but also a desire to limit Muslims' civil and constitutional rights (see chapters 4 and 5).

How do we prevent this anger? Among other things, we have to grapple with evangelicals' actual grievances and not be "distracted" by claims of racism and fascism—particularly because such a distraction is hugely counterproductive. In the European context, sociology professor Göran Adamson says that when the Left belittles the concerns of populist voters and labels them ignorant or racist, they "merely fuel the flames of anti-elitist anguish among [a] large section of the population." What's more helpful, he says, is to "approach the electorate with a less self-righteous attitude, ensuring that their voices are being acknowledged."

The Daily also came to this conclusion in its five-country examination: "The defenders of liberal democracy are going to have to really find ways to respond to these conservative needs. They're going to have to find a way to paint a vision of the future that speaks to people and that pays attention to people. . . . Liberal democracy is not going to win that battle if it doesn't change, if liberals don't take a very hard look at themselves." Chua advises similarly in the American context when she notes that "white identity politics has . . . gotten a tremendous recent boost from the Left, whose relentless berating, shaming, and bullying might have done more damage than good." Similarly, in his *New York Times* piece, WHO CAN WIN AMERICA'S POLITICS OF HUMILIATION? Thomas Friedman wrote:

> People will absorb hardship, hunger and pain. They will be grateful for jobs, cars and benefits. But if you make people feel

humiliated, they will respond with a ferocity unlike any other emotion, or just refuse to lift a finger for you. As Nelson Mandela once observed, "There is nobody more dangerous than one who has been humiliated."

By contrast, if you show people respect, if you affirm their dignity, it is amazing what they will let you say to them or ask of them. Sometimes it just takes listening to them, but deep listening— not just waiting for them to stop talking. Because listening is the ultimate sign of respect. What you say when you listen speaks more than any words.

It can be hard to listen openly without voicing judgment. When white Christians talk about being the "new minority," they ignore the reality of smaller, far more marginalized groups in the United States. Even with demographic shifts, white evangelicals are a quarter of the population, whereas Jews constitute 2 percent and Muslims 1 percent. And even with smaller numbers, white evangelicals do not face the systemic disadvantages in housing, employment, and education that racial, sexual, and other denigrated groups face. So, to hear them complain about "persecution" can be hard to bear for many who have experienced much more tangible and urgent suffering.

But empathy is crucial to forward progress. More in Common notes that each side has its own stories of oppression and victimhood, but "tribalism makes conversations about these issues harder, because it robs individuals of their humanity and reduces them to members of in-groups and out-groups." To build connection across difference, Brené Brown says, again, that we have to "zoom in." We have to be willing to "intentionally be with people who are different from us" and "learn how to listen, have hard conversations . . . and be more curious than defensive." Speaking purely pragmatically, if we mock or berate conservative Christians for feeling like the "new minority," they'll feel like the new minority even more.

There is some evidence already that honest listening works in the Christian-Muslim context. One focus group study shared with me privately found that conservatives respond favorably to Muslims when Muslims "acknowledge their concerns and make them feel heard." This chapter was my first foray into "zooming in" and acknowledging the concerns of many Christians. The next chapter looks at how these concerns play out in the religious freedom arena.

Religious Freedom Under Attack

IT WAS A HOT SUMMER day in 2014. I was teetering at the edge of a small, square platform, holding onto my spot next to my colleagues Adele Keim, Angela Wu Howard, Kristina Arriaga, and Lori Windham. Lori was at the podium, six microphones thrust near her mouth, a sign wedged beneath them proclaiming in large letters: #ReligiousFreedom #WomenInControl. The message echoed the signs being waved around us—hot pink proclamations like WOMEN FOR RELIGIOUS FREEDOM. Behind us loomed a frieze of the United States Supreme Court.

My then law firm, the Becket Fund for Religious Liberty, had just won the landmark case *Burwell v. Hobby Lobby Stores, Inc.*

Hobby Lobby, a crafts company owned and operated by a devout Christian couple, David and Barbara Green, had contested the part of the Affordable Care Act (ACA) that required employers to cover twenty FDA-approved contraceptives in their employee insurance plans. The Greens objected to covering four drugs on the list that could prevent a fertilized egg from implanting in a woman's uterus. This, they said, constituted abortion, and facilitating abortion in any way, including paying for these drugs, violated the Greens' religious beliefs.

As I would explain a few hours later in an interview for Al Jazeera America, the Greens weren't trying to stop their female employees from using these IUDs and drugs. They just couldn't pay for them, as it would make them complicit in something their religion said was sinful. The Court ruled in Hobby Lobby's favor because there was no need to force the Greens to violate their religion—the government had already come up with an alternative route for getting these drugs to any employee who wanted them. "A win-win solution!" I said.

A nonwhite, American Muslim woman defending Hobby Lobby on a Qatari-owned television network? That's a stark disruption of our tribal mega-identities. Brown-skinned religious minorities are traits of the liberal mega-identity, and religious cases brought by white conservative Christians indisputably belong to the conservative mega-identity. The rights of each tribe are seen as in tension with one another: for marginalized minorities to have rights, white conservative Christians have to be stopped from asserting their own claims.

How did religious liberty become so tribalized?

* * * *

IN MANY WAYS, of course, *Hobby Lobby* was inherently political. The fight over sexuality is an old one in American politics. Professor Marie Griffith writes in *Moral Combat: How Sex Divided American Christians & Fractured American Politics* that our public debates over sexuality have been "so numerous, so ferocious, so religiously inflected" that they are "immune to definitive resolution."

But as this chapter will explore, the current battle is different in important ways. First, as we explored in chapter 1, conservative white evangelicals (as a subset of white Protestants broadly) are experiencing dramatic demographic shifts. Once highly influential in American culture, conservative white Protestants went from winning to losing the culture, and now often feel like they are struggling just to carve out a space for themselves. Alongside this is the rise of what journalist Christopher Caldwell calls the "civil rights approach to politics," which helps disparaged groups articulate their grievances in the language of rights.

Consider how this works with racial shifts. While white tribalism is partly a continuation of the centuries-old tradition in which white male Protestants dominated America, today, many conservative white Americans say that white identity politics has been foisted onto them by the Left. In this view, the Left encourages everyone else in America—black, Asian, Hispanic, Jewish, Muslim—to celebrate his or her racial and ethnic identity, but, Amy Chua says, the Left also tells white Americans that "they must never, ever do so." The problem, though, is that "tribal instinct is not so easy to suppress," particularly when it's combined with a fast-changing—and fast-browning—America. Together, the suppressed tribal instinct and feelings of demographic threat have produced tense tribal dynamics.

Ezra Klein agrees. Citing Ashley Jardina's book *White Identity Politics*, he says, "White political identity is conditional." When whites don't feel threatened, they don't exert their political identity. But it "emerges in periods of threat and challenges—periods like this one. Demographic change, the election of the first black president, and the downstream cultural and political consequences of both have 'led a sizeable proportion of whites to believe that their racial group, and the benefits that group enjoys, are endangered. As a result, this racial solidarity now plays a central role in the way many whites orient themselves to the political and social world.'" (Again, though, Jardina also found that whites can rally around their racial identity without also attacking nonwhites.)

Identity politics have implications for rights, too. In *The Age of Entitlement: America Since the Sixties*, Caldwell argues that the Civil Rights Act of 1964—the main purpose of which was to rectify racial injustice—created "a structure of judicial and bureaucratic supervision and redress" that today has expanded so much that it has become a "rival constitutional system." That is, an ever-expanding list of minorities today demands equality under the civil rights system, and their claims are privileged over freedoms of speech and press protected by the original Constitution. The dominance of the civil rights system also means that, to protect their interests, people must frame their issues in civil rights terms. White identity politics is a result of this, Caldwell says, because in this new conception of rights, "group identities are the only ones that count."

This also applies to religious group identities. With the end of Christian America has come a shift away from traditional Christian values. In January 1996, 59 percent of Americans believed the government should protect traditional values. By 2014, this percentage had dropped to 41 percent. The demographic shift has led traditional Christians to feel like they are a group "despised and degraded," and like other despised groups in a civil rights regime, they defend their interests using the language of civil rights. Caldwell uses *Hobby Lobby* as an example: "Civil rights had been devised for blacks. But its remedies proved useful to a widening circle of groups that, at the time of its passage, had not seemed similarly ill treated: First immigrants. Then women. Then gays. Then, in the *Hobby Lobby* case that came before the Supreme Court in 2014: Christians."

To be clear, minority Christian sects such as Mormons, Jehovah's Witnesses, and the Amish have long made legal arguments in favor of protecting religious liberty, but it wasn't until recently that conservative white Christians generally began to see themselves as a "minority" in need of civil rights protections. This idea of a "new minority" is unsettling for many, given the realities of truly marginalized groups. Similarly unsettling is white Christians' use of civil rights, which were originally formulated to address the deep inequalities faced by blacks. But as Caldwell emphasizes, "a terrible irony of civil rights" is that "members of *any* group that felt itself despised and degraded could defend its interest this way."

Christian conservatives tried to avoid it. Andrew Lewis, in *The Rights Turn in Conservative Christian Politics*, says that traditionally liberalism spoke about rights, while religious conservatives often resisted liberalism's demand that moral arguments be reduced to rights discourse. But that's no longer the case. We have seen a monumental change away from adopting biblical principles as the guide for public discourse, toward replacing them with rights. As Lewis writes, conservative Christians have transitioned from "morality to liberty" in much of their politics.

It's a "seismic shift" but one that was inevitable, given the increasing role of rights in American law and politics. Plus, liberals used the rights discourse to secure victories against conservative traditionalists who were focused on morality. "[W]omen gained access to birth control and abortions . . . gay sex was decriminalized and gay marriage was legalized." These victories, Lewis says, activated the culture wars in American politics.

Abortion advocacy helped precipitate the shift. Until and throughout much of the 1970s, most evangelicals supported a limited right to abortion. For example, the Southern Baptist Convention (SBC) differed in this respect from the more staunchly pro-life National Association of Evangelicals (NAE). But during that decade, individual Southern Baptists increasingly shifted toward the NAE's position, and then in the late 1970s and early 1980s, the "momentum metastasized," leading the SBC to fully adopt the NAE's anti-abortion position. Today, evangelicals lead the movement to end legalized abortion.

With this transition came a new approach to rights. In the late 1970s and 1980s, it helped them speak of abortion in terms of the fetus's "right to life" (terms Catholic anti-abortion activists had been using since the 1930s). In the '80s and '90s it inspired cases under both the Free Speech Clause of the First Amendment and the Equal Access Act of 1984, which forbid public schools from receiving federal funds if they, among other things, don't allow religious students to conduct meetings on campus. Over time, these efforts helped professionalize the movement and cultivate the lawyers corps. Today, the movement is going strong, buoyed by the rise of identity politics and demographic shifts that have left white evangelicals feeling like a despised minority.

Abortion continues to provide much of the substantive frame for these claims. The *Hobby Lobby* case is a classic example of this: the Greens won protections for their anti-abortion beliefs by using the Religious Freedom Restoration Act (RFRA). Enacted in 1993, RFRA was at the time understood—even by evangelicals—as protecting those who lacked political capital. By the end of the '90s, evangelicals began to see themselves as precisely those types of people. Following the 2010 ACA contraceptive mandate, and feeling powerless against it, evangelicals realized RFRA could help them protect their own interests, too.

The abortion-related cases also helped train religious conservatives to speak of their rights in the gay marriage context. Leading evangelicals like Russell Moore and prominent Catholics like Ryan Anderson drew on the legacy of the pro-life movement to argue for the legitimacy of dissenting voices on gay rights, too. Speaking at an ERLC conference, Anderson noted that pro-lifers had earned respect for their perspective by couching it in natural law and natural rights arguments. He went on to say, "Government ultimately should respect the rights of all citizens. And a form of government that's respectful of free association and free contracts and free speech and free exercise of religion would protect citizens' rights to live according to their beliefs that marriage is a union of a man and a woman."

And indeed, this is what Christians argued in the 2018 Supreme Court case *Masterpiece Cakeshop v. Colorado Civil Rights Commission*, which involved a Christian baker who refused on religious grounds to bake a wedding cake for a gay couple. Of course, this and similar cases haven't just provided legal fodder—Lewis writes that "public attitudes and elite rhetoric" transformed the "legal cases to national politics." As conservative Christians in these cases play defense, the offense, in their view, is becoming angrier and ever more ruthless. And because the attack on Christians (the in-group) is almost entirely coming from the opposing party (or political out-group), group dynamics are activated, and many conservative Christians today embrace religious liberty as a partisan tool.

Let's see how that transformation happened with *Hobby Lobby* and *Masterpiece*.

* * * *

WHEN THE ACA contraceptive mandate was enacted in 2010, requiring employers to provide all FDA-approved contraceptives in their employee insurance plans, both Protestant and Catholic organizations that objected to paying for some or all of these drugs used RFRA to protect their interests. Under both the federal and state RFRAs, religious individuals or groups can ask the government to not apply a certain law to them because doing so would force them to violate their religious freedom. In religious liberty law, these are called "exemptions," meaning the religious entity is exempt from a law that everyone else has to follow.

To qualify for an exemption, religious actors have to show that the law they are challenging places a "substantial burden" on their "sincerely held religious belief." Once they demonstrate that, the government has to show it has really good reasons (what the law calls "compelling government interests") to stop them from engaging in particular religious practices. It also has to show that there's no better way to serve the government's interests than restricting the religious practice. Together, these standards make up the "strict scrutiny" test.

The test carefully balances the interests of the religious claimant and the government. No side gets an automatic win, and religious people do not get to use it as a trump card. RFRA instead levels the playing field in court for people with deep religious convictions to be able to argue their case.

When Hobby Lobby won at the Supreme Court, it successfully proved its case under the RFRA standard. First, no one in the case disputed that the Greens' religious beliefs were sincere (because the ruling was limited to "closely held" corporations, the owners' religious beliefs were the ones evaluated). Devout Christians, the Green family believes that "it is by God's grace and provision that Hobby Lobby has endured," so they always strive to run the company in a way they think is consistent with biblical principles. The stores are closed on Sundays and only operate sixty-six hours per week, based on the Greens' religious beliefs that their employees should have the opportunity to spend Sundays with their families. Similarly, they have applied Christian teachings on respect and fairness by increasing their employee wages for several consecutive years and starting full-time workers at 90 percent above the federal minimum wage. Christian teachings have also prevented the Greens from engaging in certain conduct. For example, I noted earlier that the Greens do not drink alcohol and also do not facilitate others' drinking alcohol, so they turn down requests from other businesses to rent the Hobby Lobby trucks to transport alcohol.

So when the Greens said they couldn't pay for IUDS and two drugs required under the ACA (medications believed by the Greens to be abortifacients) because doing so would violate their religious beliefs about abortion, no one in the lawsuit doubted that the Greens were sincere. The Greens passed the first part of the test with flying colors. Then they showed that the government's burden was substantial. If Hobby Lobby did not comply with the mandate, it faced massive fines—as much as $1.3 million per day, or approximately $475 million per year.

When it was the government's turn to show that it had a compelling interest in making the Greens pay for the four abortifacients, and that there wasn't any other way to serve this interest, it failed to do so. A slew of Christian nonprofits had also objected to the contraceptive mandate, and the government had come up with a way to get the drugs to these nonprofits' employees without directly involving the nonprofits themselves—the nonprofit fills out a form and submits it to the government, which prompts the insurer or a third-party organization to provide the coverage instead. The Court in *Hobby Lobby* said that if the government can do that with nonprofits, it can also do it with closely held corporations (that is, corporations with a limited number of shareholders) like Hobby Lobby. Referring to this workaround as an "accommodation," the Court made clear that "the effect of the HHS-created accommodation on the women employed by Hobby Lobby . . . would be precisely *zero*. Under that accommodation, these women would still be entitled to all FDA-approved contraceptives without cost sharing." Even Planned Parenthood acknowledges on its website that after the *Hobby Lobby* decision, the government made sure that "health insurance companies . . . directly provided birth control at no cost to [Hobby Lobby] employees."

To many supporters, the case seemed like a good balance between competing interests. The *Atlantic*'s Emma Green said neither side "gets to be 'right' in this case. No one's religious beliefs can trample someone else's health needs, and even if the government can't force closely held private companies to pay for contraceptives, these companies can't stop their employees from being on birth control." *Hobby Lobby*, she said, is a "balancing act, not a bludgeon—and certainly not an attack on women's rights." Others said it was a straightforward application of the RFRA legal standard. As one writer noted in *Forbes*, "You can bet on hand-wringing and outrage about judicial activism and political motives behind the 5–4 U.S. Supreme Court decision in the *Hobby Lobby* case but, in fact, this case was all but decided in 1993 when Congress passed the Religious Freedom Restoration Act (RFRA)."

But as the writer predicted, much of the public discourse was about political motives. Outlets from MSNBC to *Politico* to the *Washington Post* lamented the "war on women." In HOBBY LOBBY OPENS A NEW FRONT IN THE 'WAR ON WOMEN,' Karen Finney wrote, "It's unacceptable that in 2014, the Supreme Court would legalize a form of discrimination against women." The National Organization for Women said, "Displaying a shocking disregard for women's health and lives, the Supreme Court ruled today . . . that corporations may, in the name of religious 'beliefs,' strip contraception from their employer-based health plans. . . . A 'belief' that works to the detriment of a specific demographic group that has historically experienced discrimination is no more than a religious mask for bigotry."

One writer for *Rewire News Group* said that the goal of "much of the right" was "depriving women of contraception and asserting employer ownership over their private lives." *Hobby Lobby*, critics decried, "was never about religious liberty, but about taking religious and reproductive freedom away from women." To this day, many Americans remain appalled by the Supreme Court's willingness, as they see it, to empower the Greens to interfere with their female employees' personal lives and to subordinate those employees' right to birth control to their own religious preferences.

Legal critics took aim at RFRA. Even though the ACLU had been at the forefront of advocating for RFRA when the statute was enacted in 1993, after *Hobby Lobby* was decided, the ACLU pulled its support for RFRA. In the *Washington Post*, Louise Melling, the deputy legal director of the ACLU, called RFRA "discriminatory": "RFRA is being used as a vehicle for institutions and individuals to argue that their faith justifies myriad harms—to equality, to dignity, to health and to core American values." Her solution was for Congress to adopt the Do No Harm Act, which would amend RFRA "to ensure that federal law protects religious liberty but does not let religion be used—or misused—to harm others."

It's worth noting, however, that while Melling and others backing the Do No Harm Act claim that RFRA has become a tool for an increasingly powerful religious right, the empirical data paints a more nuanced picture. In a 2016 paper, legal scholar Christopher Lund noted that the majority of RFRA cases have little to do with sexual morality or the culture wars: "Whatever else can be said of them, RFRA and state RFRAs have been valuable for religious minorities, who often have no other recourse when the law conflicts with their most basic religious obligations." In a 2018 study, attorneys Luke Goodrich and Rachel Busick reviewed over ten thousand court opinions for religious freedom wins in the previous five years, and in some cases, ten years. They found that "religious minorities are significantly overrepresented in the cases relative to their population, while Christians are significantly underrepresented." They also found that RFRA has been underenforced. Also in 2018, law professors Stephanie Barclay and Mark Rienzi demonstrated that *Hobby Lobby* did not make it significantly less likely that the government would lose religion cases and religious claimants would win. And a 2019 empirical analysis of every federal district court RFRA decision since *Hobby Lobby* found that "while there was an uptick in contraceptive mandate cases following *Hobby Lobby*, RFRA is rarely used, and where litigants bring RFRA claims, they are mostly for individuals with minority religious beliefs."

Still, proponents continue to push the Do No Harm Act. As Melling noted, the statute is relevant not just to *Hobby Lobby*–type cases; it is also meant to prevent Christians' use of RFRA in cases involving LGBTQ individuals. Those cases turn on a disagreement about the nature of marriage. Melling and others see marriage as a legal relationship, whereas many traditional religious believers see it as primarily a religious relationship. Culturally, those two conceptions of marriage are entangled, which in recent years has led to conflicts. Law professor Douglas Laycock explains that Christian conservatives who are "focused on the religious relationship refuse to participate in same-sex weddings or commitment ceremonies.

Some churches will not make their space available, many clergy will not perform the ceremony, and some individuals in the wedding business will not assist with the ceremony or the reception. Conservative Christian counselors will not counsel same-sex couples. Catholic adoption agencies will not place children with same-sex couples."

Among the wedding vendor cases, *Masterpiece* is the most well-known example, and the only case heard by the Supreme Court so far. In 2012, years before Colorado or the Supreme Court legalized gay marriage, Jack Phillips, a Christian baker in Lakewood, Colorado, declined to create a custom wedding cake for a gay couple, Charlie Craig and David Mullins. Phillips was fine with the couple buying a premade cake off his shelf but felt that making a wedding cake specifically for the occasion would implicate him in the celebration of the union, which in turn would violate Phillips's religious beliefs.

When Phillips refused, Craig and Mullins filed a charge with the Colorado Civil Rights Commission alleging discrimination on the basis of sexual orientation. The commission ruled in favor of the gay couple and ordered Masterpiece to not only make a cake for them but also change its policies to bring them in line with the antidiscrimination law, train its staff, and provide quarterly reports to the commission that it was complying with the law.

Phillips sued the commission, saying that its order violated his rights to free speech and religious liberty because it punished him for refusing to make a cake that he could not make without violating his conscience. On free speech, he said that "custom-designed wedding cakes constitute artistic expression" and deserve protection under the Free Speech Clause of the First Amendment. On religious liberty, he acknowledged that in certain cases, the government has the duty to "prevent discrimination that 'deprives persons of their individual dignity.'" But he also said the commission could not prevent discrimination if it meant depriving Phillips of his constitutional rights. He said in his brief that he doesn't discriminate against people because of their race, religion, or sexual orientation. He's happy to "create his custom art for everyone, including LGBT patrons, but he declines all requests (regardless of the requester's identity) to create custom artistic expression that conflicts with his faith."

The Supreme Court decided the case in 2018. It said that the Colorado Civil Rights Commission had treated religion with overt hostility, and that this hostility violated the "First Amendment's guarantee that our laws be applied in a manner that is neutral toward religion." One commissioner described religion as "one of the most despicable pieces of rhetoric that people can use to . . . hurt others" and compared Phillips to people who in the past used their religious beliefs to defend slavery and the Holocaust. The Court said, "To describe a man's faith as 'one of the most despicable pieces of rhetoric that people can use' is to disparage his religion in at least two distinct ways: by describing it as despicable, and also by characterizing it as merely rhetorical—something insubstantial and even insincere."

But what about wedding vendors who didn't face such overtly hostile government officials—would they be permitted to turn away gay couples? The Court said nothing about that, sidestepping the issue everyone was wondering about. (At the time this book went to press, the Supreme Court was considering another case involving LGBTQ rights and religious objections, this one involving Catholic Social Services, which did not want to certify gay couples as foster parents.)

While many commentators understood the Court's ruling as narrow, Phillips's lawsuit was widely discussed as an attempted assault on antidiscrimination laws. The ACLU said it was about "licensing discrimination not just against lesbian, gay, bisexual, and transgender people, but against anyone protected by our nondiscrimination rules." In its view, the case was not about a cake but about "turn[ing] people away because of who they are or whom they love. They might as well have posted a sign in the shop saying 'No cakes for gays.'" About these types of cases generally, the *Daily Beast*'s headline, LET'S CALL 'RELIGIOUS FREEDOM' BY ITS REAL

NAME: POISONOUS, ANTI-LGBTQ BIGOTRY, captured the sentiment. About the conservative white evangelicals who bring these claims, *Huffington Post* summed it up: EVANGELICALS REAFFIRM THEIR LGBT IGNORANCE AND BIGOTRY.

After the *Masterpiece* decision, Phillips faced additional lawsuits. Autumn Scardina, a transgender woman, asked Phillips to make a cake celebrating her gender transition. Scardina requested a custom-designed cake with pink on the inside and blue on the outside. When Phillips refused, she filed a charge with the Colorado Civil Rights Commission. The Colorado Civil Rights Commission again sued Phillips for discrimination but ended up dropping its suit. Scardina persisted; she had her personal lawyers file a separate lawsuit against Phillips, seeking more than $100,000, in addition to legal fees. According to Phillips's attorney, Scardina's cake request had been "a setup right from the outset . . . All the way back in 2012, when the first case began, Scardina sent Jack harassing emails attacking his faith, calling him a bigot and a hypocrite." Scardina's case is still pending.

Masterpiece and *Hobby Lobby* were deeply polarizing. What's more: those challenging the cases were aligned with the Democratic Party, and those defending it were aligned with the Republican Party. In 2018, PRRI found that "59 percent of conservative Republicans favor allowing business owners to claim religious exemptions from serving gay and lesbian customers," while 76 percent of Democrats are opposed. The cases catalyzed the mapping of religious freedom onto the partisan divide, so that today, how we define religious liberty (specifically, whether we think it should protect conservative Christians' beliefs about sexuality) is increasingly a function of our tribal identity.

* * * *

"DO YOU THINK religious institutions like colleges, churches, charities should they lose their tax-exempt status if they oppose same-sex marriage?"

CNN anchor Don Lemon asked, his eyes inquisitive as he scanned the 2020 Democratic presidential candidates assembled before him during CNN's candidates' forum on LGBTQ issues.

Then candidate Beto O'Rourke was quick and decisive in his response: "Yes," O'Rourke replied. "There can be no reward, no benefit, no tax break for anyone, or any institution, any organization in America, that denies the full human rights and the full civil rights of every single one of us.

"And so as president, we are going to make that a priority, and we are going to stop those who are infringing upon the human rights of our fellow Americans."

Five years before O'Rourke's statement, Donald Verrilli Jr., a US solicitor general in the Obama administration, had hinted that tax-exempt status was going to be an issue. During oral arguments in *Obergefell*, Justice Alito asked whether Verrilli thought a religious college should lose its tax-exempt status if it opposed same-sex marriage. Verrilli responded, "It's certainly going to be an issue. I don't deny that." His statement in 2015 sent shock waves across conservative Christian America because of his willingness to use state power against Christian institutions. By the time O'Rourke crystallized it, conservative Christians were no longer surprised—though their anxiety about state power is stronger than ever.

In the intervening years, several Democrats had expressed skepticism, even disdain, about conservative Christians' religious claims. At a January 2019 event at the liberal Center for American Progress, Representative Ilhan Omar called these claims mere covers for bigotry and discrimination. In December 2018, Senators Mazie Hirono and Kamala Harris asked Brian Buescher, a nominee for the federal court in Nebraska, to resign from the Knights of Columbus. They feared his membership in the Catholic organization would impede his ability to "fairly judge matters relating to reproductive rights." In 2017, Senator Dianne Feinstein told then appellate judge nominee Amy Coney Barrett, "The dogma lives loudly within you, and that's a concern." In both cases, the senators also had in mind conservative religious liberty claims about abortion, contraception, and gay rights.

In 2016, Martin R. Castro, then chairman of the U.S. Commission on Civil Rights, summed up the Democrats' positions in the commission's *Peaceful Coexistence* report: "The phrases 'religious liberty' and 'religious freedom' will stand for nothing except hypocrisy so long as they remain code words for discrimination, intolerance, racism, sexism, homophobia, Islamophobia, Christian supremacy or any form of intolerance." He said that conservatives who bring traditional religious liberty claims are Christian nationalists who seek to "give one religion dominion over other religions, or a veto power over the civil rights and civil liberties of others."

There are two dynamics at play here: The first is the polarizing effect of the derisive rhetoric. The second is the overlap of the polarization onto the partisan divide.

Christian conservatives feel the culture is aligned against them, that it not only misunderstands their motivations but also despises them and seeks to restrict Christians' practices. Prominent liberal scholars have described conservatives' legal strategy as the "weaponization of the Free Exercise Clause"—that is, the use of religious freedom to attack others' rights—but conservatives see themselves as taking a *defensive* posture.

The polarized discourse does, however, have a radicalizing effect. Professor Marc DeGirolami considers it the natural result of "anti-Christian identity politics." He notes that the *Peaceful Coexistence* report levels its "most critical comments . . . at those cases and laws in which particular Christian scruples and beliefs were accommodated" and bestows its "highest praise . . . on those cases in which particular Christian scruples and beliefs were not accommodated." As DeGirolami sees it, "the cases cited by the commission make clear that no religion is in need of more vigorous monitoring for its 'supremacist' tendencies than Christianity."

This derision has tribalized conservative Christianity. DeGirolami writes:

> Anti-Christian American identity politics, like their pro-Christian counterpart, render compromise extremely unlikely. They are a singularly effective means of entrenching and exacerbating political polarization, as those with traditional Christian views on matters of sexuality and morality are no longer simply fellow citizens with different opinions, but fundamentally wicked and anti-American.

It's the same dynamic we explored in chapter 2, this time with respect to religious liberty. Chua says, "When groups feel threatened, they retreat into tribalism. They close ranks and become more insular, more defensive, more punitive, more us-versus-them." Klein says the same: "The simplest way to activate someone's identity is to threaten it, to tell them they don't deserve what they have, to make them consider that it might be taken away. The experience of losing status—and being told your loss of status is part of society's march to justice—is itself radicalizing." Christians, in this sense, have become radicalized on the topic of religious freedom.

Consider the responses to O'Rourke's statement. Conservative commentators called it "extreme intolerance," "religious bigotry," "religious profiling," and "religious discrimination" against Christians. When the ACLU came out against RFRA in the wake of the *Hobby Lobby* decision, *Reason* published a piece called THE ACLU NOW OPPOSES RELIGIOUS FREEDOM BECAUSE CHRISTIANS NEED IT. It reflected the general conservative sentiment with the ACLU's "disappointing retreat on principles" and "singular disdain for Christian belief." In many conservatives' view, the ACLU is "just another lefty advocacy organization—rather than a true defender of civil liberties."

Four years later, many Christian conservatives described the attacks on Jack Phillips as anti-Christian bigotry. The *Washington Times* ran a headline announcing, ANTI-CHRISTIAN BIGOTS IN COLORADO CALL RETREAT. David French wrote in the *National Review*, PROGRESSIVE ANTI-CHRISTIAN BIG-OTRY CARRIES A STEEP LEGAL COST. James Dobson's Focus on the Family was keeping tabs: MASTERPIECE CAKESHOP: 2; COLORADO ANTI-RELIGIOUS BIGOTRY: 0. When Phillips's attorney, Kristen Waggoner, was disinvited from a speaking engagement at Yale Law School, one writer asked in *USA Today*, SO YALE LAW SCHOOL ENDORSES ANTI-RELIGIOUS BIGOTRY NOW? Phillips even got a book deal by the conservative Regnery Publishing. The book description reads, "*The Baker* is Jack's firsthand account from the frontlines of the battle with a culture that is making every effort to remove God from the public square and a government denying Bible-believing Christians the right to freely exercise their religious beliefs."

Because these identity politics are being played out in relation to conservative religious liberty cases, in recent years the attack on Christians is conflated with an attack on religious liberty generally. In 2012 and 2014, Public Religion Research Institute measured the percentage of Americans who think religious liberty is under threat. When asked, "In America today, do you believe that the right of religious liberty is being threatened, or not?" 54 percent in May 2014 said yes. That number was 39 percent in March 2012 and 50 percent in November 2012. The percentage of Americans who completely agreed with the statement "The right of religious liberty is being threatened in America today" increased from 18 percent in June 2012 to 28 percent in July 2014. An August 2020 survey by the University of Chicago Divinity School and AP-NORC found that across the United States' largest religious denominations, evangelical Protestants were "especially likely to perceive risks to their freedom to worship." Headlines by conservative groups capture the prevailing sentiment: the evangelical university Biola, the *Christian Post*, the US Conference of Catholic Bishops, and the conservative Heritage

Foundation, among others, have put out pieces on "current" or "continuing" threats to religious liberty.

The attacks are coming largely, if not entirely, from Democrats, so the polarization maps onto the political divide. The Republican Party has seized on conservatives' feelings of threat and increasingly used religious liberty to consolidate support from religious conservatives—and conservative white evangelicals in particular. Even before Trump was elected, he and the other Republican presidential candidates vied throughout the 2016 campaign for the role of religious defender. Candidate Ted Cruz called the election the "religious liberty election," stating that religious liberty issues were front and center in determining who the next president would be. At a campaign event in the chapel of Iowa Wesleyan University, conservative activist Bob Plaats asked the candidates how they would preserve religious liberty. Candidate Bobby Jindal responded, "It is wrong for our government to discriminate against Christians," then referenced Jack Phillips and the Christian groups fighting the ACA contraceptive mandate: "It is wrong for our government to force these businesses to choose between going out of business or violating our sincere beliefs." Earlier that day, when Cruz spoke at a conference organized by the Network of Iowa Christian Home Educators in the state capital, he lamented, "We've seen religious liberty under assault."

Politico's coverage of the 2015 Faith and Freedom Coalition's Road to Majority conference noted, "Most of the 2016 hopefuls managed to impress evangelical and other conservative Christian voters by championing religious freedom." Cruz "tore into what he framed as the Obama administration's assault on religious liberty—a prominent theme at the conference." Jindal "blasted big business for making an 'unnatural alliance' with liberals who opposed controversial religious freedom measures." Scott Walker "reiterated his support for religious liberty." The losers, *Politico* said, were people like Marco Rubio, whose "address . . . was poorly tailored for a crowd spoiling for a champion of religious freedom."

As for candidate Trump, throughout his first campaign he promised that the "first priority of my administration will be to preserve and protect our religious liberty." And after his election, he kept his promise by instituting the expansive religious liberty protections his conservative Christian supporters wanted. In May 2017, President Trump issued an executive order directing the Department of Health and Human Services (HHS) and other federal agencies to exempt religious organizations from the contraceptive mandate. In November 2018, the government issued a new rule formally exempting all religious objectors from the contraceptive mandate and leaving in place the accommodation that delivered the drugs to employees without involving the religious employer. Under Trump, the Department of HHS opened a new Conscience and Religious Freedom Division, the Department of Justice (DOJ) instituted the Religious Liberty Task Force, and the State Department held several global conferences on combatting international religious freedom violations.

During the COVID-19 shutdown, as some conservatives felt embattled by state and local orders to close churches, church closures became the new "flash point" in the religious liberty culture wars. When the coronavirus outbreak first affected the United States, tribalization and political divides were so entrenched that the virus was almost immediately politicized. And the lockdown measures, once they affected churches, also became politicized under the religious liberty aegis.

Trump stepped in, threatening to overrule states that refused to open houses of worship. The DOJ entered the fray, filing numerous statements of interest on behalf of churches suing state and local authorities. Bill Barr put out a strong statement in defense of religion, noting that "in recent years, an expanding government has made the Free Exercise Clause more important than ever." When the Centers for Disease Control and Prevention (CDC) issued its first guidelines on reopening, Roger Severino, the head of HHS's conscience division, complained that the CDC treated religious conduct as especially "dangerous or worthy of scrutiny than comparable secular behavior." The guidelines were too prescriptive, he said, and that violated religious rights: "Governments have a duty to instruct the public on how to stay safe during this crisis and can absolutely do so without dictating to people how they should worship God."

Christians weren't the only ones worried about religious restrictions; in November 2020, the Orthodox Jewish group Agudath Israel of America challenged limits on religious gatherings and won its case at the U.S. Supreme Court. But Christian groups led the charge, particularly in the early months of the shutdown. At the state level, leaders like Republican lieutenant governor Dan Forest of North Carolina told Christian pastors that the Left was using stay-at-home orders to "hurt the church": "There is no doubt that there are people that are on the left that are using this to pull certain levers to see how far that they can go, How far are they able to push? How long can they keep churches shut down? How long will Christians be silent on this matter before they stand up?" Trump appointee Judge Justin Walker was similarly severe in his language; describing the Louisville mayor's restriction on drive-in Easter church services, he wrote, "On Holy Thursday, an American mayor criminalized the communal celebration of Easter."

Consider one example of this rhetoric's efficacy: Reverend R. Albert Mohler, one of the key leaders of the Southern Baptist Convention, titled his blog on the Louisville case more than an idle threat: REAL ASSAULTS ON RELIGIOUS LIBERTY EMERGE IN THE PANDEMIC. Three days later, the *Washington Post* reported that Mohler—highly critical of Trump in the 2016 election—had switched positions and planned to support Trump in 2020. Jonathan Merritt wrote in *Religion News Service* that the switch was the "crowning flip-flop of Mohler's career." But Mohler was clear about his reasons: abortion, Trump's Supreme Court nominees—and religious liberty.

* * * *

TO RECAP THE chapter so far, religious liberty became tribalized first, because dramatic demographic shifts led Christian conservatives to embrace the rights discourse and use religious liberty to defend their beliefs and practices in a fast-changing America; second, their court cases were heavily disparaged, almost entirely by Democrats, while Republicans seized on Christians' perceptions of threat and leveraged religious liberty to further polarize conservative Christians from Democrats. Altogether, this has led to the mapping of religious liberty onto political divides.

In its new, tribalized form, religious freedom discourse exhibits many of the same problems experts have identified with polarized political discourse generally. Jia Tolentino in *Trick Mirror* says it is "basic social physics" to make friends by "having a mutual enemy: we learn this as early as elementary school—and politically, it's much easier to organize people against something than it is to unite them in an affirmative vision." Today, our politics have taken this basic tendency to the extreme, and the media plays a big role in it. What used to be opinion journalism has become "identity journalism": the work, filtered through our chosen social channels, reinforces our identity.

But it's much easier to change an opinion than an identity. Because our identity ties us to our community, giving it up comes with significant costs, and we will go to great lengths to hold onto it. Group identity is so powerful that in many cases, even facts don't work to change our positions. More in Common found that the more politically engaged a person is, the more time he or she spends watching and listening to media that portray the other side as extreme. In turn, these people are more likely to mischaracterize the beliefs of the other side. Similarly, in a section of his book called "How politics makes smart people stupid," Klein cites a number of scientific studies that found people willing to ignore facts that challenged their political positions.

For example, in a study led by Yale professor Dan Kahan, the scientists surveyed a thousand Americans for their political views, then tested them for their math skills. Then they presented a brainteaser, a math problem about how well a skin cream worked. The test was designed to trick the participants; only if they carefully ran the numbers would they get the answer right. The scientists found that participants who were good at math solved the problem correctly, regardless of whether they were liberal or conservative.

Next, the scientists presented a politicized version of the same problem. Instead of making the brainteaser about skin cream, they made it about banning people from carrying concealed handguns in public. The question compared crime data across cities that banned and did not ban handguns. This time, the participants who were good at math stopped answering on the basis of math and switched to ideology instead. Liberals solved the math problem well when the answer "proved that gun-control legislation reduced crime." But if they were presented with a version of the problem where the math "suggested gun control failed, their math skills stopped mattering. They tended to get the problem wrong no matter how good they were at math."

So, their math skills failed in the face of ideology. Even more startling: Kahan and his group of researchers found that (1) partisans with weak math skills were 25 percent more likely to get the right answer if it fit their ideology; and (2) partisans with strong math skills were *45 percent* more likely to get the answer right if the answer fit their ideology. Klein explains it this way: "the smarter the person is, the dumber politics can make them."

More broadly, Klein says the studies show that, "Perhaps there are some kinds of debates where people don't want to find the right answer so much as they want to win the argument. Perhaps humans reason for purposes other than finding the truth—purposes like increasing their standing in their community or ensuring they don't find themselves exiled by the leaders of their tribe." Political psychologists Milton Lodge and Charles Taber call it "motivated reasoning," or "the process by which individuals rationalize their choices in a way that is consistent with what they prefer to believe, rather than with what is actually true." It's like how we react to cognitive dissonance; dissonance is disturbing and unpleasant, so we go to great lengths to make it stop, often by "reasoning" our way out of it. It's not the same as inventing a conflict, Lilliana Mason says, but it's fairly close to it. We have a certain idea about our opponents and our brain prefers not to revise that idea.

Brené Brown gets at this when she laments how often Americans today engage in these sorts of invented conflicts. She talks about it in relation to lying. Lying is a defiance of truth, whereas now there's a tendency to dismiss the truth wholesale. With people sorted into their tribes, many feel the need to weigh in on an issue even if they don't have all the facts. "We don't even bother being curious anymore because somewhere, someone on 'our side' has a position. In a fitting-in culture . . . curiosity is seen as weakness and asking questions equates to antagonism rather than being valued as learning."

Our group identity, in this way, encourages black-and-white portrayals, and it makes civility much more difficult. "'Civility is claiming and caring for one's identity, needs, and beliefs without degrading someone else's in the process . . . [It] is about disagreeing without disrespect . . . Civility is the hard work of staying present even with those with whom we have deep-rooted and fierce disagreements.'" In the religious liberty context, it works to transform *Hobby Lobby*, *Masterpiece*, and other conservative Christian cases into unambiguous examples of bigoted Christians oppressing marginalized minorities. Professor DeGirolami explains the conservative perspective: "Once Christians who hold positions that do not conform to contemporary orthodoxies become the symbols of what must be vanquished, it is no longer possible even to speak together with them, let alone to negotiate over legal arrangements."

The reality, of course, is that many of the Christians who don't "conform to contemporary orthodoxies" are far more complex than the caricatures (as are Americans across the political spectrum). We met Brian and Blake in chapter 1—conservative Christians who lean away from Christian nationalism but also hold traditional beliefs about marriage. Researchers Whitehead and Perry note that while Blake "strongly affirms the separation of church and state, believes our culture should accommodate gays and lesbians, and was classified as a rather weak Accommodator on our Christian nationalism scale, he personally feels homosexuality is a sin and fears restrictions on his freedom." When they interviewed Blake about *Masterpiece*, he responded with a sense of threat:

> You hear stories of saying like homosexuality is a sin and being prosecuted for a hate crime. That hasn't happened yet, and I'm not sure how far away we are. That would probably be the thing I'm most concerned about is limiting speech, religious speech in that way and considering things hate speech that are Christian, like biblical things. Telling someone they're a sinner and going to hell could be something like that considered hate speech.

Blake does not want to outlaw gay marriage, again, because of the separation of church and state, but he does fear that his freedom as a Christian "to publicly disapprove of homosexuality—either verbally or simply by not offering service to facilitate same-sex marriage—could be under attack." He thinks gay Americans have a right to get married, but he does not think that all Americans must necessarily endorse it.

Matthew from chapter 2 told me something similar:

> My wife and I do not hate gays (or any minorities) at all . . . the truth is, I couldn't care less what their orientation is. The problem

is many don't want to be accepted . . . they want to be endorsed. Conservatives must . . . bake wedding cakes, cater weddings, and provide any other service that may shock their sensibilities.

Brian, Blake, and Matthew don't want to impose their views on the public square, but they do want space to live out their beliefs. Political scientists Andrew Lewis and Andrew Whitehead drew that same distinction for me; in Lewis's words, "These more pluralistic types see that religious life is threatened and want to see religion protected . . . They are more open to pluralism, because protection not domination is the main goal." They don't want to "weaponize" religious freedom against others; they only want to defend their own practices.

It's true, unfortunately, that many Americans have interacted with a different type of Christian. One person (a devout Christian himself) told me, "In my experience, Christian conservatives are pretty open about not wanting [LGBTQ individuals] to have any civil rights. Inasmuch as civil government aligns with their religious values, they want the government enforcing their values." But what he's describing is Christian nationalism, not Christian conservativism, and they function in two very different ways.

We learned in chapter 1 that increasing religiosity creates open-mindedness toward Muslims, nonwhites, and immigrants. I quoted Whitehead, who said, "If you took a carbon copy of me, and my level of Christian nationalism stayed the same level, and all you increased or decreased was my religious practice—as you increase my religious practice, I would actually feel less threatened by Muslims. So, these things aren't one and the same."

But the same religiosity factor that creates openness to some minorities *also* correlates with traditional beliefs about marriage, family, and sexuality. That religiosity works this way suggests that "bigotry" can't be an accurate way of describing religious Christians who hold traditional sexual views; at minimum, it conflates conservative Christians with Christian nationalists (for whom domination *is* the main goal) and other actors who employ religion with ill intent.

As the Harvard psychologist Gordon Allport explained it, hateful attitudes toward religious and racial minorities dissipate with higher levels of religious commitment because those attitudes aren't authentic to the religion to begin with. In contrast, traditional beliefs about gender and sexuality *are* authentic—or what he calls "elemental"—to traditional Christianity. Archbishop William Lori described these beliefs as part of the "demands" of faith. Even though "society often tends to reduce religious teachings to a series of unpleasant, countercultural moral prohibitions," moral rules are actually critical elements of the "moral transformation" required of traditional Christians. Russell Moore also says that for those who hold to a traditional Christian ethic, religion cannot "morph and change" to keep up with secular culture. This explains the 2019 findings of political scientist Jeremiah Castle that among evangelicals, the more religiously committed they were (measured by rates of church attendance), the more likely they were to support the religious claims in *Hobby Lobby* and *Masterpiece*.

Several prominent gay rights advocates understand this and are speaking up in defense of Christians. In his *Atlantic* piece THE STRUGGLE FOR GAY RIGHTS IS OVER, the international gay rights activist James Kirchick observes:

> We gay people are expected to be grievously offended by the behavior of Jack Phillips, the owner of Masterpiece Cakeshop. But many, if not most, of the gay people I know can live with the fact that a baker in Colorado does not approve of our relationships. America is a land of some 330 million people, and I do not require every small-business owner across the country to reject two thousand years of religious teaching in order to pursue my happiness.

Elsewhere, a broad coalition of gay rights groups for years worked with conservative Christians on the proposed Fairness For All (FFA) federal legislation, which carefully balanced the interests of the LGBTQ community and religious objectors in employment, housing, and public accommodations. In the employment context, for example, religious entities would be permitted to limit their hiring to people who abided by traditional beliefs about sexuality. In the public accommodations context, FFA would ensure the term didn't extend to, for example, a church-organized spaghetti dinner; if government officials started counting every event that was open to the public as a "public accommodation," it could control who was or wasn't allowed there. In drafting FFA, the religious and gay rights activists understood that traditional religious beliefs about sexuality run deep for many people, and they strove to find solutions that work for everyone.

FFA grew out of similar work with the Utah legislature. The religiously conservative state of Utah (the majority of residents belong to the Church of Jesus Christ of Latter-day Saints, also known as the Mormon Church) enacted a pair of laws in 2015 that balanced LGBTQ rights and religious freedom. One measure bans anti-LGBTQ discrimination in housing and employment but also protects the ability of religious organizations to maintain their beliefs and practices through careful accommodations. Another measure ensures equal access to marriage licensing at governmental offices but also protects people who work there but have a traditional, religious definition of marriage.

The legislation was passed months before the Supreme Court decided *Obergefell* but at a time when same-sex marriage was spreading rapidly across red states. The Mormon Church foresaw that Utah would adopt same-sex marriage imminently and worked to prevent what it knew would be inevitable conflict with traditional religious understandings of marriage. The Church called for legislation to "protect vital religious freedoms for individuals, families, churches and other faith groups while also protecting the rights of our LGBT citizens in . . . housing, employment and public accommodation." Leaders of the Utah state legislature were spurred to action; as Representative Gregory H. Hughes, then speaker of the Utah House explained, "We had not heard that before, and we had not heard that with such specificity, and we took notice."

The idea behind the legislation is to carve out a live-and-let-live option. As one proponent of the FFA approach explained, "When religious liberty and LGBT interests collide, instead of incivility and driving toward a winner-take-all result, we should embrace civility, protection of core rights for all, and reasonable compromise."

Adopting this "politics of compromise" helps people understand and not resent each other. One PRRI poll found that 77 percent of Utahans support LGBTQ protections. Peter Wehner and the openly gay author Jonathan Rauch wrote in the *New York Times*: "Why the high enthusiasm for gay rights in conservative, heavily Mormon Utah? No mystery," then went on to describe the 2015 laws.

In that same piece, titled WE CAN FIND COMMON GROUND ON GAY RIGHTS AND RELIGIOUS LIBERTY, the authors advocated for the FFA approach. Writing just days after the Supreme Court, in *Bostock v. Clayton County*, extended federal employment protections to LGBTQ individuals, Wehner and Rauch reflected on the deep concerns many religious conservatives had about what *Bostock* meant for religious hiring. They wrote, "In an era when Americans are deeply polarized and angry at one another, convinced that those on the other side politically are wicked and unreasonable, there is a better way forward on the fraught issue of gay rights and religious liberty." FFA is that "better way" because it "builds new alliances, develops new solutions, and turns conflict into cooperation." At its heart, FFA and its Utah counterpart reflect the basic idea that religious objections to same-sex marriage are not fundamentally about hate and should be taken more seriously.

When Chai Feldblum, a Georgetown law professor and "the first out lesbian EEOC commissioner," wrote in support of the *Masterpiece* decision, she said her own upbringing in an Orthodox Jewish home helped her understand the deep significance of religion in people's lives. This, in turn, helped her understand why the Supreme Court ruled for the baker in *Masterpiece*, even as it emphasized that "gay persons and gay couples cannot be treated as social outcasts or as inferior in dignity and worth." Religion and LGBTQ rights need not be in conflict, she writes, and advocates on either side of the issue who opt for extreme positions fail to see the "deeper point of our constitutional democracy"—to live in a pluralistic society where people with different beliefs can coexist with peace and dignity. Two law professors, Douglas Laycock and Thomas Berg, also noted that the Court ruled in favor of the Christian baker based on the Free Exercise Clause, and not on his free speech claim: "Exclusive reliance on free exercise narrows the opinion to religious exercise, excluding simple bigots." There's something different about religion, something that separates religious views from "bigotry."

In a separate piece, Professor Berg highlights the vast social contributions made by religious organizations, many of them conservative. "Traditional religions are a lot more than one allegedly discriminatory belief might suggest." The numbers show that if conservative Christian organizations were forced to go out of business or reduce their size because they didn't accommodate same-sex marriage, "a crisis of the first magnitude would exist in the nation's social safety net." Catholic Charities USA is second only to the federal government in the number of people it serves: 8.3 million people in 2016. The evangelical Salvation Army shelters ten million people every night and provides fifty-five million meals a year. Catholic hospitals and healthcare facilities care for one in six hospital patients. Faith-based organizations provide nearly 60 percent of emergency shelter beds in homeless shelters. And when it comes to adoption, the CEO of the National Council for Adoption said that if faith-based adoption agencies were to shut down, "'the whole [adoption] system would collapse on itself.'"

Importantly, these religious service organizations are uniquely effective *because* they are religious. Government or large, secular social service agencies can't do what these faith-based agencies do. Pulling from survey evidence, Berg explains that "nonprofit church-owned hospitals 'save more lives, release patients from the hospital sooner, and have better overall patient satisfaction ratings.'" Faith-based adoption agencies are especially effective in placing special needs kids. In education, disadvantaged students fare significantly better in Catholic schools than in public schools.

And in most, if not all, cases, the organization will not stay in business if it is required to change its policies on same-sex marriage. Berg quotes the general counsel of the evangelical World Vision: "'We are not just another humanitarian organization, but a branch of the body of Christ. . . . The key to our effectiveness is our faith, not our size.'"

As such, it serves the common, or civic, good to prevent the government from crippling these organizations with fines and other penalties if these Christians, for example, refuse to hire an employee who is in a same-sex marriage. Religious organizations don't need to contribute to society in order to be protected under the Constitution, Professor Berg says, but their significant contributions strongly counsel that we let them serve.

Consider also the positions of James Kirchick and law professor Andrew Koppelman, both of them outspoken supporters of gay rights. Kirchick asked the premier gay-rights group, Human Rights Campaign (HRC), "for statistics on the number of LGBTQ people annually denied employment, housing, or service at a hotel or restaurant due to their sexuality or gender identity." HRC was unable to provide him with any. Instead, HRC referred Kirchick to a poll in which 63 percent of LGBTQ individuals self-reported "discrimination in their personal lives." The phrasing is vague enough, Kirchick notes, to encompass everything from a "stray homophobic comment heard on the street to being fired," and is thus unhelpful in determining how much of the problem can be fixed by government action.

According to Kirchick, "blanket discrimination against gay people simply on the basis of their sexual orientation is not widespread." He goes on to quote Koppelman, who has found that:

> Hardly any of these cases have occurred: a handful in a country of 300 million people. In all of them, the people who objected to the law were asked directly to facilitate same-sex relationships, by providing wedding, adoption, or artificial insemination services, counseling, or rental of bedrooms. There have been no claims of a right to simply refuse to deal with gay people. Even in the large number of states with no antidiscrimination protection for gay people, I am unaware of any case where a couple was unable to conduct a wedding.

Koppelman goes so far as to say that there is no practical need to include sexual orientation in laws that protect against discrimination. He acknowledges that gay couples being turned away by wedding vendors experience "dignitary harm" (what the ACLU's Louise Melling describes as the "harm of being rejected because of who you are, because you are a member of a class long disfavored and long subject to discrimination"). But, Koppelman says, in a country that protects free speech, it's not the government's business to protect people from dignitary harm: "The dignitary harm of knowing that some of your fellow citizens condemn your way of life is not one from which the law can or should protect you in a regime of free speech."

There are, of course, scholars and activists who disagree with Berg, Kirchick, and Koppelman. (For example, Melling agrees that Christians are generally good people and well intentioned in their objections to same-sex marriage, but says LGBTQ rights should still trump religious rights.) And it is, of course, perfectly fair to criticize the policies of the Christian Right. But outside of legal and scholarly discourse, a robust discussion about the various facets of the issue is not the norm.

Many conservative Christians have also not explained their position well; a speaker at a conference I once attended noted that because conservative Christian beliefs were long dominant in America, they never had to explain themselves; "but the fact is now they have to, otherwise the misunderstandings will bulldoze them." In the absence of Christians' own explanations, politicians have controlled the narrative. Arthur Brooks makes the same point about conservatives broadly; in *The Conservative Heart*, he says conservatives are driven fundamentally by compassion but never express their positions in the language of compassion. To help others understand them, conservatives have to put their hearts first and lead with a "statement of moral purpose."

Of course, in our tribal environment, even good arguments or compassionate language might not work, because people are more interested in winning the debate than finding the right answer. And winning the argument requires reducing conservative Christians to villains.

The message is clear: conservative Christians are evil, and they must be resisted at all costs. (The caricature is of Christians specifically; as I'll explore in the next chapter, if a Muslim baker declined to bake a wedding cake for a gay couple, the optics would be very different.) Together with other factors like demographic shift and political leveraging, this caricaturing creates the perfect storm for religious freedom to become a partisan tool.

****

AS A PARTISAN tool, religious liberty serves as a shield to protect the in-group—and hurt the out-group. Many Christian conservatives rally around Jack Phillips or *Hobby Lobby* not just because of the religious issue at hand but also because they have to fight the liberal out-group.

That includes fighting anyone thought to be allied with the out-group. There is now a growing body of both anecdotal and empirical evidence that in this in-group/out-group dynamic, Muslims are often the main targets of that hostility. We turn to that next.

PART III

❧

THE OUT-GROUP ATTACK

CHAPTER 4

Competing Victimhood

"MY THING IS, YOU GOTTA start standing up before you get too angry and out of control in this country, folks. And in [the US], the Muslims are treated better than the Christians and white people."

It was March 2019, and black conservative radio host Jesse Lee Peterson was commenting on the February 2019 massacre of fifty Muslims by a white supremacist in Christchurch, New Zealand.

"White people are getting angry rather than speaking up prior to anger. . . . You've got to start standing up before you get your anger out of control in this country."

In his own (extreme) way, Peterson captured the essence of a weaponized vulnerability. In chapter 1, I explained the basics of intergroup bias; that is, the in-group lashes out against the out-group when it feels threatened. Chapters 2 and 3 explained how and why conservative Christians feel threatened. The same intergroup dynamics likely also apply to the Left's hostility toward the Right. I did as the conflict transformation experts advise: I acknowledged conservative white evangelicals' unacknowledged vulnerability. I "zoomed in" on them as people and went beyond the headlines to understand their positions—which, I hope, will let us have "hard conversations in a soft place." In chapters 4 and 5, I move on to those hard conversations. This is where I, in the words of Brené Brown, "speak truth to bullshit." I look at how Christian vulnerability (and the partisan manipulation of it) drives anti-Muslim hostility.

At the core of that hostility is a perception of Muslims as the dangerous out-group—not just religious and racial outsiders but political ones, too. In our polarized climate, these categories merge together in part because of our "mega-identities"—the expansion of our political identities to include race, religion, ethnicity, gender, neighborhood, personal prefer-ences (favorite grocery store, favorite drink, favorite car . . . the list goes on). Muslims have in essence become part of the liberal mega-identity, and the protection of their rights is now a "liberal" thing to do and a conservative thing to resist.

But how did we get here?

* * * *

I'm Donald Trump and I approve this message.

(A grainy image of Barack Obama and Hillary Clinton standing side by side appears on the screen)

The politicians can pretend it's something else, but Donald Trump calls it "radical Islamic terrorism."

(Obama and Clinton are replaced by an image of people on stretchers behind photos of the gunman from the San Bernardino shooting)

That's why he's calling for a temporary shutdown of Muslims entering the United States, until we can figure out what's going on.

(A US battleship launches a cruise-missile strike. Bombs drop on ISIS territory. Masked terrorists appear in front of Arabic script)

He'll quickly cut the head off ISIS—and take their oil!

(Somber piano melody set to a video of North African migrants crossing the Morocco-Spain border into Spain)

And he'll stop illegal immigration by building a wall on our Southern border that Mexico WILL pay for.

(Trump at one of his rallies)

We will make America. Great. Again!

This was Trump's first campaign television ad in 2016, and it made perfectly clear what he was about—and who he was against.

Trump made good on his promises. Days after his inauguration, he issued Executive Order 13769, blocking citizens from seven majority-Muslim states from entering the United States. Dubbed by many as the "Muslim ban," thousands of protestors flooded airports in major US cities. Protests continued for days as air passengers were detained or sent home. The American Civil Liberties Union (ACLU) raised more than $24 million over a single weekend from Americans demanding that constitutional rights be vindicated in court. That number grew to $79 million in the following three months.

In time, the travel ban made its way through the courts. Each challenge prompted more edits, until finally travel ban 3.0 made it to the Supreme Court. The Court decided the case a few weeks after ruling in favor of Jack Phillips in *Masterpiece*. Recall that in *Masterpiece* the Court had based its decision on the fact that the commissioners had treated Phillips's religion with hostility. "The Commission's hostility was inconsistent with the First Amendment's guarantee that our laws be applied in a manner that is neutral toward religion," the Court said on June 4, 2018. Based on that language, media commentators immediately started speculating about the Court's imminent decision in *Trump v. Hawaii* (the travel ban case), positing that if the Court cared so much about hostility toward religion, surely it would strike down the travel ban.

After all, Trump had a long history of anti-Muslim statements. As a layperson in 2011, he tweeted that the Qur'an teaches "tremendous hatred," which "absolutely" creates a "Muslim problem." When he ran for president, he made the "Muslim problem" central to his campaign. In December 2015, he praised an author for acknowledging "Muslim problems." He later declared, "I think Islam hates us," and clarified during an official presidential debate that "I mean a lot of them. I mean a lot of them." He also insisted time and again that Muslims in America celebrated the September 11 attacks. He backed up his statements with policy proposals, such as "a total and complete shutdown of Muslims entering the United States," warrantless surveillance of American Muslims, closing American mosques, and creating a registry of all Muslims in the United States. In calling for the systematic exclusion of Muslims from the freedoms other Americans enjoy, Trump also suggested that he would consider internment camps for Muslims: "I would rule it out, but we would have to be very vigilant. We're going to have to be very smart." Immediately after he was elected, Trump put his words into action. In preparing for the travel ban, he summoned his adviser, Rudolph Giuliani, to "put a commission together" to "show me the right way to do it legally."

Surely then, commentators mused, the travel ban case was an open-and-shut matter of unconstitutional antireligious discrimination. So, when the court on June 26, 2018 upheld the travel ban despite evidence of prejudice far more egregious than the evidence in *Masterpiece*, many Americans were shocked. In THE SUPREME COURT CARES ABOUT RELIGIOUS ANIMUS—EXCEPT WHEN IT DOESN'T, Daniel Mach of the ACLU wrote:

> The wildly divergent results in those two high-profile cases—*Masterpiece Cakeshop v. Colorado Civil Rights Commission* and *Trump v. Hawaii*, the Muslim ban case—send troubling mixed messages, which threaten to undermine religious freedom, fairness, and equality for all . . . the court's aggressive efforts to root out anti-Christian animus by the Colorado Civil Rights Commission were notable, especially in light of its decision . . . to ignore far more compelling and egregious religious hostility in the Muslim ban case.

The legalities of the case are complex, and reasonable people can differ as to whether the court decided correctly. Among other things, the justices who voted to uphold the travel ban said they had to do so because of the "presidential avoidance canon." Because of the president's "unique role in the separation of powers, the law applies differently to the president than it does to anyone else." Who gets to enter and not enter the country is well within the realm of executive, or presidential, authority, and the court, like other courts and the judicial branch of government generally, could not interfere with that or even comment on it extensively.

But legalities aside, what matters for our present discussion is how the contrast between *Masterpiece* and the travel ban decision was received by the Americans who had rallied against the ban. The perceived hypocrisy was made even starker when the religious liberty groups who had supported Phillips went silent on the travel ban. Reporters wondered about it in pieces like the *Washington Post's* WHY MANY RELIGIOUS LIBERTY GROUPS ARE SILENT ABOUT THE SUPREME COURT'S DECISION ON PRESIDENT TRUMP'S TRAVEL BAN. Even if these groups thought the Court had sound legal basis for its ruling, why weren't they at least speaking out about the president's anti-Muslim animus? Another *Washington Post* writer thought these groups were silent because "to take a stand against the 'Muslim ban' is also a stand against Trump, who remains popular among conservatives and white evangelicals, and for the rights of foreign Muslims, who are often vilified by conservative Christian activists." These were early signs of an emerging narrative that in Trump's America (including under his Supreme Court picks), Christians are favored over Muslims.

That story was back in the news when, in February 2019, Alabama executed Domineque Ray, a Muslim death row inmate, without accommodating his request to have an imam in the room with him. The clergy allowed in the execution chamber were limited to the ones on staff, but the prison employed Christian clergy only. Ray challenged the prison's denial on religious liberty grounds. His case made it to the U.S. Supreme Court, which ruled against him and permitted the execution to proceed without the imam. The decision shocked many Americans, leaving them wondering, in the words of the *New York Times* editorial board, IS RELIGIOUS FREEDOM FOR CHRISTIANS ONLY?

The debate about whether Christians are favored over Muslims is in many ways a subset of the bigger fight over religious liberty inaugurated by the *Hobby Lobby* decision. In that case, the conservative Christian owners of Hobby Lobby were pitted against women as a vulnerable group. In *Masterpiece*, again, it was a conservative Christian against a vulnerable gay couple. In each case, the loser was some sort of minority. With *Trump v. Hawaii* and the Ray case, Muslims took center stage as the vulnerable minorities whose rights were being trampled on by powerful, conservative Christians (who supported both the Trump administration and the conservative justices who ruled against the Muslims in both cases).

In this way, then, Muslims are yet again proxies for a fight between conservatives and liberals. The dispute is not at its core about protecting a particular Muslim or Muslim religious practices generally; indeed, it has little to do with where most American Muslims actually stand on social issues. Instead, it is about positioning Muslims as one of many other minorities who are in conflict with conservative Christians.

The Left now increasingly draws attention to what it calls "progressive" religious liberty claims, which it sets up as a counter to "conservative Christian hegemony." For example, the Law, Rights, and Religion Project at Columbia Law School in 2019 issued the report *Whose Faith Matters? The Fight for Religious Liberty Beyond the Christian Right*. The report sets out to offer "a sweeping account of religious liberty activism being undertaken by numerous progressive humanitarian and social justice movements and uncover how right-wing activists have fought for conservative Christian hegemony rather than 'religious liberty' more generally." By doing this, it "challenges the leading popular narrative of religious freedom." Among the cases the report features is a suit by Samantha Elauf, a Muslim woman who sued the clothing store Abercrombie & Fitch for its refusal to hire her because she wore a headscarf. The report also features *Trump v. Hawaii*; the Ray case; *Holt v. Hobbs*, involving another Muslim prisoner; *Tanzin v. Tanvir*, which was brought by three Muslim men who alleged that the

FBI placed them on the No-Fly List when the Muslim men refused to spy on their religious communities; and *Hassan v. City of New York*, in which a group of Muslims sued the city of New York for its secret police program targeting Muslims. The report also discusses a range of other Muslim religious liberty matters.

The discussion about these cases is by itself extremely important—but in this report, the cases served the function of pitting "progressive" religious claims against conservative Christian claims. Muslims were on the first team, Christians on the second. And the dichotomy isn't limited to the report; political scientists have found that Americans' political positions—or tribes—influence which religious rights they support. In one study by professors Daniel Bennett and Logan Strother, respondents were told that the government had blocked a house of worship. The house of worship was first described generically, then described as an evangelical church, then a mosque. When Bennett and Strother compared how respondents felt about protecting the house of worship, they learned that if you liked Muslims more than evangelicals, you were more interested in protecting the mosque. On the flip side, only 40 percent of respondents who felt more warmly toward evangelicals wanted to help the mosque.

In another study, Andrew Lewis looked at how people respond to religious liberty claims differently depending on how the information is presented to them. Respondents first read about Muslim truck drivers who had to choose between transporting alcohol in violation of their religious beliefs or losing their jobs. Respondents then learned that either a well-known liberal or a conservative law firm was representing the truck drivers in court.

Lewis found that Democratic respondents were more supportive of the religious freedom claims when they were told a liberal law firm represented the drivers. They were also more likely to support conservative Christian claims after they were exposed to religious freedom claims by Muslims.

As for conservative respondents, they were less likely to shift attitudes in support of Muslims but were marginally more likely to support them if a conservative law firm, rather than an institution like the unambiguously liberal ACLU, was defending the Muslim claimants.

The contest has become so marked that one religious liberty lawyer noted its influence on litigation tactics. Attorney Luke Goodrich wrote in *The Hill*:

> Unfortunately, in our polarized moment, groups like the ACLU have developed an allergic reaction to the Free Exercise Clause. They know strong free exercise protections will protect traditional Christian beliefs—like when Hobby Lobby declines to pay for contraception, or a baker declines to participate in a same-sex wedding—and they don't like that result. So they put all their eggs in an Establishment Clause basket—hoping that by winning under the Establishment Clause, they can prevent blatant discrimination against religious minorities without also protecting traditional Christian beliefs.

A *Vox* piece discussing the legal issues in the Muslim case *Tanzin v. Tanvir* made a similar point about progressives' discomfort that a victory would ultimately help conservative Christians:

> If the Supreme Court holds [in favor of Tanvir], the biggest winner is unlikely to be religious minorities like Tanvir. Rather, the biggest winner is likely to be the Christian right . . . *Tanvir*, in other words, presents a deeply fraught conflict between the goal of protecting religious minorities and the goal of rooting out many other forms of discrimination. It's also likely to put many civil rights advocates in the awkward position of hoping that Tanvir loses his case.

In sum, the Left wants to protect the religious rights it prioritizes without also supporting conservative Christian claims. And as I explore in more detail in chapter 5, many conservatives take a similarly selective approach to religious liberty. Indeed, the flip side of liberals protecting Muslims is Christian reluctance to protect Muslims, and it's all tied up with the politics of vulnerability. The Left thinks Christians are favored over vulnerable minorities, and the Right thinks its own vulnerability is overlooked in favor of minorities.

The Right perceives a double standard in the Left's treatment of Christianity versus Islam. Many conservative Christians believe that the Left would support religious liberty claims made by Muslims but object to the same claims made by Christians. In a widely circulated video, conservative comedian Steven Crowder enters a Muslim bread bakery in Dearborn, Michigan. Crowder poses as a gay man looking for a wedding cake for his upcoming wedding and tries to place the cake order, but the baker declines the request. Crowder's point with the video is to show that while Christian bakers like Jack Phillips are excoriated by liberals, Muslim bakers with the same objections as Phillips are left alone. (There is no actual evidence, however, that the Left supports a Muslim cake baker who refuses service on the basis of his or her religious beliefs. Even the Crowder video proves nothing; the baker who turned down Crowder's cake request did so because his bakery only bakes bread.)

Commenting on the Crowder video, radio host Rush Limbaugh said, "This is an attack on Christianity. They don't care what the Muslims are doing. They don't care that there's anti-gay bigotry in Dearborn, Michigan. Doesn't matter. It's not about that. . . . This is about shifting power. This is about taking power away from an existing majority—in this case the white, Christian majority . . ."

Or as one conservative explained it to me, the perception on the Right is that "the Left hates Christianity and opposes our religious claims because they want to rub our faces in the dirt. Meanwhile, for the Left, Islam is the better—the *best*—religion." Given these tribal dynamics, the Right responds with even fiercer hatred of Muslims. Think of it in terms of the ancient proverb, "The enemy of my enemy is my friend." In the Right's view of Muslims, it's "The friend of my enemy is also my enemy." There isn't even room to acknowledge that Muslims are actually facing religious discrimination in the United States. Indeed, many of the same commentators who claim Christians are "persecuted" in America decry a "false" Muslim "victimhood."

A June 2018 poll by Morning Consult exposed the tribalism on an even more granular level. It found that white evangelicals are more likely to support religious business owners refusing services to LGBTQ individuals if the business owner is a Christian, Jew, or Mormon—but less so if the business owner is a Muslim. Even as conservative white evangelicals are struggling against liberals to secure this right, they are adamant about cutting out Muslims.

Trump knew to play on these frustrations. In the midst of the coronavirus pandemic when many houses of worship were subject to state stay-at-home orders, Trump pushed the theory that Democratic officials were going to treat mosques better than churches.

> I would say that there could be a difference . . . I've seen a great disparity in this country. I've seen a great disparity . . . I would be interested to see that because they go after Christian churches, but they don't go after mosques . . . I am somebody that believes in faith . . . our politicians treat different faiths very differently . . . I don't know what happened with our country, but the Christian faith is treated much differently than it was, and I think it's treated very unfairly.

FactCheck.org, a project of the Annenberg Public Policy Center at the University of Pennsylvania, found that several social media posts propagated this idea of preferential treatment for Muslims. It looked specifically at a widely circulated Facebook post claiming a "double standard" favoring mosques over churches. The post said, "City officials allow MOSQUES to stay open . . . while arresting Christian pastors like Tony Spell in Baton Rouge Louisiana for busing in poor minority children to feed them at Sunday service. Double standard anyone?????" The post was littered with factual inaccuracies, which FactCheck clarified, and as writer Tim Murphy notes, "It's sort of a weird premise. . . . Activists from New York City to Murfreesboro, Tennessee, have tried to block Muslim residents from even *building* mosques; mosques have been subjected to (sometimes unconstitutional) surveillance; and the current president of the United States ran for office on literally banning Muslims from entering the United States."

But the stark inaccuracies didn't stop the idea from spreading. In 2016, then presidential candidate Marco Rubio criticized President Obama for talking about Islamophobia during a mosque visit. "Look at today—he gave a speech at a mosque. Oh, you 'know, basically implying that America is discriminating against Muslims." He dismissed the severity of anti-Muslim discrimination by comparing it to sports rivalries: "We can disagree on things, right? I'm a Dolphin fan, you're a Patriot fan." When he was questioned about these comments at a Republican presidential debate, Rubio elaborated. "My problem with what he did is, he continues to put out this fiction that there's widespread discrimination against Muslim Americans."

He went on to make the inevitable comparison with anti-Christian discrimination:

> I do believe it is important to recognize, you want to talk about religious discrimination in America. I don't think Barack Obama's being sued by any Islamic groups, but . . . We are facing in this country Christian groups and groups that hold traditional

values who feel and in fact are being discriminated against by the laws of this country that try to force them to vie to violate their conscience.

Critics were quick to debunk Rubio's claim that anti-Muslim discrimination is a "fiction." Writing in February 2016, Philip Bump of the *Washington Post* noted, "The FBI keeps records on hate crimes in the United States, the most recent year of data being 2014. In 2014, there were 1,140 victims of hate crimes based on religion. Of that total, the majority were targeted for being Jewish. The next most commonly targeted religion? Muslims."

But facts have nothing to do with the Christian sentiment. It's about political tribalism pure and simple. Chua in *Political Tribes* writes, "One group's claims to feeling threatened and voiceless are often met by another group's derision because it discounts their own feelings of persecution—but such is political tribalism." The feeling of vulnerability becomes the reality in this situation. In 2020, the University of Chicago Divinity School and the AP-NORC found that while half of Americans believe that American Muslims' religious freedom is threatened at least somewhat, only about three in ten white evangelicals said the same.

The finding was not new. In 2019, Pew reported that Democrats and those who lean Democratic "are more likely than Republicans and Republican leaners to say Muslims face at least some discrimination in the U.S. (92% vs. 69%). . . . At the same time, Republicans are much more likely than Democrats to say evangelicals face discrimination (70% vs. 32%)." In 2017, the Rasmussen Reports found that "fifty-six percent (56%) of Democrats . . . believe most Muslims in this country are mistreated, a view shared by only 22% of Republicans." Also in 2017, PRRI found that Democrats were four times as likely as Republicans to believe that Muslims faced greater discrimination than Christians did. Among white evangelicals specifically, 57 percent said that anti-Christian discrimination is widespread in the United States, while only 44 percent said the same thing about anti-Muslim discrimination.

In 2016, after candidate Trump promised to bar Muslims from entering the United States, the *Washington Post* and ABC News asked Americans "whether or not they thought Muslims in the United States experienced discrimination based on their religion." Seventy-three percent said yes, and 59 percent of those said that the discrimination was unjustified. Eighty-three percent of Democrats thought Muslims experienced discrimination. In contrast, more than a third of Republicans thought Muslims experienced no discrimination.

There are likely multiple phenomena at play here. First, again, Christian conservatives cannot acknowledge Muslim suffering because it challenges their own group's identity as persecuted. It's also probably the case that many of the Republican and white evangelical respondents had little knowledge about court cases and hate crime statistics. More likely, they were relying on what they read in their preferred news outlet and/or how they felt the culture was aligned, which in turn is communicated to them through their own political and religious circles. Polls from before the 2016 presidential election found that fewer white evangelicals thought they faced more discrimination than Muslims. An October 2016 PRRI survey found that 56 percent of white evangelicals believed Muslims faced more discrimination than evangelicals did. By February 2017, that number had dropped twelve percentage points. The political rhetoric was working.

Then there's the faith element. David Nirenberg of the University of Chicago Divinity School says certain faith communities exist in "communication bubbles" that reinforce to believers that their religious freedom is imperiled. The Pew Research Center found that in 2012, only 18 percent of white evangelical Protestant churchgoers reported hearing about attacks on religious liberty from the pulpit; in a 2016 survey, that number went up to 43 percent. Along with preachers, conservative Christian advocacy firms and Christian talk radio often about the threats to conservative

Christianity—and say little or nothing about what Muslims are experiencing. Our informational environment drives our opinions and, in this case, helps underscore a competing victimhood.

Even more troubling: when Muslims *are* mentioned, they're portrayed as threats. We see that in poll results, too. An ABC News poll found that a third of Republican respondents who thought that Muslims face discrimination said the discrimination was justified.

****

PROMINENT CONSERVATIVES HAVE a couple of theories about why liberals defend Muslims. The first is the usual conservative lament about political correctness, that is, it is a way for liberals to stigmatize dissent and control the way people think about a range of marginalized groups. The second theory goes further—according to some very prominent commentators, liberals defend Muslims in order to "recruit" them to the Left's grand plan to destroy Western civilization and the traditional Judeo-Christian ethos of America (more on that later).

About political correctness, More in Common found that Americans feel pressured to self-censor about Islam and Muslims more than any other topic—a full 66 percent said they felt this way. Seventy-eight percent of "traditional" and 88 percent of "devoted conservatives" believe that "many people nowadays are too sensitive to how Muslims are treated." And in their view, liberals are to blame for it: traditional conservatives complained that liberals treat Muslims as a "protected class," and devoted conservatives felt they "are being forced to accept liberal beliefs" about Islam. Or as the columnist and talk show host Dennis Prager concluded in his *National Review* piece WHY IS ISLAM TREATED BETTER THAN OTHER FAITHS? "There is only one possible reason, and that is political correctness—Western elites bending over backwards on behalf of Muslims and Islam in ways they never would for another religion."

In this, conservatives agree with commentators like Bill Maher and Richard Dawkins, who say complaints about "Islamophobia" are attempts to shut down legitimate criticism of Islam. On his HBO show, *Real Time with Bill Maher*, Maher castigated liberals for treating Muslims as a "protected species": "If we talk about them at all, or criticize them at all, it's [as if we're] somehow hurting or humiliating Muslims. It's ridiculous." Michelle Malkin in the *National Review* referred to it snidely as "Islam*faux*bia." James Kirchick calls it the Muslim win in the "Rock, Paper, Scissors of PC Victimology." He says the same about Obama's rejection of the phrase "Islamic terrorism." Naturally, then, Trump took up the cause; as one *Vox* headline noted, TRUMP LOVES SAYING "RADICAL ISLAMIC TERRORISM."

The dynamic has particular resonance in the Christian-Muslim context. The *American Conservative*'s Barbara Boland says the Left has a selective "allergy to language." Writing about the April 2019 church bombings in Sri Lanka by Islamist suicide bombers, Boland lambasts Barack Obama, Hillary Clinton, and Julian Castro for tweeting their condolences to "Easter worshippers" instead of "Christians." She wasn't the only one:

> "We're actually called Christians not 'Easter worshippers' wouldn't hurt to maybe just say that," *National Review* writer Alexandra DeSantis tweeted, as conservatives throughout the Twitter[verse] became incensed over the phrase. Breitbart called the tweets a "sympathy snub" that showed Obama and friends "could not bring themselves to identify the victims of the attacks as 'Christians.'" A *Washington Times* op-ed called the phrase anti-Christian.

The Left has an "inability to call things what they are," Boland says, and it uses this handicap in pernicious ways. Liberals won't acknowledge Christians' suffering, but they will refrain from using "Islamic terrorism" to protect Muslims from feeling attacked. Ignoring the fact that Muslims constitute just one percent of the American population, Boland frames her point in global terms: "There are nearly two billion Muslims in the world, but the Left insists on seeing them as a persecuted minority."

One conservative columnist compared liberals' response to the Christchurch mosque shooting and the Sri Lanka church bombing. He described a "hierarchy of victimhood" that places Christians at the bottom and Muslims on top:

> To get a sense of the depth of the double standard, consider this: Alexandria Ocasio-Cortez, the Twittersphere's favourite socialist, tweeted about the Christchurch massacre 14 times; she tweeted about the Sri Lanka atrocity not once.

> She isn't alone. Tweeters have compared and contrasted well-known liberals' and leftists' response to Christchurch and their response to Sri Lanka.

> They found that these people tweeted and posted and condemned far less after Sri Lanka than they did after Christchurch.

Former Trump counselor Kellyanne Conway also called out Ocasio-Cortez (AOC) for her silence. Pastor Darrell Scott, a board member of the National Diversity Coalition for Trump, said AOC was silent on the Sri Lanka attacks because she couldn't "weaponize them against Trump." In all of these examples, the purpose is to pit attacks on Christians against attacks on Muslims and other minorities the Left defends in order to prove the Left's victim bias.

Some Christian conservatives have even coined the term "Christophobia" to talk about Christian persecution and, in some cases, to compete with claims of "Islamophobia" (and "phobias" of other minorities, such as "homophobia"). The term fuels further judgments; writer Court Anderson complains, WHY WON'T THE MEDIA SAY "CHRISTOPHOBIA"?

Popular commentators aren't alone in drawing these comparisons. Both Johnnie Moore Jr., president of the Congress of Christian Leaders, and Tim Schultz, president of the center-right group First Amendment Partnership, told me it's become a common refrain for conservative evangelicals to respond to negative media coverage with, *Imagine if it were Muslims.* When news headlines declare conservative Christians "bigots" for insisting on a traditional definition of marriage, or when the *New York Times* prints Katherine Stewart's headline THE ROAD TO CORONAVIRUS HELL WAS PAVED BY EVANGELICALS, Christians respond, Imagine if it were Muslims these newspapers were talking about. For example, one reviewer of Stewart's book *The Power Worshippers* (which discusses a range of Christian conservative religious claims and legal cases), wrote:

> Imagine if we replaced the word "Christians" with the world [sic] "Muslims"—how quickly the author would be (rightly) criticized for such false and blanketed statements against an entire community based on their religious beliefs. It's always interesting to see the ones screaming for tolerance are the most intolerant of differing views. The book is filled with hateful ramblings, distorted information, and illogical claims. It's really sad that in today's society we cannot openly express and discuss our views without being unjustly and unfairly labeled.

The comment reflects both the siege mentality ("we cannot openly express and discuss our views without being unjustly and unfairly labeled") and a concern about the disparate treatment of Muslims and Christians. The two often go hand in hand, Schultz told me. He works with state legislatures to help pass religious freedom protective laws, so his interaction with conservative Christians is far ranging.

Given my work, I'm aware of the spectrum of positions among American Christians. . . . Among the average churchgoer, there's a sense of Christianity being scorned by American elites. They realize that the things they took for granted are no longer possible and there's a cultural decline in Christianity. At the same time, they feel that if you're a Muslim, those things don't apply in the same way. So, they conclude that elite culture has a specifically anti-Christian animus.

"It's a partial story, or a half-truth," Schultz acknowledged. Indeed, empirical data paint a very different picture. The Media Portrayals of Minorities Project at Vermont's Middlebury College analyzed 26,626 articles from 2018 that were published in the *New York Times, Washington Post, Wall Street Journal,* and *USA Today* and found that news coverage of Muslims was "far more negative than that of other minority groups." Even when the researchers removed articles related to terrorism, foreign conflicts, or Islamist groups, "stories about Muslims are still more negative than stories about any other group." A separate study found that violent attacks committed by Muslims receive 357 percent more coverage than attacks committed by others. Stated another way, a non-Muslim attacker has to kill on average seven more people than a Muslim attacker does to get the same media coverage.

Still, it is true that liberals are uneasy with anti-Muslim speech. In a study published in 2016, a group of political scientists at Brigham Young University (BYU) measured Americans' levels of unease with and willingness to sanction negative speech about different religious groups. They found that Democrats "express the greatest unease—and the greatest willingness to sanction those who make the disapproving comments—with statements about Jews and Muslims."

But they also found that Republicans exhibit "exceptionally low levels of discomfort with and unwillingness to sanction negative comments about Muslims." In a polarized culture, where our mega-identities rule, if liberals sanction anti-Muslim speech, conservatives make sure not to. It's not that Republicans are above sanctioning speech, they just don't do it for Muslims—partly because Democrats do that, and Republicans don't want to be like Democrats.

The BYU researchers found exactly these group dynamics: "partisans of different stripes express strikingly distinctive patterns of concern." They also found that the groups differed the most on the Muslim question: Muslims "most readily experience the effects of group-based religious bias." Republicans "sanctioned disparaging statements about every religious group but one: Muslims. Whereas more than 70% of Republicans sanctioned statements about all other religious groups . . . only 38% of Republicans sanctioned commentators making statements about Muslims."

The researchers used social identity theory to explain their findings. Depending on which group you belong to, you face different social costs when you sanction negative speech about Muslims. For Republicans, the social costs—repudiation by their tribe—are highest for sanctioning anti-Muslim speech. For Democrats, the social costs for the same thing are much lower, and the social benefits much higher.

Here again, group members might be falsely enforcing unpopular norms—for example, some Republicans may be open-minded but in order to throw off suspicion from their in-group they will eagerly take the opportunity to express close-minded views. A particularly apt example of this: when current US senator Josh Hawley (R-MO) was a candidate for Missouri attorney general, his Republican opponent took out an ad lambasting Hawley for representing the Muslim prisoner Gregory Holt at the Supreme Court. Holt had challenged his prison's grooming policy, which prohibited him from growing a short beard in accordance with his religious beliefs. The Becket Fund for Religious Liberty, where Hawley worked at the time, represented Holt and won a unanimous decision for him. The religious claim was, on all counts, uncontroversial, but because Holt was Muslim and had expressed extremist views, his case became a flashpoint in the political race. Hawley's reaction? He disavowed his work on the case and said his name had been mistakenly placed on the Supreme Court brief. The political costs were just too high for Hawley to stand by his work.

A series of studies conducted between November 2015 and June 2016 also highlight these costs and benefits. The University of Maryland conducted three national polls measuring Americans' views about Islam and Muslims. The last survey was done just days after the June 2016 Pulse nightclub shooting in Orlando, Florida, where a Muslim attacker killed forty-nine people and wounded fifty-three others. The polls found that Americans' attitudes about Muslims improved between each of the three surveys, even after the Orlando shooting.

But the positive upward movement depended on one's party affiliation. Republicans stayed relatively fixed across all three polls, whereas Democrats' views rose by twelve points. Commenting on the findings in 2016, Shibley Telhami of the Brookings Institution noted the political context:

> Because GOP candidates have used the issue of Islam and violence as a political weapon against their Democratic opponents and President Barack Obama, the emphasized link between Islam and violence has become associated with GOP candidates, especially Donald Trump. To agree with the view that Islam and terrorism are tightly linked, in other words, is to take Trump's side of the political divide. On the one hand, this means that his core supporters will likely embrace his opinions, and the poll results indeed show that Trump supporters bucked the national trend. On the other hand, those who oppose him have the tendency to reject his view in part because it's his and because he is using it for political gain. It's less about Islam and Muslims, and more about taking political sides.

That last line—"it's less about Islam and Muslims, and more about taking political sides"—gets at the fact that Muslims are treated or even seen less as Muslims and more as proxies in a liberal-conservative fight. Favorable views of Muslims are traits of the Democratic mega-identity, and negative views are traits of the Republican mega-identity. As Telhami explained again a year later, this time well into the Trump presidency, "The more one side emphasized the issue—as happened with Trump on Islam and Muslims—the more the other side took the opposite position."

Telhami's explanation also gets at the difference in costs and benefits to each group. For Democrats, protecting Muslims means winning against Republicans; for Republicans, winning requires denigrating Islam and Muslims. Recall Tajfel's findings from chapter 1: People exhibit discriminatory intergroup behavior in a way that creates the biggest gap between their group and the out-group. Above all else, it is the winning that is important to them. Lilliana Mason explains it this way: "The danger of mega-partisan identity is that it encourages citizens to care more about partisan victory than about real policy outcomes. We find ways to justify almost any governmental policy as long as it is the policy of our own team. What is best for America . . . is secondary to whether our party's team gets what it demanded."

To be fully loyal to their party, people are willing to change their positions and "mold their political opinions to their party." Sometimes that requires adopting caricatured perceptions of the other party or imaginary conflicts of interest. Mason writes, "Partisan conflict today is characterized by an exaggerated and poorly understood difference between the parties, based in both genuine and imaginary conflicts of interest." We see that in the way conservatives explain the relationship between Muslims and the Left—the Democratic Party isn't just the other team but is instead a fundamental threat that seeks to destroy everything conservatives hold dear, and it uses Muslims to further that agenda.

For example, Rod Dreher at the *American Conservative* thinks "progressive culture is happy to support Islam insofar as it can be used as a club to bash Christians." Prominent conservative commentator Ben Shapiro goes even further, arguing in his piece WHY THE LEFT PROTECTS ISLAM that liberals "recruit" Muslims as one of many minority groups in order to destroy Western civilization: "The Left believes that the quickest way to destroy Western civilization is no longer class warfare but multicultural warfare: Simply ally with groups that hate the prevailing system and work with them to take it down. Then, the Left will build on the ashes of the old system." More in Common also found that conservatives "celebrate" those who maintain "traditional Judeo-Christian and American . . . values, such as Evangelicals" and "distrust those they view as threatening them, such as Black Lives Matter activists, feminists and Muslims." It's liberals and Muslims (and others) against America, conservatives, and Christians.

In 2009, political scientists Kerem Ozan Kalkan, Geoffrey Layman, and Eric Uslaner noted that while "prejudice toward most minority groups has declined in recent decades . . . Muslims are an exception: they are viewed much less favorably than most other religious and racial minorities." In their "Bands of Others" study, the researchers also noted that religious and racial outsiders are eventually accepted by the in-group, but cultural outsiders—people who exhibit behaviors different from the mainstream or who are thought to hold different values—have a harder time being accepted. Kalkan et al. hypothesized (and proved) that a big reason Muslims aren't accepted is because they belong to both of these "bands of others"; Muslims are considered both racial and religious outsiders and "behavioral" outsiders. About the latter, the researchers wrote that even though Muslims are "generally well integrated into American society," they are also "disproportionately foreign born . . . and their religious practices and teachings are clearly 'strange' from the standpoint of the Judeo-Christian tradition." (In identifying these factors of "otherness," the study found that the 9/11 attacks and fears about terrorism didn't explain anti-Muslim attitudes in the United States.)

Other studies suggest that "strange" means more than just "different." A 2016 survey by the Pew Research Center found that almost half of all American adults believe that some American Muslims are anti-American. A 2017 Pew poll found that half of American adults believe that Islam does not have a place in "mainstream American society," and almost half (44 percent) think there is a "natural conflict between Islam and democracy." In 2019, Pew wrote that "attitudes toward Muslims are tied to politics, even after taking education, age, and other demographic factors into account," and found that Democrats are more accepting of Muslims than are Republicans.

In many ways, Democratic congresswoman Ilhan Omar represents the full amalgamation of traits that conservatives find threatening. She is unapologetically progressive in her politics, visibly Muslim in her head-scarf, and unabashed in her criticism of the United States. Along with Muslim congresswoman Rashida Tlaib and two other progressive congress-women, Ayanna Pressley and Alexandria Ocasio-Cortez, Omar is part of the "Squad" that President Trump and his supporters scorned. Referring collectively to all four women, Trump tweeted in 2019, "The 'Squad' is a very Racist group of troublemakers who are young, inexperienced, and not very smart," and said these women need to "go back" to the "crime infested places from which they came."

The tweet implied elements of un-Americanness and anti-Americanness—themes conservatives associate with Omar often. A November 2019 opinion piece by Sam Kumar titled CONGRESSWOMAN ILHAN OMAR'S ANTI-AMERICANISM catalogues some of the statements (taken out of context) that have solidified the perception for conservatives.

> Congresswoman Ilhan Omar of Minnesota, a member of the so-called Squad, endorsed Sen. Bernie Sanders for presi-dent, claiming that Sanders will fight against "Western imperi-alism" . . . She referred to the attacks of 9/11 as "some people did something." She accused Jewish-Americans of dual loyalty

with the "It's all about the Benjamins" tweet. Then there is the tweet saying, "(M)ay Allah awaken the people and help them see the evil doings of Israel."

She blamed the U.S. for the terrorist attack on the Kenyan mall that killed 70 people and wounded 200 more. She wanted a Minnesota judge to show leniency to a man who tried to obtain [sic] fake passports to go fight for ISIS. She blamed the U.S. for the Venezuelan coup. She supported the terrorist organization Hamas as they fired rockets at Israel. She complained about the way Americans pronounce "Al Qaeda." She made the false claim that U.S. forces killed thousands of Somalis during the "Black Hawk Down" mission and included the hashtag "#NotTodaySatan" . . . At every turn, Omar has sided with people who march down the streets and chant "Death to America!" while burning our flag.

The piece goes on to draw the predictable partisan contrast.

Omar, unfortunately, is not the only person in the Democrat Party who thinks poorly of America . . . not a single flag was on stage during the October Democrat presidential debate . . .

Contrast that with the Republican party. Disrespect the flag or the anthem and you will be persona non grata within the party. Chants of "U-S-A" rain down from the rafters at our rallies. We sing along with the national anthem and we are proud to do so. In the Republican party, patriotism, including respect for the flag and anthem, is nonnegotiable.

Trump also wove these points together seamlessly. Recall his statement at the coronavirus briefing about church and mosque closures, including during Easter and Ramadan. I edited the earlier quotation; here's what he said in full:

> I would say that there could be a difference. And we'll have to see what will happen. Because I have seen a great disparity in this country. I've seen a great disparity. I mean I've seen a very strong anti-Israel bent in Congress with Democrats. It was unthinkable seven or eight or 10 years ago, and now they're into a whole different thing. Between Omar and AOC—I saw AOC plus three, add them on. You have, the things that they say about Israel are so bad. And I can't believe it. Just a minute. So I would be interested to see that. Because they go after Christian churches but they don't tend to go after mosques. And I don't want them to go after mosques! But I do want to see what their event is—. I just had a call with imams. I just had a call with ministers, rabbis. We had a tremendous call with the faith leaders. No, I don't think that at all. I am someone that believes in faith. And it matters not what your faith is but our politicians seem to treat different faiths very differently. And they seem to think and I don't know what happened with our country, but the Christian faith is treated much differently than it was, and I think it's treated very unfairly.

When *Mother Jones* reported on Trump's remarks, it found the bit about Israel and the Squad a "weird digression . . . from a question about a religious holiday to a rant about Democratic critics of the Israeli state." But, in fact, mentioning Israel reminded the audience of Representative Omar's past comments and Trump's run-ins with the Squad, further underscoring the Right's perception not just that Democrats favor Muslims but that they favor them in order to further an anti-American agenda.

* * * *

THIS PORTRAYAL OF Muslims as integral to the Left's destruction of the America (indeed, the civilization) conservatives defend can affect even people who aren't Christian nationalists. Andrew Lewis told me, "Those who are constantly inundated with perspectives that Christianity is threatened (even if they are not necessarily hostile to other religious faiths) are more likely to accommodate Christian nationalist views on their own side. Trying to push back against nationalism from your team and religious discrimination on the other team is a difficult path to follow." In other words, it is difficult for many non-nationalists to both resist liberals' attacks on their Christian practices and also resist Christian nationalists' push to privilege Christianity. So they accommodate the rhetoric and tactics of the Christian nationalists even if they are more open to diverse faiths.

There's evidence that people adopt views in this way. In 2011, Marc Hetherington and Elizabeth Suhay published a study about "authoritarianism," a personality type that sees the world as black-and white and society as fragile, and seeks to impose hierarchy, order, and uniformity. Hetherington and Suhay tested the connection between the authoritarian personality type and perceptions of threat from terrorism and found that people who score high on authoritarianism don't "become more hawkish or less supportive of civil liberties in response to a perceived threat of terrorism"; they hold these positions even in the absence of threat. But people "who are less authoritarian adopt more restrictive and aggressive policy stands when they perceive a threat from terrorism. In other words, many *average Americans* become susceptible to 'authoritarian thinking' when they perceive a grave threat to their safety." (emphasis mine)

Diana Mutz made similar findings in her 2018 study on social dominance orientation (SDO), a trait closely related to authoritarianism, and which indicates a desire to dominate the out-group. She tested the relationship between threats to one's status and support for Trump and found that people who felt their status was threatened experienced an increase in SDO, which in turn led them to support Trump. Once again, it was the average American who changed the most: "There is no evidence that those high in preexisting SDO were especially likely to defect to Trump. . . . Instead, it is the increase in SDO, which is indicative of status threat, that corresponded to increasing positivity toward Trump."

Similarly, Lewis posits that the perceived threat to Christianity leads otherwise non-nationalist Christians to accommodate Christian nationalists even if they fundamentally disagree with their values. For Christian nationalists, the threat is to America's identity as a Christian nation. For those who lean away from nationalism, the perceived threat is about their own ability to live according to their Christian beliefs.

Importantly, Lewis says, "All of this is wrapped up in partisanship, as partisan leaders prime these responses—both out-group intolerance and in-group protection. In some eras, partisans have played homage to protecting Christians from losing ground to secularism or liberals. But now partisans on the Right are increasingly emphasizing both secularism and liberalism, as well as Islam and other foreign religions." This explains Mutz's findings, too—Trump's deft use of the victim narrative helped attract voters who were experiencing status threat. On the campaign trail, he told them in the clearest terms, "We will have so much winning if I get elected that you may get bored with the winning."

In a nutshell, then, authoritarianism and SDO are triggered by a perceived threat and people respond by protecting the in-group and excluding the threatening outsider. Lewis calls it "activated vulnerability." Brené Brown calls it "weaponized belonging."

And, again, this is true not just for people high on the authoritarianism or SDO scale—it's true of the many, many Americans who are perceiving a threat to their status. This is what Ezra Klein is getting at when he points to "what happens in moments like this one, moments when a majority feels its dominance beginning to fail. The answer, attested to in mountains of studies and visible everywhere in our politics, is this: change of this magnitude acts on us psychologically, not just electorally."

The implications are serious. Intergroup bias at its most innocuous includes stereotyping and prejudice. At its worst, it results in discrimination or explicit disfavoring of the out-group. In some countries, it goes as far as genocide. The Pew Research Center in 2009 found this pattern in countries across the world. Specifically, it found a correlation between government restrictions on religion and social hostilities: the more a government limited religious beliefs and practices, the more social unrest there was.

In the United States, conservative Christians feel that their rights are under attack. They saw it in the Affordable Care Act mandate requiring religious employers to pay for contraception and abortifacients. They saw it in the hostile words of the commissioners in *Masterpiece*. And they sense from the public debate that if a Democratic president is elected, they will face additional restrictions. All of these restrictions count as "government restrictions" for purposes of Pew's study. (I once moderated a panel discussion that included Brian Grim, one of the authors of the Pew study. An audience member asked him whether he would count restrictions on Christian wedding vendors as a "government restriction" on religious exercise. Grim said yes.)

With government restrictions on the rise, conservatives feel threatened, and their vulnerability manifests in social hostilities—with Muslims bearing the brunt. An August 2017 poll by the Annenberg Public Policy Center of the University of Pennsylvania found that almost one in five Americans believe that under the US Constitution, American Muslims do not have the same rights as other American citizens. A 2015 poll by the Associated Press-NORC Center for Public Affairs Research found that Americans favor protecting religious liberty for Christians over other faith groups, ranking Muslims as the least deserving of this right. Eighty-two percent voted in favor of protecting religious liberty for Christians, while only 61 percent said the same for Muslims.

A 2011 Faith Matters survey connected this anti-Muslim posture to demographic threat. Respondents were first asked whether religion was gaining or losing influence. They were then asked if that was a good thing or a bad thing. They were later also asked whether they would support the building of a mosque in their community. The results: those who saw religion as losing influence were less supportive of the mosque, and especially so if they also thought the loss of religion was a bad thing. In other words, anti-Muslim sentiment is related to feelings of threat around the changing face of America.

Similarly, researcher Saeed Khan in 2016 compiled extensive data linking state anti-Muslim legislation and legislation targeting other progressive issues. His study connected support for so-called anti-sharia bills (bills that restrict Muslim religious arbitration) with support for policies restricting voter access and abortion rights, anti-immigration proposals, and bans on same-sex marriage. If a lawmaker supported legislation in one of these areas, there was an 80 percent chance of support in one of the other areas. Anti-Muslim sentiment tracked particularly closely to Voter ID and Right-To-Work-related bills, which, Khan notes, "lends credence to the idea that the current legislative agenda is about preserving power."

Based on his findings, Khan says "it is unhelpful to view Islamophobia as an isolated phenomenon in America." Instead, we have to situate it in the "general malaise affecting a significant portion of the population, that is, the so-called 'culture wars.'" This "deep anxiety around the changing demographic nature of American society and the approaching demographic tipping point . . . is the wider domestic context in which anti-Muslim prejudice and animus operate." While Shapiro and others argue that the Left is using Muslims to further its multicultural agenda, many on the Right position themselves against Muslims as a way of protecting a Judeo-Christian vision of America.

That Muslims' rights have become a casualty of our current polarization makes stark the dangerousness of our current "ferocious polarization of everything." In Klein's words: "Viscerally and emotionally, the stakes of politics we have evolved to sense is whether our group is winning or losing, whether the out-group is gaining the power to threaten us or whether our allies are amassing the strength to ensure our safety and prosperity. As our many identities merge into single political mega-identities, those visceral, emotional stakes are rising—and with them, our willingness to do anything to make sure our side wins."

CHAPTER 5

Conspiracies and Demagoguery

YOU MET HIM EARLIER, BUT let me reintroduce you to Frank Gaffney Jr., who had this to say about me at the National Religious Broadcasters' NRB 2020 Christian Media Convention in February 2020:

> We do not support Sharia supremacists themselves or their enablers or their apologists.
>
> And it pains me beyond words that this program that will be coming up after the attorney general's remarks, you have such an

individual who will be presented to you, I'm afraid, as someone who is a perfect example of moderate Muslims and a perfect interlocutor for us in interfaith dialogue and bridge building and the like . . .

I hope that you will not be misled into believing this individual. I've nothing against her personally. But this individual and what she stands for—and most especially what she is doing with organizations like the Council on American-Islamic Relations (one of the most aggressive Muslim Brotherhood front organizations in the country)—must not be endorsed, even implicitly, by this organization.

I had hoped that she would not be given a platform. She is. I trust you will listen attentively. But I hope that you will not give her yourselves a platform.

Gaffney is the founder of the virulently anti-Muslim organization Center for Security Policy and a prominent player in the billion-dollar propaganda machine that instigates fear and hatred of Muslims. Everything he says about me, down to his precise words and references—"interfaith," "bridge building," "Muslim Brotherhood"—have been carefully calculated over many years to alarm Christian audiences.

The fearmongering is centered on two manufactured falsehoods: First, Muslims are going to destroy America by fundamentally altering its Christian foundations. Second, this destruction is made possible by the Left. Time and again, the professional propagandists manipulate Christian vulnerability and portray Muslims as traits of the liberal mega-identity.

Unfortunately, despite the far-fetched nature of their claims, they are influential among masses of evangelicals and other Christian conservatives. Their talking points show up on Fox News and other conservative media outlets, and they're repeated by Republican politicians across the United States (a 2018 investigative piece recorded instances in forty-nine states, and the remaining state—Utah—quickly caught up). After Trump's 2016 election, Gaffney and others have moved in closer to the White House, too. And average Americans are taking it all in. Many are suspicious of interfaith exchanges because of ideas like Jeanine Pirro's, who said on her Fox show, "Muslims . . . have conquered us through immigration. They have conquered us through *interfaith dialogue*." (emphasis mine) The antagonism has morphed into something almost impenetrable; when mere dialogue is made to seem sinister, bridging the Muslim-Christian divide becomes so much harder.

In this chapter, I will take you into the world of conspiracy theories and trace their impact on Muslims' religious rights. Ezra Klein notes, "To the extent that it's true that a loss of privilege *feels* like oppression, that feeling needs to be taken seriously, both because it's real, and because, left to fester, it can be weaponized by demagogues and reactionaries." The case of anti-Muslim propaganda is a perfect example of this phenomenon; I show here what happens when we don't take Christian vulnerability seriously and leave it to fester.

* * * *

Teachers for Trump Facebook Page

Muslims are commanded to imitate Mohammed. Mohammed stole from, raped and killed thousands. This is what Islam means by "peace." Let's stop Islamic supremacy. #ItsNotAReligion

Evangelicals for Trump Facebook Page

(Commenting on the April 2019 fire that destroyed significant portions of the famous Notre Dame church in Paris, France, and suggesting possible Muslim involvement)

The Mainstream Media Ignores the case of three (3) Muslim jihadist women who planned to burn down the Notre Dame cathedral. Just an "accident," once again.

"ONE OF THREE women allegedly involved in a foiled plot in 2016 to blow up a car packed with gas canisters near the Notre Dame cathedral in Paris was today sentenced to eight years in prison by a French court for earlier offenses."

Veterans for Trump Facebook Page

Public Enemy #1: George Soros undermines Republics and Western Civilization by funding 1) open borders to likely Democrat voters; 2) Thousands of projects attacking Jews/Israel and Christian morality & people in Europe, America, the Middle East, Africa and Asia.

While he cleverly cries "victim" of anti-Semitism, he is secretly funding anti-semitism along with Islamists.

The *Google English Dictionary* defines *Islamist* as "an advocate or supporter of Islamic militancy or fundamentalism." But the above Facebook posts and others like them move fluidly between Muslims, Islam, and Islamists, and depict them as one and the same. Soros, a billionaire philanthropist and Democratic Party backer, is falsely presented as the primary benefactor. He is said to have these Muslims on his "Leftist-Islamist payroll," which he also purportedly uses to fund a range of other individuals whom the conspiracy theorists find irritating—such as the teen survivors of the February 2018 Parkland School shooting in Florida, a few of whom became prominent advocates of gun control and nonviolence in schools and earned the ire of the political Right.

The Facebook pages cited above have distinct audiences: teachers, evangelicals, veterans. Still others are titled "Jews & Christians for America" and "Blacks for Trump." But in 2019, the investigative website *Snopes* discovered that a network of similarly themed Facebook pages (a total of twenty-four, with a combined 1.4 million followers) could be traced back financially to one person: Kelly Monroe Kullberg. She is neither Jewish nor black nor a veteran. She is a white evangelical author and activist. Kullberg has founded multiple evangelical organizations, including the Veritas Forum—which, interestingly, has in recent years helped foster Muslim-evangelical dialogue—as well as Christians for a Sustainable Economy and the American Association of Evangelicals. That last organization in 2016 issued an open letter to Christians and Christian leaders warning them that "wealthy, anti-Christian foundations, following the lead of billionaire George Soros's Open Society Foundation, fund and 'rent' Christian ministers as 'mascots' serving as surprising validators for their causes."

These protests about Soros, his "Leftist-Islamist" payroll, open borders, fake news, and so on, are rooted in the idea of cultural Marxism, the tenets of which I explain below. In a piece for the *Guardian*, journalist Jason Wilson explains that those who believe there is a cultural Marxist conspiracy use the concept of "cultural Marxism'" as a catch-all to "account for things they disapprove of—things like Islamic immigrant communities, feminism," and so on. In the midst of the coronavirus pandemic, the conspiracy theories extended even to mask wearing and social distancing; a widely followed writer of the *Gateway Pundit* tweeted in June 2020:

> "Social distancing" is an Islamo-Marxist idea.
>
> You can only be out in public with your family members (Islam)
>
> You have to cover your face when you go out in public (sharia for women)
>
> No parties, no fun, no weddings, no gatherings (Islam, Marxism)

As many responded on social media, the claim was ridiculous to the point of being funny. (In fact, Muslims love parties, fun, and weddings so much that many Muslim cultures typically have weeklong celebrations for weddings!) But for Islamo-Marxism conspiracy theorists, everything they disapprove of can be traced back to this supposed partnership.

The theorists' explanation of how it's all connected "depends on a crazy-mirror history, which glancingly reflects things that really happened, only to distort them in the most bizarre ways." The manufactured idea is that when the socialist revolution failed to extend beyond the Soviet Union, Marxist thinkers expanded their reach indirectly through cultural institutions like universities, the government, and media. According to the conspiracy theorists, Marxists also decided that it wasn't enough to destroy capitalism; they needed to destroy social conventions around family, sexuality, and gender hierarchies, too. For this, the Marxists engaged in psychological manipulation, made even more powerful once they supposedly took over universities and Hollywood. These institutions, the conspiracists say, enforced ideas like feminism, gay rights, and even political correctness—all in an effort to "destroy traditional Christian values and overthrow free enterprise."

Another writer, this one in the *EU Reporter*, explains it this way:

> Contrary to classical Marxism, cultural Marxism sees the society as the battleground between the "exploited" and the "exploiter." In other words, the conflict is no longer class based but between the majority and the socially marginalised groups. Followers of cultural Marxism generally advocate LGBT rights, the foundations of feminism, ethnic minorities, and so on, but they also have a point of attachment to the Islamists.

> While Christianity is in their view an exploiting force to be looked down upon, the adherents of Islamism are generally seen as belonging to the "exploited" camp and hence deserving of

leftist support. Although theoretically, such reconciliation between cultural Marxism and Islamism must be a logical impossibility, in practice, and in spite of their fundamental differences and diametrically opposing views on a vast range of issues from women rights to transsexuals, homosexuals, and so on, the two worldviews have managed to forge a deep connection to each other.

"Cultural Marxism" helps rationalize the siege mentality even as it struggles to fuse seemingly contradictory ideologies. Wilson says it "allows those smarting from a loss of privilege to be offered the shroud of victimhood, by pointing to a shadowy, omnipresent, quasi-foreign elite who are attempting to destroy all that is good in the world." For many of the conspiracists, Gaffney foremost among them, the "shadowy, omnipresent, quasi-foreign" role is filled by the Muslim Brotherhood, an Islamist organization. Gaffney claims that the Brotherhood seeks to replace the US Constitution with a caliphate based upon sharia law, and that it controls American mosques and civic organizations in furtherance of this goal.

Peter Beinart in *The Atlantic* writes, "If you squint hard enough, you can see how Gaffney reaches his conclusions. The group [Muslim Brotherhood] was created in Egypt in 1928 with the purpose of spreading Islam globally and reviving the Caliphate." And in the 1960s, some of its members reportedly helped found the Muslim Students Association, from which some of today's American Muslim organizations spring. But, Beinart writes, "If you stop squinting, the conspiracy theory looks absurd. . . . Although 'some U.S. Muslim organizations were founded by or with the assistance of the Muslim Brotherhood decades ago, for most of them, these links are ancient history.'" To fully grasp Gaffney's absurdity, it's helpful to understand his approach as a type of modern-day McCarthyism. One can be concerned about the Brotherhood, but to say it controls most American Muslims is akin to saying the American Communist Party controls most of Washington and Hollywood.

Still, the propagandists are obsessed with the Brotherhood and with discrediting American Muslim civic groups by drawing tenuous links. Their favorite target is the Council on American-Islamic Relations (CAIR), a civil rights advocacy organization. In his NRB comments about me, Gaffney falsely smeared CAIR as "one of the most aggressive Muslim Brotherhood front organizations in the country."

Naturally, then, CAIR plays a central role in the presumed cultural Marxist agenda. The theory about the alliance is propagated far and wide, many times with the help of Christian funding. Kelly Kullberg from the *Snopes* report is not alone in this work. One report tracked funding from seemingly benevolent charitable foundations to projects dedicated to promoting anti-Islam, anti-Muslim rhetoric. The top two funders were Christian Advocates Serving Evangelism, Inc. and the National Christian Charitable Foundation, which collectively represent $48.1 million, or 54 percent of the $89.5 million contributed by the "mega-funders of Islamophobia." (The researchers acknowledge that in some cases, these foundations are not ideologically aligned with their donors and are instead exploited by donors who want to anonymize their donations to anti-Muslim special interest groups.) The conservative Christian Heavenly Father's Foundation gave $1.2 million to the American Family Foundation, which has said on its radio program that American Muslims have no First Amendment rights: "Islam is clearly the religion that Satan is promoting to be the counterfeit alternative to Christianity," and "the threat to our freedoms comes not from radical Islam but from Islam itself."

Among others, Christian fund recipients who propagate anti-Muslim fear include Foundation for Advocating Christian Truth, Global Faith Institute, Freedom of Conscience Defense Fund (FCDF), and the Christian Action Network. The Global Faith Institute says it works "with churches, schools, and civic organizations across the country to educate them about Islam and the civilization jihad taking place in our schools, churches, and government. Its mission is to give a voice to the victims of Islam, expose the *real* war on women, and protect the US constitution and our Judeo-Christian values." Meanwhile, the Christian Action Network put out a report called *The Secret Agenda of New York City's Muslim Patrol Cars*, in which it alleges that Muslim Community Patrol & Services was created to "enforce sharia law on citizens." (I discuss FCDF in detail below.)

A separate investigative report examines the organizations and key propagandists that receive funding for anti-Muslim messaging—for example, Pamela Geller and Robert Spencer, the cofounders of the Stop Islamization of America organization, and Brigitte Gabriel, the founder of ACT for America. A major grantee, identified by both reports, is Gaffney's Center for Security Policy (CSP). This is the organization that describes most explicitly what it has at various times called "Islamo-Leftism," the "Leftist-Islamist alliance," or the "Red-Green Axis." Anders Breivik, the Norwegian terrorist who in 2011 killed more than ninety people in Sweden with the motive of "Christian war," quoted Gaffney seven times in his manifesto. Breivik said his actions were "gruesome but necessary" to save Europe from Marxism (which he equated with liberalism and multiculturalism) and "Muslimization." He vowed to wage "brutal and breathtaking operations" to defeat the alleged "ongoing Islamic Colonization of Europe." (Brievik isn't the only violent actor to be so motivated. The *New York Times* found in 2017 that nearly one in ten attacks globally is committed by attackers who identify as white, Christian, and culturally European. These attackers seek to defend "their privileged position in the West" from threats "by immigrants, Muslim and other religious and racial minorities.")

CSP-funded author Jim Simpson wrote two books on the subject: *The Red-Green Axis: Refugees, Immigration and the Agenda to Erase America* and *The Red-Green Axis 2.0: An Existential Threat to America and the World*. The "Red" points to the red in the Communist hammer and sickle flag, and implicitly connects the political Left, communism, and socialism. The "Green" points to the green often found in the national flags of majority-Muslim countries; green symbolizes Islam. According to Simpson, this axis of Islam and liberalism endeavors to re-create America and fundamentally alter its culture—a process he calls "civilization jihad."

Of the two, liberals are the ones in control. The various theorists disagree on this point, but for Simpson, the Left is the architect of the alliance and Muslims merely the pawns. The alliance utilizes three main tools to take over America: deception, immigration, and interfaith dialogue. On deception, Simpson says the Left supports various minority groups only as a means of achieving their ultimate goal of a "permanent progressive majority." In an interview on the *Debbie Aldrich Show*, Simpson explained, "None of those issues, my body my rights, none of those issues matter to the Left. What matters to the Left is power. And they're doing anything and everything they can to amass it."

On immigration, Simpson says increasing the flow of Muslims—including Muslim refugees—into the country helps the Left both solidify its voter base and generate social instability.

> There is a method to their madness: *it is the Left's goal to build a "permanent progressive majority" ruling class.* The open borders agenda is a perfect vehicle. Millions of needy poor become bought and paid for Democrat voters once citizenship is obtained. And erasing American culture, traditions, and adherence to rule of man-made law inspires calls for still more government to solve the manufactured crisis.

Immigration introduces "exotic and incompatible" populations into the country, which Simpson says allows Muslims and liberals to wage the warned-about civilization jihad.

As for the apparently nefarious use of interfaith dialogue, Simpson was invited to discuss that threat in September 2019 at an event organized by a Baptist church in Detroit. Called "9/11 forgotten? Is Michigan surrendering to Islam?" the two-day event sought to uncover how the interfaith movement is sabotaging America. The event was ultimately cancelled because of backlash from political leaders and community organizations, but a group called Sharia Crime Stoppers stepped in and created a webinar to feature Simpson's remarks. There, Simpson extolled the Baptist church as an exception among evangelicals: "In many ways, evangelicals have been asleep. This church is an exception, and [this pastor] is a target."

He goes on to explain that Muslims and the Left use interfaith dialogue "to subvert our society and encourage terrorism. The minute you sit down with them, you're opening the door, because now you've made yourself susceptible to their very well-thought-out strategy. Our churches and synagogues are the last holdouts against this tidal wave of virulent corruption, subversion of our culture and our entire society," and if evangelicals permit interfaith dialogue, they allow the enemy to penetrate those holdouts.

In a 2017 piece titled WHEN EVANGELICALS BECOME USEFUL IDIOTS FOR ISLAMISM, Simpson explains that the "Christian church has not escaped" the Left's agenda to create "ungovernable anarchy."

> In fact, it has become a major target. The Left, in concert with
> its allies among atheists, Islamists, and the homosexual lobby,
> is engaged in a multi-front war to destroy what remains of our
> nation's Christian bedrock. One of the fronts in this war comes
> under the innocuous heading "Interfaith Dialog." It sounds so
> compelling: a mutually beneficial outreach for "differing faith
> traditions" to find common ground and join forces to mend the
> fractious divisions between Muslims, Christians, Jews, and for
> that matter, practically everyone else.

> But that is not what is accomplished . . . those in the forefront of this battle, like the Council of American Islamic Relations (CAIR) and the hundreds of other Muslim Brotherhood front groups, are determined to use every tactic at their disposal to deconstruct our laws, our Constitution and our religious and secular institutions, to replace them with the Islamic version, Sharia law . . .

There are other tale-tellers spinning stories about "Islamo-leftism." CSP-funded writer Matthew Vadum gets into it in his book *Team Jihad: How Sharia-Supremacists Collaborate with Leftists to Destroy the United States.* David Horowitz, well known for his anti-Muslim advocacy, wrote *Unholy Alliance: Radical Islam and the American Left.* Andrew McCarthy, a former assistant US attorney and a columnist for the *National Review,* proposes a similar theory in *The Grand Jihad: How Islam and the Left Sabotage America.*

Their claims are patently exaggerated, even fantastical. But they are influential even among mainstream audiences, perhaps for the same reasons Christian conservatives are driven to accommodate nationalist beliefs. Recall from chapter 4 that the portrayal of Muslims as integral to the Left's destruction of America can affect even people who aren't Christian nationalists; it can be difficult for these Christians to both resist liberals' attacks on their Christian practices and also resist Christian nationalists' push to privilege Christianity. So, they accommodate the rhetoric and tactics of the Christian nationalists even if they are more open to diverse faiths.

Those same fears can draw average Americans into Gaffney and others' web of conspiracies. There's evidence of it already. Consider the voices spreading the ideas: McCarthy, a columnist at a mainstream conservative publication and Ben Shapiro, with his almost three million followers on Twitter and vast audience at the *Daily Wire.* Remember, Shapiro, too, posits that the Left "protects Islam" in order to "destroy Western civilization" through "multicultural warfare."

Even President Trump is in on it. When Paul Sperry, the author of *Muslim Mafia: Inside the Secret Underworld That's Conspiring to Islamize America* tweeted about Democrats favoring mosques over churches, Trump not only retweeted him but also defended the tweet at a White House briefing. This same president, with his evangelical base, brought the previously outlying Gaffney into the center of power. Beinart in his March 2017 piece THE DENATIONALIZATION OF AMERICAN MUSLIMS notes that Washington conservatives used to ridicule Gaffney's claims and stigmatize him for making them. But things changed quickly after Trump's election.

In 2003, after Gaffney attacked two Muslim staffers in the Bush White House, anti-tax crusader Grover Norquist banned him from his influential "Wednesday meeting" of conservative activists. In 2011, according to sources close to the organization, the American Conservative Union informally barred Gaffney from speaking at CPAC, the ACU's signature event. In 2013, the Bradley Foundation, which had backed the Center for Security Policy since 1988, cut off funds. That same year, Gaffney lost the *Washington Times* column he had been writing since the late 1990s. As late as December 2015, *The Daily Beast* declared that, "Frank Gaffney has been shunned by pretty much everyone in conservative intellectual circles."

Yet less than 18 months later, America is led by a president, Donald Trump, who has frequently cited the Center for Security Policy when justifying his policies toward Muslims. Trump's chief strategist, Steve Bannon, has called Gaffney "one of the senior thought leaders and men of action in this whole war against Islamic radical jihad." Trump's Attorney General, Jeff Sessions—who has said "Sharia law fundamentally conflicts with our magnificent constitutional order"—in 2015 won the

Center for Security Policy's "Keeper of the Flame" Award. Trump's CIA Director, Mike Pompeo, has appeared on Gaffney's radio program more than 24 times since 2013. Sebastian Gorka, who runs a kind of parallel National Security Council inside the White House called the Strategic Initiatives Group, has appeared on Gaffney's radio program 18 times during that period. He's called Sharia "antithetical to the values of this great nation" and recently refused to say whether he considered Islam a religion.

With colleagues and advisers like these, it's no wonder that Trump parrots the Gaffney talking points. Gaffney speaks often of Muslims and Muslim institutions as "Trojan horses." Trump used that precise metaphor in June 2016, the day after the Pulse nightclub shooting, when he said refugees and immigrants "could be a better, bigger more horrible version than the legendary Trojan horse ever was." He also said his Democratic opponent would be the one to let the Trojan horse in: "Altogether, under the [Hillary] Clinton plan, you'd be admitting hundreds of thousands of refugees from the Middle East with no system to vet them, or to prevent the radicalization of their children." And he threw in an additional allegation of Muslim deception, claiming that American Muslims knew what the Pulse shooter was planning and did not alert authorities: "They know what's going on. They know that he was bad . . . But you know what? They didn't turn [him] in."

Gaffney's and Simpson's false warnings about interfaith dialogue have resonance, too. Enough for Jeanine Pirro to warn about it on Fox. Enough, too, for a group of religious engagement experts to caution against using "interfaith" in any of my conversations with conservative Christians. When I asked what key terms I should avoid in Muslim-Christian engagement, I received answers like: "TERMS TO AVOID: Interfaith—sounds liberal; "Don't say interfaith—it's seen as liberal"; "Avoid the term 'interfaith' with Christians"; "Evangelical Christians get nervous about the word 'interfaith.'"

Part of the resistance is theological. "Interfaith" is mistaken for the idea that all religions are equally valid, and any such project threatens to challenge evangelicals' theological beliefs. As some of the respondents to my question explained, "Evangelicals are afraid of compromising." Kevin Singer from Neighborly Faith told me evangelicals believe they have to give up something in order to accept religious diversity, and his job is to show them "Nope, you don't. Bring it all." I understand the fear—claims to absolute truth are not unique to Christianity; they are an aspect of many religions.

But the respondents also noted that evangelicals have a "fear of hidden motives/agendas." They are, perhaps, wary of becoming one of Simpson's "useful idiots for Islamism." This is what Simpson, Gaffney, and others seek when they propagate their extreme theories; they feed information to a group of people already feeling vulnerable against the Left and minorities. With these conspiracy theories planted in their minds, conservative white evangelicals (and others) can "rationalize their choices in a way that is consistent with what they prefer to believe, rather than with what is actually true." About other areas of tribalism, Klein writes, "Much of the data is wrong or irrelevant. But it feels convincing. It's a terrific performance of scientific inquiry . . . if our search is motivated by aims other than accuracy, more information can mislead us—or, more precisely, help us mislead ourselves." The same can be said here.

****

MSNBC NEWSCASTER: The idea of Muslim law taking over in a place like Oklahoma where the wind comes sweeping down the plain may seem pretty remote, but still some state lawmakers there have decided it's time to make sure it never happens.

They're hoping to get a question on the November ballot that would ask voters whether it should be illegal for state courts to consider anything but US federal and state law when it comes to deciding cases. Republican Rex Duncan is one of the lawmakers backing the vote on the amendment that some call "Save Our State."

(Duncan's friendly face appears on the screen, a small smile tugging at the edges of his lips)

NEWSCASTER: What do you want to save your state from?

DUNCAN: Well, we want to save it from an attack on its survival, its future. Contessa, you know, Oklahomans recognize that America was founded on Judeo-Christian principles and we are unapologetically grateful that God has blessed America and blessed Oklahoma. And State Question 755, the Save Our State Amendment, is just a simple effort to ensure that our courts are not used to undermine those founding principles and turn Oklahoma into something that our founding fathers and our great-grandparents wouldn't recognize.

NEWSCASTER: Do you believe that there is imminent danger of judges considering sharia law when deciding cases?

DUNCAN: It's not just a danger. It's a reality. Every day, liberals and . . . um . . . just . . .

NEWSCASTER: *(Incredulity seeping into her voice despite her best efforts)* "Reality?" Wait, has that happened in your state of Oklahoma?

DUNCAN: It has not. This is a preemptive strike to make sure that liberal judges don't take the bench in an effort to use their position to undermine those founding principles and to consider international law or sharia law. The other part of the state question is to prohibit all state courts from considering international law or sharia law when deciding cases, even cases of first impression.

NEWSCASTER: I'm sorry, Mr. Duncan. But less than 1 percent of your population is Muslim, so where would that threat come from?

DUNCAN: It's a growing threat, frankly. And this again is a preemptive strike. They understand that this is a war for the survival of America. It's a cultural war. It's a social war. It's a war for the survival of our country. And other states while they've looked away too long, looked the other way, and kowtowed to political correctness, have lost an opportunity perhaps to save their state. I believe Oklahoma voters at a margin greater than 90 percent will approve this state amendment, and when we do, other red states and maybe even some lesser blue states will decide whether their states are worth saving, too.

NEWSCASTER: Are you worried about other kinds of religious fundamentalism creeping into the decisions judges make when it should really be based on secular law?

DUNCAN: It oughta be based on state law and federal law and any effort by any source to do anything else . . . frankly it's the face of the enemy, it's the face of the enemy. We need to call it what it is. And Oklahomans are going to do that, and they are going to show other states what it looks like to take a leadership role in saving their own future and sanctity of their state court system.

Duncan's mention of "sharia" is designed to alarm viewers, but the reality is that sharia is not a threat to the United States. There is a lot to be said here, but the CliffsNotes version is that contrary to anti-sharia agitators talking a big game about trying to save America from an existential threat, the legal effect of anti-sharia laws is to intervene in the rather humdrum matter of whether American Muslims can legally conduct their family matters (marriage, divorce, inheritance), business disputes, and internal community matters according to their own religious tradition. This type of religious arbitration, utilized by many different religious groups, is limited to civil law matters and does not extend to criminal law issues. Faith-based arbitrators also cannot in any way violate people's rights as American citizens or exceed the authority granted to them by civil law and the parties, regardless of what their religions may teach.

As a separate matter, the above exchange with Duncan also reveals the central themes of this book: Christian vulnerability, the twinning of the Muslim and liberal threat, and for good measure, a complaint about political correctness, too. Note that Duncan thinks "liberal judges" are the vehicle for this sharia takeover, and that the judges' goal is to undermine America's founding principles, which he describes as "Judeo-Christian." Even the name of the amendment is telling—it's the "Save Our State" Amendment. This "cultural war," "social war," "war for the survival of our country" is about preserving a Judeo-Christian America against the Left's assault, and "sharia" makes for the perfect veneer.

Indeed, Gaffney loves to use "sharia" to promote the idea of a nefarious Muslim plan to take over the United States. Unlike Simpson, who thinks the Left uses Muslims as pawns in its grand plan, Gaffney believes that Muslims are the ones in control, strategically deceiving the Left to conquer the world. This difference of opinion changes the angle each takes.

For example, in a 2018 episode of his podcast, *Secure Freedom Minute*, Gaffney says American Muslims running for office "are sharia-supremacists—or, at a minimum, they're currying support from those who are." While Gaffney sometimes concedes that not all Muslims are bad and that Muslims are frequently the victims of violence perpetrated by other Muslims, his conclusion is always that Americans have to reject Muslims wholesale because any Muslim can be a threat in hiding. In a conversation with Sam Faddis, a retired CIA operations officer, Gaffney says the obligation on Americans to work against Muslims is not an "a la carte menu that you can choose or not choose. [Wholesale rejection] goes with the program." In this view, *any* Muslim might be using a friendly cover to deceive Americans into believing he or she is good.

Others in Gaffney's network echo this idea of deception. In Gaffney's January 2020 interview with Robert Spencer, who has been described as "one of America's most prolific and vociferous anti-Muslim propagandists," Gaffney asks what the "sharia supremacists" have in mind as their ultimate end state. Spencer responds, "[They have a] universal global vision . . . Conversion, subjugation, or death." Spencer and Gaffney posit that this "conversion" and "subjugation" don't happen in the open but, again, hide in "Trojan horses"—that is, any and all Muslims are potential foes.

The sheer breadth of these claims should give Gaffney's audience pause. But for those looking for a grand solution to their sense of siege, it feels convincing. Gaffney and others are masters at proof texting (the use of isolated, out-of-context quotes to support one's position) with quotes from Islamic scholars and Qur'anic verses; they even make sure to sprinkle in Arabic terms. To use Klein's words, it's a "terrific performance," or mimicry, of scientific inquiry.

And it has very real effects. As I explain below, Gaffney also uses the Trojan horse metaphor to describe American mosques and motivate vicious anti-mosque protests. On the matter of the so-called sharia threat, the Oklahoma anti-sharia ballot initiative was just one of 217 such measures across the United States. It all started with David Yerushalmi, who in 2006 started a nonprofit called the Society of Americans for National Existence, and proposed on the organization's website a law that would make observance of Islamic law (which he likened to sedition) "a felony punishable by twenty years in prison." His efforts stagnated for a bit, but when the Tea Party emerged three years later, Yerushalmi had his opening. With Gaffney's help, he began writing a model statute called American Laws for American Courts, which would prevent state judges from considering arbitral rulings that violate American constitutional rights—in other words, they told judges to do what judges already do. To date, Yerushalmi's model statute has been virtually cut-and-pasted into bills considered in forty-three states, and twenty bills have been enacted.

But the statutes weren't his primary goal: his purpose instead was to "spread fear about Muslims living in America and to portray them as untrustworthy and out of step with American values. 'Even if these bills do not become law they help to subject Muslims to surveillance and other forms of exclusion and discrimination.'" He says Muslims will use sharia—which, in his words, is not religious law but a "legal-political-military doctrine"—to annihilate Western civilization as we know it today. The anti-sharia movement thrives on the idea of "creeping sharia," that is, the United States and all of our fundamental rights are at risk every time we let any Muslim engage in even the most minute aspect of Islamic law and tradition. In this conception, in order for America to protect itself, Muslim religious exercise must be prohibited.

In the most literal terms, then, Yerulshami, Gaffney, and others in their network have set up a battle between Muslims' rights and Judeo-Christian America. Often the propaganda references saving the US Constitution, which in the view of these theorists (many of whom would qualify as "Christian nationalists" according to studies by Whitehead and Perry and others) is based on Judeo-Christian foundations and encapsulates that tradition. The First Amendment's religious freedom provisions pose a pesky obstacle to this fearmongering, but the theorists have a solution for that, too: deny Islam is a religion.

Partisan leaders have been repeating that claim for years. In 2011, Allen West, a former US congressman from Florida, said, "Islam is a totalitarian theocratic political ideology; it is not a religion. It has not been a religion since 622 A.D." Also in 2011, Jody Hice, US representative from Georgia's Tenth Congressional District, said, "Most people think Islam is a religion, it's not. It's a totalitarian way of life with a religious component. . . . That's why Islam would not qualify for First Amendment protection. . . . Islam and the Constitution are oceans apart." John Bennett, a Republican lawmaker in the Oklahoma state legislature, said in 2014, "Islam is not even a religion; it is a political system that uses a deity to advance its agenda of global conquest." In 2015, Andrew C. McCarthy chimed in with a piece in the *National Review*. "'Islam' . . . should be understood as conveying a belief system that is not merely, or even primarily, religious."

Retired Lieutenant General William "Jerry" Boykin, an adviser to Ted Cruz's 2016 presidential campaign, has claimed that Islam "should not be protected under the First Amendment." Former national security adviser Michael Flynn told a 2016 ACT for America conference in Dallas, "Islam is a political ideology" that "hides behind the notion of it being a religion." In July 2019, John Andrews, founder of the Western Conservative Summit and a former Colorado Senate president, stood on the Summit stage, under a banner proclaiming the importance of religious liberty, and said, "The simplistic approach of simply granting unconditional 'freedom of religion' to a religion that doesn't believe in freedom—and never doubt me, Islam does not—that approach is civilizational suicide, friends."

The idea that Islam, which has more than 1.8 billion adherents worldwide, is not a religion was even deployed in a 2010 legal challenge to county approval of building plans for a mosque in Murfreesboro, Tennessee. The plaintiffs argued that Islam is not a religion but rather a geopolitical system bent on instituting jihadist and sharia law in America.

Because Islam is not a religion, the argument went, the mosque construction plans should not benefit from the county or federal laws that protect religious organizations.

In that case, the local court ruled against the mosque, but the Tennessee appellate court overturned the ruling and the mosque prevailed. But other mosques continue to face challenges. Sometimes, the opposition resorts to violence. In 2011, a mosque in Wichita, Kansas, suffered more than $100,000 in damages because of an arson attack. In 2012, portions of mosques in Joplin, Wisconsin, and Toledo, Ohio, were set on fire. In 2016 the same Joplin mosque had its roof burned down, and then a month later, the entire mosque was burned down. In 2017, fires raged at five mosques, burning down properties in places like Ypsilanti, Michigan; Victoria, Texas; and Bellevue, Washington.

In other cases, challengers attempt to prevent the very existence of a mosque. That is the story of New Jersey's Islamic Society of Basking Ridge. When local Muslims outgrew their makeshift prayer space and decided to build a place of their own, they had to endure two lawsuits, five years, and thirty-nine public hearings before they could finally move ahead with construction. At public hearings, those opposing the mosque would use the language of land use—criticisms about drainage, parking, landscaping, the size of the facility, and the number of people expected to attend services. But even as the mosque submitted revised plan after revised plan, addressing each subsequent set of land use concerns, opponents found more things to complain about. They even got the town government to adopt a new ordinance increasing the minimum plot size needed to build houses of worship.

The tactics come straight out of Gaffney and CSP's handbook, titled *Mosques in America: A Guide to Accountable Permit Hearings and Continuing Citizen Oversight.* The guide advises readers "to express questions and reservations in a manner appropriate to the relevant civic forum's purpose" and avoid "expressing alarm as hysteria," as that could be "used to characterize the entire oversight effort as racially biased and ignorant." In other words, cloak your intentions well.

But it's near impossible for many of these adversaries to hide their true intentions. The New Jersey mosque was founded by Mohammad Ali Chaudhry, who served first as deputy mayor in 2003 then mayor in 2004 of Bernards Township in Basking Ridge. He was also elected to the township committee in 2001 and again in 2005, each time for a three-year term. Despite his unquestionable dedication to the well-being of Basking Ridge—a community *The Guardian* describes as "wealthy and well-educated"—he quickly became the subject of suspicion and disparagement when he began the process of building the mosque in 2011. In the course of the mosque's resulting lawsuit against the town, lawyers found racially charged emails shared between town officials. On a national level, activists smeared him as a "terrorist sympathizer." Some residents of Basking Ridge even received an anonymous letter titled "Meet Your Neighbor" that alleged Chaudhry's "serene, grinning" demeanor was mere deception—a classic Gaffney rebuttal against all Muslims, regardless of their character or actions.

The story in Basking Ridge has been repeated across the United States for decades, with an upsurge during Trump's 2016 campaign and presidency. Fourteen mosque disputes were documented in 2016 alone. Even today, mosques continue to face long approval processes, with public hearings dominated by hours of statements by local residents expressing concerns about terrorism and "the role of mosques in terrorist training." They repeat Gaffney's imagery of mosques as Trojan horses for terrorists. Neighborhood associations echo Gaffney, Simpson, and others when they assert that a mosque will "subvert the Constitution of the United States." Outside public sessions, objectors take to the street in loud and fiery protest. In many cases, the fury of the debate is highly disproportionate to the size of the Muslim community at issue.

In all cases, the central idea is that Islam is against everything Americans stand for. As one scholar describes it, mosque projects across the United

States have come to serve "as proxies for a number of more complex struggles commonly reduced to simple dichotomies: Islam versus the West, Islam versus Judeo-Christian culture, and the culture wars between 'red' and 'blue' America."

That proxy fight, persistent and worsening as vulnerabilities run high, isn't limited to mosques or religious arbitration. It rages fiercely in our public schools, too.

＊＊＊＊

ON JULY 10, 2017, attorney Charles LiMandri joined Christian radio host Kevin Conover to talk about his lawsuit against the San Diego Unified School District over its "anti-Islamophobia initiative." The school district created the initiative in partnership with CAIR after the district received complaints from Muslim students about being bullied.

> **LIMANDRI:** We believe the whole bullying thing is a pretext because in conjunction with that, they want to change the curriculum to be more favorable in putting Islam in general and Muslims in particular in a more favorable light to faculty and students. And, again, they are relying on materials by CAIR.
>
> *(Side conversation on how Islam isn't really just a religion but also a political ideology)*
>
> **LIMANDRI:** We feel that it is propaganda and at least a subtle form of indoctrination, which is going to include even having Muslim prayer rooms at some of the schools.
>
> **CONOVER:** Now, this is amazing to me, because you constantly hear people saying, hey separation of church and state and so

forth and so on, they're saying hey we've got to keep religion separate and yet here we're seeing in the city schools, which are hardly conservative—

LIMANDRI: No, they're very Leftist—

CONOVER: And so, it's strange because typically they would cry separation of church and state, and yet here you're saying they'll potentially have Islamic prayer rooms.

LIMANDRI: That's part of the plan. They're also saying they'll put Muslim holidays on the school calendar. Now, for a long time because of the so-called separation of church and state, I mean, you couldn't even say Merry Christmas. Now, because the Muslims want to have Ramadan celebrated, they're being forced to recognize that there's such a thing as Christmas and Easter that are on the school calendar, but of course you have to refer to them as Winter break and Spring break. You can't even talk about Christmas and Easter vacation . . . anyway—

CONOVER: It's *such* a double standard.

LIMANDRI: No question about it. And that's why there's been pushback.

(Conover and LiMandri discuss the case timeline)

LIMANDRI: [The school board] had people from CAIR coming in as early as February of this year, soon after the election, I think kind of as a reaction, "Okay you conservatives voted for President Trump, we are going to show you what we can do with our power. And if you are going to have things like immigration reform, we're going to make sure that the people that you think . . . raise potential concerns with regard to immigration, that we're going to bend over backwards to overly accommodate them in response." That's the impression that I get. It was kind of a knee-jerk political reaction by the Leftist members of the school, at least in terms of the timing.

LiMandri and Conover went on to discuss the matter for almost an hour, during which they also alleged that devout Muslims are commanded by the Qur'an to wage war and decapitate infidels, and that it is core to Islam that "women are second-class citizens." Christianity, in contrast, "elevated women more than any other political or religious beliefs," LiMandri asserted. "Absolutely," Conover exclaimed, "we don't discriminate based on sex or race or anything else."

The conversation then turned to America's Founding Fathers. LiMandri said, "All that makes Christianity unique and perfectly well disposed for democratic government, which is why our Founding Fathers embraced it and recognized that religion and morality were essential to government." Conover and LiMandri then both agreed that when the founders were thinking of religion and morality, they were referring solely to Christianity.

The exchange is revealing for many reasons. For one, it again reveals a deep sense of Christian angst in the face of secularizing changes in American society and public schools specifically. Much of that angst can be traced back to the U.S. Supreme Court's 1962 decision in *Engel v. Vitale*. The Court said it was unconstitutional for state officials to compose an official prayer and encourage public school students to recite it. The following year, in *Abington School District v. Schempp*, the Court prohibited school-sponsored Bible readings in public schools. These two decisions were widely seen as dismantling Protestantism as the given American faith tradition, "kicking God out of the schools," and helping usher in the past half century of culture wars.

These exaggerated responses mistake the actual court rulings. The Court simply prohibited *school-sponsored* prayers; students can still pray in public schools, as long as they don't disrupt school activities or interfere with others' rights. While the rulings did result in some school administrators banning perfectly legal religious activities, on the whole, student religious expression in public schools today is more robust than at any time since the 19th century. Charles Haynes, a prominent expert on religion in schools, says, "Far from being 'kicked out,' God goes to school today through the First Amendment door." Still, in the years since *Engel*, the purported "removal" of school prayer has been connected to a variety of social ills, from drug addiction to school shootings and even to America's decline.

And with those grandiose claims have come a variety of nonprofits and initiatives designed to "put God back in schools." One initiative called Project Blitz is coordinated by three conservative Christian political groups: the Congressional Prayer Caucus Foundation, which focuses on religious freedom; the National Legal Foundation, a nonprofit Christian law firm; and WallBuilders, a nonprofit dedicated to protecting the "moral, religious and constitutional foundation upon which America was built" ("WallBuilders" is a biblical reference drawn from the book of Nehemiah meant to emphasize grassroots work). Project Blitz's playbook proposes "Legislation Regarding Our Country's Religious Heritage," such as bills that require public schools to display IN GOD WE TRUST in areas visible to students. South Dakota in 2019 adopted one such law, stating that "in God we trust" fosters patriotism and comforts students during times of difficulty. Similar laws have been approved by Louisiana, Arkansas, Tennessee, Florida, Alabama, and Arizona.

There has also been a recent wave of "Bible literacy" bills in state legislatures that would require or encourage public schools to offer elective classes specifically about the Bible's literary and historical significance.

Some of the lawmakers supporting these bills say they want to "restore traditional values in schools." A separate type of bill, such as Ohio's Student Religious Liberties Act, instructs schools to protect student religious expression "in the same manner and to the same extent" as they do for secular speech (something experts point out is already protected by the First Amendment). Even though Ohio lawmakers deny any connection to Project Blitz, a nearly identical bill is outlined in Project Blitz's strategy document.

Trump, too, responded to the post-*Engel* panic—and, naturally, used it to stoke partisan divides. On January 16, 2020—National Religious Freedom Day—Trump issued what he called "new" religious liberty guidance. Among other things, the guidance required school districts to remove any obstacles that might impinge on a student's right to pray in school. This "new" guidance did not propose changes to existing law or regulations; it simply reinforced existing protections previously issued by Presidents Bill Clinton and George W. Bush. Still, Trump said he—uniquely—was defending school prayer from "the far left."

> In public schools around the country, authorities are stopping students and teachers from praying, sharing their faith or following their religious beliefs. It is totally unacceptable. . . . Tragically, there is a growing totalitarian impulse on the far left that seeks to punish, restrict and even prohibit religious expression.

Trump also took the opportunity to remind his evangelical base about their lost cultural dominance. The (alleged) absence of prayer, he said, is "something that, if you go back ten years or fifteen years or twenty years, it was unthought of that a thing like that could even happen—that anybody would even think of something like that happening." Trump, with his religious liberty policies, will win back the American evangelicals once knew.

His statement dovetails perfectly with another relevant theme of the LiMandri-Conover exchange that has been recurrent in Christian nationalist rhetoric: "Leftists" are to blame for the alleged removal of Christianity from public schools. They are anti-Trump and anti-conservative—and in LiMandri's telling, the liberals on the San Diego school board used the anti-bullying initiative to stick it to conservatives after Trump's win. The actual Muslims benefiting from the initiative are mostly just a sideshow.

It is true, as we have seen throughout this book, that Muslims are in many ways symbols of anti-Trump defiance, and pro- and anti-Muslim attitudes are proxies for bigger issues in the liberal-conservative divide. But combined with LiMandri's allegations of Muslim "indoctrination and propaganda" and other references to "Leftists" and a "double standard," the theory seems to be that the Left is using Muslims toward a particular cultural goal. It is reminiscent of Simpson's claims of "civilization jihad"— the Red-Green axis re-creating America and fundamentally altering its Judeo-Christian culture. As LiMandri put it, "We believe the whole bullying thing is a pretext because in conjunction with that, they want to change the curriculum to be more favorable in putting Islam in general and Muslims in particular in a more favorable light to faculty and students."

In fact, combatting purportedly pro-Islam and anti-Christian public school teachings is a central project of ACT for America, an organization run by anti-Muslim activist Brigitte Gabriel in close consultation with Gaffney. ACT has nearly 17,500 volunteers, seventeen staff members, and half a million "warriors" devoted to creating a "safer America." One of its main programs, a nationwide textbook review program, looks for evidence in public school textbooks of statements deemed "too sympathetic to Islam."

According to its report *Education or Indoctrination? The Treatment of Islam in 6th Through 12th Grade American Textbooks*, "too sympathetic" includes statements like "During the Crusades, Christians conquered the city [Jerusalem] for a time until the Muslims recaptured it" and "The armies of the First Crusade defeated the Muslims and held the Holy Land for about 100 years. Later, Muslims took back their lost lands. Seven more Crusades followed, but Muslims held on to the Holy Land." ACT says these statements offer a "Muslim revisionist perspective" on history. It objects to the depiction of Christians as the "initiators of the aggression" and the reference to Muslims taking back "their lost lands." Since its inception, ACT has succeeded in removing historical statements like these from Texas textbooks.

LiMandri's reference to "propaganda" and "indoctrination" also connects to Simpson's claims about interfaith dialogue. That is, education about Islam is ultimately a front for a sinister Islamo-leftist agenda. Conservative advocacy group American Center for Law and Justice (ACLJ) has challenged a range of public school lessons on Islam that its website describes as "Islamic indoctrination." In a 2016 piece that begins with the sentence "Islamic indoctrination in public school is occurring right here in our backyard," an ACLJ staffer says that schools in several states "are reportedly forcing students to learn the Five Pillars of Islam—the creed one must learn to convert—and teaching students that Allah is the *same God* worshipped by Christians." Students and parents are outraged, she writes, particularly because Christianity "barely gets covered."

With ACLJ's help, parents and students have objected to school lessons on Islam, which is taught in cultural and historical terms alongside other religions in various social studies courses. In a Georgia case, parents objected to a worksheet that tested students on various Muslim beliefs. They objected in particular to the fill-in-the-blank sentence "Allah is the [blank] worshipped by Jews & Christians," the correct answer being "same God." In Maryland, a student challenged another fill-in-the-blank sentence, this one about the Islamic creed. Students had to answer that, according to Islam, "There is no god but *Allah* and Muhammad is the *messenger* of Allah" (the words in italics being the correct answers). After the complaining student lost her case in appellate court, she took it to the U.S. Supreme Court, which declined to hear the case in October 2019. In New Jersey, the same fill-in-the-blank sentence, given as homework after students watched a brief cartoon video on the five pillars of Islam, ignited complaints that landed the parents on Fox's *Tucker Carlson Tonight.* The discussion there alleged that the school district "was suppressing discussion about Christianity while proselytizing Islam."

In Virginia, plaintiffs objected to lessons on Arabic calligraphy, which was, like Chinese calligraphy, taught as part of a world geography course. The teacher showed students a picture of the Islamic creed written in Arabic. She didn't ask students to translate the statement or recite it; she simply asked them to try writing the curves and dots of the Arabic script. That was too much for some parents, who flooded the school administration with emails and calls. Some even organized an in-person protest, leading to a school security lockdown with the students still inside. Kimberly Herndon, who organized the protest, said the calligraphy lesson was a form of indoctrination, accusing the teacher of "[giving] up the Lord's time. She gave it up and gave it to Mohammed."

The *Atlantic*'s Emma Green recounts a number of similar controversies in her 2015 piece THE FEAR OF ISLAM IN TENNESSEE PUBLIC SCHOOLS. In Williamson County, Tennessee, parents objected to lessons in a seventh-grade course on world geography and history. As part of a unit on the "Islamic world" up to the year 1500, students were taught the basic tenets of Islam, which school board member Beth Burgos said was "indoctrination." Burgos submitted a resolution that social studies should cover all religions equally, "except to the extent necessary to accurately reflect the Judeo-Christian heritage expressed by our Founding Fathers."

In neighboring Maury County, the school board submitted a resolution to the state board of education questioning whether the tenets of Islam had to be taught as part of a world history class. In another Tennessee county, White County, the group Citizens Against Islamic Indoctrination placed an ad in the local paper featuring all-caps text:

ISLAMIC INDOCTRINATION IS IN SCHOOLS ACROSS OUR STATE AND OUR NATION.

In all cases, a core objection was that Islam was being treated more favorably than Christianity, by which they partly meant that Islam needed to be presented through the lens of violence. As one thirteen-year-old student complained, "I am being taught in class that Islam is a peaceful religion, yet there are many historical and modern-day examples of violent killings and persecution in the name of Allah and Islam." Meanwhile, the parents who pushed back against these protests were accused of working for Obama and George Soros and not being "Christian enough, not Republican enough."

As recently as July 2020, when Democratic presidential candidate Joe Biden said he wished "we taught more in our schools about the Islamic faith" alongside "all the great confessional faiths," prominent Christian conservatives like Christian Broadcasting Network analyst David Brody tweeted, "Christianity and its history/values are being eliminated/distorted in public schools and @JoeBiden wants MORE teachings on Islam?" Conservative activist Charlie Kirk tweeted Biden's comment, then wrote that Biden didn't support prayer or studying the Bible in schools. A former Republican congressional candidate called Biden, a lifelong Catholic, "anti-Christian." In August 2020, internationally influential pastor John MacArthur even went so far as falsely claiming that Biden planned on filling his cabinet with Muslims, which, in MacArthur's view, was "as anti-Christian a statement as you could possibly make. That is a blasphemy of the true and living God." Reactionaries also took notice when Biden said "inshallah," the Arabic term for *God willing*, during the first presidential debate in September 2020; when Trump said he would release his tax returns, Biden responded sarcastically, "When? Inshallah?"

suggesting it was never going to happen. Robert Spencer, a close Gaffney ally, slammed it as "Islamopandering," another way for Biden to "demonstrate his support for the Left's favored religion, Islam."

In addition to social studies lessons, parents and state authorities have also criticized religious accommodations for Muslims in schools. In Frisco, Texas, the same state attorney general who often alleged "anti-Christian discrimination" in Texas schools and once sued a middle school principal to keep a Bible quote on a door, contested a prayer room used by Muslims at Liberty High School. Attorney General Ken Paxton sent a letter to Liberty complaining about the room, and before the school could respond, he issued an official press release in which he falsely claimed that the prayer room is "apparently excluding students of other faiths." Texas governor Greg Abbott also tweeted about the matter.

But no one goes after Muslim religious accommodations like LiMandri, who created the Project for Constitutional Rights in Education at his nonprofit, Freedom of Conscience Defense Fund (FCDF). In May 2019, FCDF—which says on its webpage that it was created to "halt the secular progressive agenda of harassment and intimidation of people of conscience"—issued a cease and desist letter threatening to sue a Washington school district to end its accommodations of Muslim students who were fasting for Ramadan. The fast requires Muslims to refrain from food and drink (yes, even water) during daylight hours, which in May 2019 was sixteen hours. The accommodations included requests such as:

Allow Muslim students to quietly slip away for prayer so as to avoid calling unwanted attention to them.

Consider the impact of your planned school activities on students who are fasting and whether they will feel pressured to break their fast before sunset.

Mention Ramadan briefly during a lesson as a way of promoting a sense of inclusivity.

This, FCDF declared, was equivalent to the school "endorsing" Islam and forcing "pro-Islam diversity" on teachers; its statement said, "The school district's so-called Ramadan 'accommodations' run roughshod over the First Amendment and are a blatant insult to students of other faiths. Under the mantle of 'diversity' and 'inclusion,' school officials have exalted Islam as the state-sponsored religion. Teachers and parents are outraged, and they should be."

FCDF demanded that the school district rescind its Ramadan policy. When the school district complied, the Fund celebrated on its website: "We applaud the courageous parents and teacher who took a stand to remind Northshore it is a public school district, not an Islamic madrasa."

The quest to stop American public schools from becoming "Islamic madrasas" includes challenging anti-Muslim bullying programs. Notably, FCDF targets anti-Muslim bullying programs while it ignores measures designed to combat, for example, anti-Semitic bullying. FCDF is currently planning a challenge to an anti-bullying program in Minneapolis, which was created in response to complaints about faith-based bullying filed by the city's large Somali-Muslim population. FCDF is also investigating a program in Seattle public schools that seeks to better inform students about Islam and its holidays and to create a safer and more welcoming environment for Muslim students.

As for FCDF's lawsuit against the San Diego school district, that was settled in March 2019. The settlement agreement specified that "guest speakers from religious organizations could not present to students on religious topics. Educators can't show a preference for one religious viewpoint over another. And religions must be taught in the context of world history, with the 'time and attention spent discussing each religion being proportionate to its impact on history and human development.'" San Diego's attorney pointed out, though, that the "district was doing everything in the agreement already, and nothing's really changing." Still, CAIR attorney Gadeir Abbas worried about what's next: "I do believe that this is the first of what's going to be many attempts to exclude the Muslim community from public schools throughout the country. This is a sign of things to come."

Abbas has reason to worry. Matthew Vadum, the CSP-funded conspiracy theorist who authored *Team Jihad: How Sharia-Supremacists Collaborate with Leftists to Destroy The United States*, urges Christian conservatives to resist school anti-Muslim bullying programs; he says these programs are the Left's tools to "eventually make it as difficult and uncomfortable as possible to criticize the faith founded by Muhammad in the 7th century after the birth of Christ."

> The political correctness that has metastasized in American culture aids Islamist groups like CAIR by requiring that no one speak ill of Islam or say anything that might stigmatize or "other-ize" a Muslim in any way. All Americans must think and say only nice things about Islam. CAIR and its ilk are determined to stamp out criticism of Islam, and they have an army of nonprofit organizations, foundations, academics, media outlets, and name-calling activists to help them.

About the San Diego program, he says:

> Under the guise of this anti-bullying program, [the school district has] fallen in with the aforementioned religious organization to set up a subtle, discriminatory scheme that establishes Muslim students as the privileged religious group within the school community. Consequently, students of other faiths are left on the

outside looking in, vulnerable to religiously motivated bullying, while Muslim students enjoy an exclusive right to the School District's benevolent protection.

Given the broader context, it is clear which "students of other faiths" Vadum is referring to. For him, the Christian students are the truly vulnerable ones, and they are being ignored.

Or to put it in Klein's words, the Christian loss of privilege *feels* like oppression, and to the extent we leave it to fester, Vadum, LiMandri, Gaffney, Simpson, and others will continue to weaponize it.

PART IV

HOW TO HEAL THE TRIBAL DIVIDE

CHAPTER 6

The Shared Burden
of Healing

IN CHAPTER 3, WHERE I referred to my defense of the *Hobby Lobby* decision on Al Jazeera America, I noted the stark disruption of tribal mega-identities. Religious and racial minorities like myself are viewed as aspects, or "traits," of the liberal mega-identity, and religious cases brought by white conservative Christians indisputably belong to the conservative mega-identity.

I try to challenge the mega-identities over and over again throughout my work. After *Hobby Lobby*, it was *Masterpiece*, and then a host of other scenarios that raised the same conflicts (Christian wedding photographers, adoption agencies, and so on). It can be an uncomfortable position to defend because the public debate is so often set up as "you're either with us or against us," forcing everyone to take sides. For those like me, who prefer to stand in the middle, to ask questions, be curious, and point out the reasonable elements of each side in an attempt to truly effect change, the experience can be frightening.

I had a lot of those frightening moments when I was on my book tour for *When Islam Is Not a Religion*. The tour afforded me the opportunity to talk about Muslims' religious liberty to conservative audiences and conservatives' religious liberty to liberal audiences, which led to some . . . interesting conversations. In some cases, the audience was politically diverse, and I had to carefully navigate a room rife with tension. On the way to one such event at the Texas Tribune Festival in Austin, I found myself tweeting from Brown's *Braving the Wilderness*: "True belonging is not passive . . . It's a practice that requires us to be vulnerable, get uncomfortable, and learn how to be present with people without sacrificing who we are. We want true belonging, but it takes tremendous courage to knowingly walk into hard moments."

In my work, I draw inspiration from a few different sources. First, the law. Yes, courts are not immune to political influence, but even the most politically charged legal case is ultimately about jurisprudence—about the relevant precedents and how they work in the case's specific factual context. Second, the philosophy that undergirds the law. In the case of religious liberty, the law protects our right to live together despite our differences. After the U.S. Supreme Court issued a series of high-profile decisions in summer 2020, former appellate judge Michael McConnell wrote in the *New York Times*:

> Some Supreme Court watchers have been quick to interpret recent decisions as skirmishes in American "culture wars"—with some decisions (on abortion and sexual orientation) siding with the cultural left and others (on religion) siding with the cultural right.

There is another way to look at them. Viewing the decisions as a whole, rather than one by one, they can be seen not as advancing left or right but instead as protecting pluralism—the right of individuals and institutions to be different, to teach different doctrines, to dissent from dominant cultural norms and to practice what they preach.

When I support those same decisions by the Court, I, too, seek to protect our right to be different—to debate and dissent and be true to our respective faiths.

I am also inspired by the power of human connection. I wrote this book during the first months of the coronavirus lockdown. With a global pandemic as my backdrop, I stayed focused on the possibility of a world where our shared human vulnerability could help us overcome our politics of vulnerability. Social scientists tell us, after all, that we are biologically wired for human connection. In our polarized times, our belief in that connection is, in Brené Brown's words, "constantly tested and repeatedly severed." Those of us who give up retreat into our bunkers, but those who hold on learn "to *feel* hurt rather than *spread* hurt."

Most of us want to hold on. More in Common says the "Exhausted Majority"—the vast majority of Americans—desperately wants to break through impasse. These Americans are not centrists or even moderates but instead hold passionately to a diverse array of views. What sets members of the Exhausted Majority apart from those on the ends of the political spectrum is that they are each willing to endorse different policies based on the "precise situation rather than sticking ideologically to a single set of beliefs."

Americans are particularly likely to want to find common ground on matters of religion. In *American Grace*, Robert Putnam and David Campbell write, "For many Americans, religion serves as a sort of civic glue, uniting rather than dividing." Even the "highly secular" and "highly religious" among us value religious diversity—not just because our Constitution insists on it but because we believe in it. Research conducted by Putnam and Campbell revealed that "by a wide margin, Americans see the value in religious diversity for its own sake."

Finally, I derive courage from religion generally, and my religion specifically. Religious polarization is not just another flavor of polarization—when it comes to the Muslim-Christian conflict, we have as external references God, holy texts, and thousands of years of religious tradition. We are reminded of our own fallibility; as much as we may think we are right, we are in the end just fumbling toward the truth.

Religion also gives us a different perspective on tribal loyalties. For example, the Qur'an says, "O mankind, indeed We have created you from male and female and made you peoples and tribes that you may know one another" (49:13). The verse is literally talking about tribes and telling us that tribal identities are not in and of themselves a bad thing. (Social scientists say this, too—recall the work of Tajfel and others who found that group loyalty boosts self-esteem.)

Even when tribal loyalties become toxic, I know not to despair because God, in that verse, says not only that it is possible to mend the divide but also that mending the divide is the very purpose of our differences. We have been made into tribes so that we "may know one another." My work on tribalism is thus focused on searching for a solution that I know exists.

This chapter is that search. I have sought to weave together empirical data, religious teachings, and personal experiences to propose a path forward. On the social science front, I look at techniques that have been proven to reduce bias against racial and religious out-groups, and which some experts think can help heal partisan rifts, too.

My analysis considers strategies to be employed by each side of the conflict. One person working in the Muslim-evangelical space told me that while he works to improve relations on both sides, he knows that "what most people in this country care about is whether evangelicals' attitudes improved—that is, whether they are more oriented toward justice and more willing to work with people different from themselves." In *Talking to Strangers*, Harvard political theorist Danielle Allen says that "the hard truth of democracy is that some citizens are always giving things up for others." More is demanded of the people we see as "winners" in any given political moment—they should step up and make the "possibility of a political friendship real."

The problem, though, is that we cannot agree on who the winner is. At any given moment, we have "a chorus of contradictory voices persuasively claiming victimhood." We've seen throughout this book how vulnerability and victimhood are claimed by both Muslims and Christians—and that there's at least some truth to both claims, even if the issues are severer on one side.

So it is not enough to put the burden of healing on just one party. Each of us has a role to play, and in fact, social scientists have devised various methods that are applicable here. I look first at tolerance and empathy as strategies the out-group (Muslims, liberals) can use to contribute to the healing process. Then I look at what the Christian in-group can do through self-affirmation, superordinate goals, and deep canvassing. In the next chapter, I will consider what partisan dealignment might look like and the risks that come with it for both sides.

****

SO FAR, I have described conservative white evangelicals and, to a large extent, conservative Christians generally as the "in-group." In this setup, Muslims—particularly as facets of the liberal mega-identity—are at the receiving end of hostility. Conservative Christians are feeling threatened because of seismic demographic and cultural changes, and when an in-group feels threatened, its vulnerability is weaponized against the out-group.

In this section, however, I want to flip the dynamics. To the extent that Christians feel like a persecuted minority in the United States, it's helpful to think through how Muslims, liberals, and others whom conservatives think—accurately or inaccurately—are positioned against them can help build bridges.

TOLERANCE

There are two main types of hostility toward the out-group: prejudice and intolerance. The difference between the two is the object of the hostility. Prejudice is a social orientation toward whole groups of people—African Americans, Mexicans, or sexual minorities, for example. There is a variety of reasons why the in-group hates or feels antipathy toward these groups, but the key feature of prejudice is that the hostility is focused on a category of people *as* people. It's the classic "us" versus "them" dynamic whereby the in-group puts itself in one social category and everyone else in an opposing social category. To reduce prejudice, social scientists have devised and tested a number of strategies—things like focusing on superordinate goals or self-affirmation and increasing contact between members of the in-group and out-group. I'll explore these strategies later in this chapter.

Here, I focus on the second type of out-group hostility: intolerance. Intolerance is about specific beliefs, practices, or ways of living that the in-group disapproves of. It can be group-based if the entire out-group endorses—or is perceived as endorsing—the disapproved belief or practice. But the focus is always on specific actions, rather than hating a category of people as people. For example, studies on anti-Muslim attitudes in parts of Europe distinguish between hostility toward all Muslims (prejudice) and opposition to traditional Muslim dress codes (intolerance).

Or, to use a more relevant example, consider what this means in the context of American debates about religious liberty and sexual freedom. While our political mega-identities lead us to see each other with contempt (what Arthur Brooks calls a "noxious brew of anger and disgust"), on the specific religious freedom issues, we can begin to figure out solutions if we see the phenomenon as more akin to intolerance—liberals disapprove of conservatives' *beliefs and practices* related to gay marriage, contraception, abortion, etc.

In devising strategies to increase tolerance, social scientists distinguish between beliefs and practices that are at least minimally reasonable, as opposed to those that are "arbitrary (e.g., use of double standards), unintelligible, and without moral value." In other words, there's a difference between racist-based hatred, pedophilia, domestic violence—which should not be tolerated—and anti-abortionists' concern for the unborn life or beliefs and practices about euthanasia and gay marriage—which can be tolerated. It might be helpful to think of this in terms of the legal strict scrutiny standard I described in chapter 3. The law accommodates religious practices that do not contravene a compelling government interest. So, for example, if religious parents want to deprive their children of a lifesaving blood transfusion due to religious objections, the government is allowed to step in and stop them. But in less extreme cases, the law carves out space for us to accommodate (or tolerate) religious practices.

In this latter case, there are two possible outcomes when an in-group disapproves of the out-group's beliefs or practices. It can decide the belief or practice is unacceptable and try to prevent it. Or the in-group can decide that some higher goal requires their tolerance; in our case study, that would be like saying, "We don't agree with you, but religious freedom gives you the right to act according to your beliefs." Liberals can decide to endure conservatives' practices, even as they continue to vehemently disapprove of them (and vice versa). Nothing about tolerance requires diluting one's own convictions. As social psychologists Maykel Verkuyten, Kumar Yogeeswaran, and Levi Adelman note, toleration is about "putting up with specific beliefs and practices that you consider wrong (i.e., you accept what you disapprove of). It involves self-restraint in order to prevent the negative attitude from becoming negative actions."

This is Professor Thomas Berg's point, too, when he argues that "civil rights and liberties ideally reduce the stakes in sociocultural conflict; they reduce each side's existential fear that a hostile majority will successfully attack their core commitments." About the *Masterpiece*-type scenarios, he notes, "If same-sex couples can marry and religious opponents of same-sex marriage can live according to their beliefs, their deep disagreement will generate less in 'malignant' bitterness and alienation." In other words: tolerance will reduce intergroup hostility.

Importantly, those who are in a position to tolerate or not tolerate necessarily have the power in that relationship, because we can only tolerate what we can prohibit. Christians who lament their persecution at the hands of liberal "elite culture" believe liberals are ultimately the decision makers. In their view, in a post-Christian America, Christians are no longer in control of the cultural narrative, and it's up to liberals to decide whether they want to tolerate traditional Christians' way of life or work to prevent it.

What might compel liberals to tolerate conservative Christian beliefs and practices? First, again, preserving a higher goal—such as religious freedom or free speech—might be reason enough to tolerate them. Americans haven't always applied religious freedom equally or fairly to all religious groups, but they have since the founding era embraced its principles robustly. Many of our Founding Fathers extolled the virtues of religion; they believed that government required morality, and that religion is an important contributor to morality. They also believed that religion leads to societal happiness, that it guarantees oaths, and is necessary for a free government—and they embraced religious liberty so that religion may flourish and society may benefit from its flourishing.

Many Americans also understand that religion runs deep for believers. Religion is critical to believers' identity, their sense of purpose in the world, and for that reason, there has to be space for religion to manifest in public rather than just in private. This general appreciation for religion and religious freedom provides an opening for cross-cutting conversations.

For example, one of my public presentations ties together cases as diverse as *Hobby Lobby*, a Muslim prisoner case, a case involving Native Americans' access to sacred eagle feathers, a case challenging the Oklahoma anti-sharia law, and the Knights of Columbus's fight to keep a statue of Jesus on federally owned (but privately leased) land. In each case, I outline how deeply and sincerely the religious believer held his or her beliefs. Then I tie the cases together so that the audience understands how the same principles of religious liberty apply across all of the scenarios, despite their vastly different fact patterns. I've been told by liberal audiences that this presentation takes them on an "emotional roller coaster" because they find themselves wrestling with—rather than outright rejecting—the conservatives' cases.

Andrew Lewis found similarly in his 2018 survey of eleven hundred men and women across all demographics and political affiliations. The purpose of the study was to understand how the general public responds to requests for religious exemptions (that is, people's request that a law not apply to them because doing so would violate their religion). Specifically, he wanted to see whether priming Americans with information about Muslims seeking religious exemptions would make them more receptive to evangelicals' claims for religious exemptions.

He presented the (real) story of two Muslim truck drivers who refused to deliver beer and alcohol based on their religious beliefs, and asked participants whether they supported the truck drivers' right to religious freedom or the company's right to fire the drivers. The case study was unique because, instead of a conservative Christian asking for an exemption, the request came from a member of a religious minority.

Unsurprisingly, Lewis found that liberals, much more than conservatives, supported the Muslim truck drivers. More unexpected is what he learned when he asked the same participants whether they would support a Jack Phillips–type small business owner. Lewis found that liberals were less opposed to the Christian same-sex marriage exemptions once they saw the issue through the perspective of the Muslims' religious freedom case.

So, the shared goal of religious freedom is compelling for many liberals. As for those who need more than that, consider that exhibiting tolerance can help reduce perceptions of threat, and if Christians don't feel threatened, they are less likely to act out with hostility on a range of matters liberals care about. Indeed, threat-reduction could benefit even liberals' gay rights advocacy. Perhaps counterintuitively, giving conservative Christians space to object to gay marriage can ultimately cultivate support for it.

EMPATHY

Coexistence with people who have widely variant beliefs and practices often requires more than tolerance. Empathy is also essential. Whereas tolerance implies "putting up with" dissenting beliefs and practices, empathy goes further in trying to understand where the other person is coming from. Dictionaries define "empathy" as the "intellectual identification of the thoughts, feelings, or state of another person" or the "ability to share in another's emotions, thoughts, or feelings." Or as one expert describes it, empathy in our engagement with others means that "what is present before the listener is not merely an argument but a person."

Brené Brown says empathy and shame are on opposite ends of a continuum. Empathy "moves us to a place of courage and compassion" and helps us "realize that our perspective is not *the* perspective." (emphasis mine) It is incompatible with judgment; when we shame others with our comments, we do exactly what empathy is designed to prevent—we create disconnection. Commentators noted this about mask-wearing during the coronavirus pandemic, finding that shaming people into wearing masks doesn't work in the long term: "Empathy works as well as shame in the short term, and works far better over the long term." Writing for the *New York Times*, science journalist Annalee Newitz recommended the approach taken by British Columbia: "Masks were recommended, but not mandatory." Individuals and businesses were allowed to "make their own decisions about how to comply." In contrast to Ontario, where "local authorities used shame tactics to enforce health guidelines," the empathetic approach emphasized mutual trust between citizens and proved far more effective in controlling coronavirus outbreaks.

Professor Berg makes a similar point about empathy in the *Masterpiece* context, "Labeling the contenders in a legitimate socio-cultural-political dispute as 'bigots' may inflame rather than calm the situation; it may simply add further charges and countercharges, in a vicious cycle." Shaming others can also drive them to engage in destructive behavior. A writer for the conservative Christian publication *First Things* describes well what this destructive behavior looks like for many of her coreligionists:

> Feeling excluded or alone can lead Christians to adopt as fellow travelers provocateurs who may scandalize the secular world, but not because they preach the faith that is "foolishness to the gentiles." Such grifting agitators are not seeking space to speak the truth, but to revel in division. They may lead people moved by real political concerns to view their opponents as permanent enemies, not our divided brothers whom we are called to pray for and convert into allies . . .

> Wallowing in fear and giving in to contempt will eventually lead us to despair. Hatred for God's people cannot coexist alongside love for him and trust in his love for us. It will destroy us, and may spill over into violence visited upon others. When our lives are shaped by fear, we cut ourselves off from the full glory of creation. . . . We see others only as they relate to us, and not as they are in their fullness.

The author goes on to exhort fellow Christians to rise above the political fray. But liberals as the relevant in-group in this context have to take steps, too, with tolerance and empathy as their tools. In contentious religious liberty debates, this means seeing the real human concerns on both sides. Justice Kennedy modeled this in his *Masterpiece* opinion, emphasizing that "gay persons and gay couples cannot be treated as social outcasts or as inferior in dignity and worth" but also saying about Phillips that "the customers' rights to goods and services became a demand for him to exercise the right of his own personal expression for their message, a message he could not express in a way consistent with his religious beliefs." The Court spoke about both parties' concerns from a place of empathy rather than labeling one party bigoted.

Professor Berg calls this approach "positive sympathy." To break the vicious cycle of condemnations and counter-condemnations, instead of shaming one or the other side of the debate, we should focus on their respective plights. This goes for both sides—conservatives and liberals both have to approach each other from a position of "positive sympathy." Again, for liberals weighing the benefits of such an approach, Berg notes, "The positive case is suited to generate understanding for the lives and claims of gay people." That is, if you want Christian conservatives to feel empathy for gay people, show a little empathy for Christians, too. Nothing about contempt is persuasive, Brooks says in *Love Your Enemies*: "No one in history has been convinced with insults."

Nicholas Kristof also gets at this in his *New York Times* piece HUG AN EVANGELICAL:

> I've argued often that gay marriage should be legal and that conservative Christians should show a tad more divine love for homosexuals.
>
> But there's a corollary. If liberals demand that the Christian right show more tolerance for gays and lesbians, then liberals need to be more respectful of conservative Christians.

Importantly, empathy does not require you to give up your own position on an issue. As proclaimed by one TED talk that went viral, "Empathy is not endorsement" (incidentally, the talk was by a gay man who actively engages with people who disapprove of his sexual orientation). To add some urgency to this imperative: Justices Thomas and Alito of the U.S. Supreme Court issued a statement in October 2020 that, in their view, *Obergefell* was wrongly decided and needs to be rethought. The time is thus particularly ripe for gay rights supporters on the Left to explore strategies that win over conservatives.

Returning to the Muslim-Christian divide, the approach of empathizing without endorsing helps there, too. It's one reason why I have sought, throughout this book, to talk about conservatives' concerns in a nonantagonistic manner. I try to choose my words carefully. Recall my efforts to avoid the term *interfaith* in my engagement with Christian conservatives. I also avoid *Islamophobia*. People working in the field have told me that evangelicals find *Islamophobia* to be shaming because it assumes that evangelicals, when they speak openly about Islam, are coming from a place of hatred rather than fear. As with conservatives' concerns about political correctness being overly restrictive, *Islamophobia* is seen as a way to squelch dissent.

During my book tour for *When Islam Is Not a Religion*, it became evident that many of the conservatives I was meeting didn't trust a book with "Islam" and "freedom" in close proximity. Many asked, "Do Muslims want to impose sharia law on non-Muslims? Do you support female genital mutilation (FGM)? What about Muslims who want to misuse religious freedom to engage in violence, or to subjugate women?" I cringed at the questions (for many reasons, but an obvious one being that they were telling a woman who had just presented herself as a devout Muslim that her religion subjugates women). But I tried not to show my annoyance, and instead communicated, "I hear you. I also fear violence. You are not a bad person for feeling scared, confused, defensive."

In other words, I make a conscious effort not to cut off meaningful conversation by making the person feel bad—or shamed—for asking the questions to begin with. I try to *empathize* with the human concerns motivating the questions. It can be exhausting, and my openness doesn't absolve them of their duty to read and learn on their own, but to heal the rift, I cannot assume ill intent.

My approach is rooted in my religion. A common refrain in the Muslim community, first articulated by a classical Islamic scholar, is "If a friend among your friends errs, make seventy excuses for them. If your hearts are unable to do this, then know that the shortcoming is in your own selves." The idea is that we should always carry a default assumption about the goodness of humans, and if anything causes us to doubt this goodness, we should be careful to look beyond the surface. It's a version of Brown's instruction to "zoom in" to the real person. The Qur'an, too, emphasizes this fact-finding when it commands Muslims to "Shun much doubt; for lo! some doubt is sinful" (49:12).

As it turns out, affirming the goodness of people is also a key social psychological method of reducing prejudice.

****

UNLIKE INTOLERANCE, WHICH has more to do with specific beliefs, practices, or ways of life, prejudice is about making entire groups of people the "other"; it's about favoring "us" and explicitly disfavoring "them." Tolerance and empathy are strategies to reduce intolerance, whereas a separate array of strategies helps reduce prejudice. Later, I'll discuss a few ways that I think both sides can embrace, but here I want to look at what specially the Christian in-group can do: self-affirmation, working toward shared or "superordinate" goals, and increasing contact with the out-group.

SELF-AFFIRMATION

As I've argued throughout this book, conservative white evangelicals feel threatened in the face of a culturally changing America. Self-affirmation theory talks about this threat as damaged self-esteem, or self-uncertainty, and is premised on the basic fact that when people feel low self-esteem, they seek alternative ways to boost it. One powerful alternative is to turn to one's group for a sense of affirmation. Studies have connected low self-esteem to American patriotism and stronger religious identification—but also to destructive ideologies that make enemies of the out-group. What's more, people who turn to their groups for affirmation want those groups to be homogenous so they can isolate themselves from the "other" as much as possible. They "'circle the wagons' of social identity," political scientist Lilliana Mason says, "in order to keep their multiple identities as aligned (and therefore impervious to outsiders) as possible." That type of sorting is political polarization at its core.

To counter this tendency, social psychologists have experimented with methods that remind people of their own self-worth, a technique called self-affirmation. People can self-affirm about their individual identity or their collective identity (for example, their membership in a racial group or their citizenship in a country). First, people report an important value or life domain—their relationships with their friends or family, making art or music, a charity they're dedicated to, etc. Second, they write an essay about this important aspect of their life or engage in some other exercise that allows them to assert how important it is to them. What the person chooses to self-affirm cannot be related to the provoking threat. For example, one cannot write about how compassionate they are after they have acted uncompassionately—that sort of self-affirmation creates more dissonance.

Even though self-affirmation should not be related to whatever is damaging one's self-esteem, it does still have to be an important aspect of one's identity. In the case of collective identity, it has to be something that reminds the person of "who we are." The point is to rewire self-identity and develop a larger view of the collective self so that one feels securer and more aware that the group's dignity and integrity are not in fact under threat.

Various studies have found that when people self-affirm, they stop responding defensively to others. For example, one study looked at Americans' responses to the 9/11 attacks. It first found that Americans generally responded in one of two ways. They either uncritically embraced their American national identity and saw the United States as a force for good in the world (the researchers labeled these Americans "patriots"), or they looked more critically at American foreign policy in the Middle East and the potential connection between the policies and the attacks (the "anti-patriots").

Next, the researchers wanted to see how people's identities as patriots or anti-patriots affected their evaluation of a report titled *Beyond the Rhetoric: Understanding the Recent Terrorist Attacks in Context*. Here's how they described the setup:

> The report argued that Islamic terrorism can be understood in terms of the social and economic forces of the Middle East. It further underscored the role that US foreign policy had played in fostering some of the social-economic conditions in the Middle East that later led to the terrorist attacks of 9/11. The arguments were credible (drawn from the writings of several prominent analysts) and buttressed with factual evidence and historical analysis. To amplify the counter-American tone of the report, it was ostensibly written by an author of Arab descent, "Babek Hafezi." To make participants' American identity situationally salient, the experimenter wore a small American flag pin on her lapel.

In the absence of self-affirmation, patriots were far more critical of the report than the anti-patriots were (there was a 34 percent variance in their openness to the report). But when the participants self-affirmed before reading the report by writing an essay about an important value unrelated to their national identity, the patriots became more open to the report. Group identity no longer affected how participants received the information in the report. "Indeed, the correlation between prior identity and openness was reduced to nil ($r = -.05$)," the researchers wrote. And, as we'll see later, if self-affirmation can lead to positive intergroup relations (or "contact"), those interactions may serve as their own source of affirmation.

Other studies have focused on scenarios like the ones we've looked at in this book where members of a Christian in-group try to protect their group by denying the prevalence of racism and religious discrimination and alleging that minority groups exaggerate claims. People who self-affirm are significantly more likely to acknowledge that the discrimination is real; they "have less need to distort or reconstrue the provoking threat and can respond to the threatening information in a more open and even-handed manner." In the religious freedom context, self-affirmation might help Christian in-group leaders resist the urge to hyperinflate threats to Christians and develop a broader awareness of discrimination against religious minorities.

It can be hard to let go of the wound, though. Author and therapist Caroline Myss has written numerous *New York Times* bestselling books on what she calls "woundology," or people's tendency to wear their wounds like a badge of honor. Wounds have a seductive power, she says, a type of "manipulative value." During her healing workshops with people who had experienced tremendous trauma, she found the participants almost competing with each other to see whose experience was more painful (not unlike the competing victimhood we saw in chapters 4 and 5). But more than that, there was an intimacy that developed between people when they shared stories of pain. Wounds help hold tribes together—something that might be at play when we consider how conservative Christians share their vulnerability with each other.

The sharing of wounds had become the new language of intimacy, a shortcut to developing trust and understanding. The exchange of intimate revelations, which had been originally developed and intended as appropriate dialogue between therapists and patients, had become the bonding ritual for people just getting to know one another. . . . This type of social authority can become very powerful, even addicting.

Myss says that many of her patients find comfort in their discomfort: "In this paradigm, pain becomes a prerequisite for remaining close to and needing one another, and healing can be seen as a positive threat to the bond. The partnership is inevitably threatened when one of them decides the time has come to release the past and move on." Yet, it's essential to move on; if we stay stuck in the "power of our wounds," we block our own transformation and fail to learn the lessons we are meant to derive from our suffering.

Hardship is, after all, not relevant for its own sake but to get us to a higher plane. That is a lesson taught by many religions, Islam and Christianity included. An oft-cited saying of the Muslim prophet Muhammad is "If God intends good for someone, he afflicts him with trials." Another version is "God tests those he loves." Experiencing difficulty makes us better people and more faithful believers. It exposes to us our weaknesses, and with that awareness, we can be more proactive in rectifying those faults in our character. It also forces us to turn to God for help, thus drawing us nearer to him. The Qur'an asks, "Do people think that on their mere claiming, 'We have attained to faith,' they will be left to themselves, and will not be put to a test?" (29:2).

Similarly, the Bible states, "Count it all joy, my brothers, when you meet trials of various kinds, for you know that the testing of your faith produces steadfastness. And let steadfastness have its full effect, that you may be perfect and complete, lacking in nothing" (James 1:2). In both traditions, trials are merely a means to transformation, and if we treat them as ends in themselves, we block that transformation.

Rooting ourselves in our religious traditions helps us to not only transcend our wounds but also self-affirm the very best parts of who we are: We were not made into tribes so that we could hate each other; we are different so that we *may know one another*. Eboo Patel, the founder and president of the Interfaith Youth Core (IFYC) and a Muslim, calls this the "theology of interfaith cooperation." The theology of interfaith cooperation requires people to interpret key sources from their own faith (historical moments, archetypal figures, religious art, the writings of significant philosophers, theologians and jurists from the tradition, etc.) in a way that weaves a "coherent narrative and deep logic that calls for positive relationships with people of diverse religious orientations" and explains the religious elements that seem to encourage negative relationships.

The evangelical-led Neighborly Faith also relies on self-affirming language to encourage conservative evangelicals to love their neighbors of other faith traditions. Cofounders Kevin Singer and Chris Stackaruk told me their consistent message to evangelicals is "Bring your whole self." "Evangelical Christians for so long have been taught that they must give up a part of their faith in order to work with Muslims or anyone of a different faith. But we want to tell Christians that you don't have to give up any part of your faith. Working with people of different beliefs is actually deeply rooted in our faith. Jesus encourages us to do this!"

Bob Roberts Jr., a pastor at Northwood Church in Texas, also emphasizes the "bring your full self" message in his Muslim-Christian program, My Neighbor's Keeper. Christianity calls believers to welcome the stranger, the refugee, and those who hold to different faith traditions, he says, but that process doesn't require hiding parts of yourself. It's about expressing your full self and letting others express their full selves, and no one getting angry about any of it. Of his close—and very public—friendship with the Muslim leader Mohamed Magid, he says, "Just seeing us goof around and laugh surprises both Muslims and Christians. We *actually* are really good friends." Roberts and Magid, like the other pastors and imams who participate in My Neighbor's Keeper, have widely divergent beliefs about Jesus and the path to salvation, but they learn to ask questions and, in Roberts's words, "move away from tribes and into a global community."

SUPERORDINATE GOALS

Roberts's language of "global community" reminded me of Patel, too, who had told me about a key IFYC strategy: "As an interfaith community, we have to create situations where people with fundamental disagreements are working together on a *superordinate goal*." "Superordinate goals" is also the name of a social science approach to reducing prejudice.

The theory was first tested by husband-and-wife team Muzafer and Carolyn Wood Sherif, both social psychologists. The Sherifs brought a group of boys with similar backgrounds to a camp called Robbers Cave. The group was split into two teams that would compete against each other to produce "intragroup solidarity and intergroup rivalry." The rivalry and solidarity were both intensified when the Sherifs intentionally favored the competition to the benefit of one group. Quickly, these two groups developed a deep sense of identity with their team (tribe) and hatred of the other, so much so that competitions often turned violent.

To turn the situation around, the Sherifs took the rival teams and focused them on a common goal, one that would benefit both teams. For example, on their way to a swimming hole, the boys' bus broke down (not really, but the Sherifs made it seem so) and the boys had to work together to get the bus out of a ditch. Working toward this shared goal increased intergroup solidarity significantly.

The Sherifs found these results in an experimental setting, but Patel used open-ended case studies to show me how Americans accomplish shared goals practically every day:

Think of the number of contexts where we do this naturally, like healthcare. We have fundamental disagreements, but we are working together on something really important. For example, let's imagine you're a heart surgeon and you're deeply committed to a particular ideological view. You're scheduled to perform this surgery and just as you're preparing, you notice the person you are performing surgery with is taking off campaign material pertaining to a candidate you hate. Do you not perform the surgery? Nobody says "yes."

Let's walk this down the chain: You're a firefighter. Would you refuse to put out a fire in your ideological opponent's house? Would you refuse to serve on a PTA with someone you fundamentally disagree with? Refuse to coach Little League with that person? Civic life in America depends on people with different views working together towards superordinate goals *all the time*.

IFYC helps college kids wrestle with these issues both theoretically and practically by having them work on community service projects with students of other faiths.

Robert Putnam's *Bowling Alone: The Collapse and Revival of American Community* considers different types of social capital, which he defines as "social networks and the norms of reciprocity and trustworthiness that arise from them." The type of social capital IFYC encourages is "bridging social capital"—"the value assigned to social networks between socially heterogeneous groups." It stands in contrast to "bonding social capital," which is born of socially homogeneous social networks. Building off these categories, Arthur Brooks in *Love Your Enemies* talks about two different types of identity: bonding and bridging identity. Unlike "bonding identity," which groups people according to shared characteristics and thus helps reinforce group identities, "bridging identity" comes from embracing people outside your tribe. Bonding identity is the "'what' about you that someone else can share," and bridging identity is the "'why' that unites you with all other people." The "why" is our common humanity and a shared goal, like Pastor Roberts's "global community" or Patel's "civic space."

Or my mantra, "Religious liberty for all." It's a version of the tolerance principles I talked about earlier, but in this case, it's utilized to combat prejudice against an entire group of people. Intolerance is about specific beliefs, practices, or ways of living that the in-group disapproves of, whereas prejudice is focused on excluding a category of people *as* people. Religious freedom as a shared goal helps reduce both prejudice and intolerance.

Mason in *Uncivil Agreement* says that superordinate goals have been hard to identify in a hyper-partisan context. Shared goals require some level of trust in the authorities; people want to know that the people in charge are working in their interest. Quoting political scientist Marc Hetherington, Mason notes that unfortunately, today, "'trust among those who identify with the party outside the White House is much lower than historical norms and, indeed, almost completely evaporated among Republicans during Barack Obama's presidency.'" It's harder and harder to find a cross-cutting issue that unifies Democrats and Republicans over and above the partisan rancor.

But religious freedom might be the cross-cutting issue we need. Recall Lewis's findings that "priming" liberals with Muslims' religious claims made them less opposed to conservative Christians' claims. "Liberals are essentially saying, 'Oh, I hadn't thought about that in this context. It's not just about the Christians, now it applies to all groups.'" In other words, liberals who are dedicated to protecting vulnerable minorities begin to understand that the goal is unachievable if Christians aren't protected, too. The implication for conservatives is that if they want liberals to support them, conservatives need to increase their own support for Muslims' religious freedom.

For superordinate goals to work, it is really important that groups are not made to feel like their identity is being threatened or minimized.

People have to be able to hold onto their distinctiveness even as they let go of their prejudices. Just as we learn to tolerate others' practices without accepting or even approving of them, so it is with working together toward shared goals. The point isn't to erase differences but to live among and with diversity.

As attorney Luke Goodrich argued in *Free to Believe*, his book for a conservative evangelical readership, evangelical Christians have a legal stake in protecting the religious freedom of Muslims. Under a section titled Self-Interest, Goodrich explains how legal cases involving widely divergent fact patterns all rely on one another. For example, the conservative Christians in *Hobby Lobby* won in large part because the court relied on *Abdulhaseeb v. Calbone*, a case involving a Muslim prisoner who was denied a halal diet in prison. The court said that just as the government had wrongly required the Muslim prisoner to choose between his faith and eating, so also the government required the owners of Hobby Lobby to choose between their faith and millions of dollars in fines. Similarly, the Muslim plaintiffs in *Tanzin v. Tanvir* relied extensively on *Hobby Lobby* to argue for a robust interpretation of RFRA and in December 2020, one of the most conservative justices on the Court, Justice Thomas, delivered a unananimous win to the plaintiffs. The same principle in reverse means that a legal loss for Muslims often leads to legal losses for Christians.

Law professor Thomas Berg also emphasized this need for consistent advocacy in a piece for *Christianity Today*, where he explained that you can't broadly exclude other religions and still expect to protect your own. In a piece titled 4 WAYS MUSLIMS' RELIGIOUS FREEDOM FIGHT NOW SOUNDS FAMILIAR TO EVANGELICALS, Berg explains that the two religious groups are both (1) unpopular; (2) criticized for using their religion as pretexts (for Muslims, it's a pretext for terrorism and for Christians, it's a pretext for bigotry); and (3) told to relegate their faith to the private sphere. The fourth similarity: false assumptions about each group help the government overregulate their religious practice. To effectively fight back against such

ASMA T. UDDIN

overreach, evangelicals and Muslims both have to demonstrate consistency and stand up for each other's rights.

The truth of the jurisprudence is that "religious freedom for some is religious freedom for none." To understand the point, evangelicals and Muslims might consider a range of hypotheticals. Evangelicals can consider a case where a Muslim woman is denied her right to wear a headscarf, and then be asked to consider a parallel matter where a Mennonite woman is prohibited from wearing her bonnet or a Jewish man his yarmulke. Another set of hypotheticals can set up challenges to houses of worship: Muslim communities across the United States routinely face attempts to block construction of mosques. They face dubious claims about noise or traffic or parking. The same arguments can and have been used against Christian churches and other facilities. A third hypothetical could explore challenges to tax-exempt status for mosques and then compare that to similar challenges for churches. By exploring these case studies together, Muslims and evangelicals might see better the shared principle across scenarios.

Beyond this, what's needed is basic legal literacy about religious freedom law (for example, the strict scrutiny standard or how cases with diverse facts rely on one another) and what precisely courts are deciding when they decide religious freedom cases (as I've described with *Hobby Lobby* and *Masterpiece*). Religious freedom comes with limits, and the law draws the line very carefully. Skeptical conservatives who distrust Muslims need to know that religion can never trump national security; skeptical Muslims need to know that the law won't permit Christian supremacy; liberals need to know that accommodating Christians' objections to same-sex marriage will not create serious access issues for LGBTQ+ individuals. Even the most conservative among Christian advocates agree that if, for example, there are limited alternative vendors in a given area, the Christian baker's religious rights can legitimately be trumped. Altogether, religious freedom as a legal tool cultivates balance and pluralism.

At its simplest, religious freedom as a superordinate goal can be thought of in purely transactional terms. It wouldn't be the only legal right that's used that way. I was presenting my arguments at a law school once when a law professor exclaimed, "Oh, you're talking about interest convergence!" Derrick Bell, a former Harvard law professor and civil rights activist, developed the interest convergence theory in the context of civil rights advocacy for blacks. According to Bell, blacks receive favorable judicial decisions to the extent that their interests coincide with the interests of whites. For example, the Supreme Court's decision in *Brown v. Board of Education*, which ended racial segregation in public schools, was not motivated by a desire to redress black suffering, Bell says; instead, the United States eliminated Jim Crow in order to improve its international image during the Cold War.

There are complexities, of course, as conservatives face competing pressures. Muslims' wins in the legal arena give Christians more legal protections, but capitalizing on white Christian vulnerability helps them win in the political arena. It's important to emphasize the tension between these two goals and the way political maneuvering ultimately hurts Christians' legal rights.

Beyond the purely transactional, a multi-faith conversation on religious freedom also helps depolarize the intergroup dynamics and create an opportunity to share vulnerability across religious and partisan lines. It makes *possible* the type of conversations that More in Common said tribalism makes *impossible*.

This is true of a wide range of Americans whom conservative white evangelicals might consider antagonistic. For example, one left-leaning Christian pastor told me that he resents being grouped in with the tribal left. He works to protect religious minorities as a key part of following Jesus and is critical about the role of white Christian supremacy in US history. At the same time, though, he promotes liberty for evangelical and conservative Christians and, like them, worries about forces that seek to minimize or even eradicate a robust religious presence in the public square. As with More in Common's Exhausted Majority, Christians like these reject the stark divisions between tribes and instead have cross-cutting identities. They endorse different policies based on the precise facts rather than ideologically hewing to a single set of beliefs. The *New York Times* describes them as having a "mutually standoffish relationship with the Democratic Party."

With American Muslims, too, a depolarized conversation on religious freedom pays dividends. Evangelical groups like the religious liberty commission of the Southern Baptist Convention as well as the National Association of Evangelicals have filed briefs in support of mosques facing hostile community pressure. These groups have received significant push-back from their constituents—but a clear idea of how all of our rights are interlinked helped them respond to their critics.

Indeed, "religious liberty for all" is the theme I emphasized at NRB, in *When Islam Is Not a Religion*, and in countless other places where I address conservative Christian audiences who I know are deeply committed to the cause of religious freedom. Time and again, when I have these conversations, I see the tension in the room ease up. Suddenly, the gentleman in the front row who had been staring me down looks puzzled instead. Some in the audience are even smiling. Everyone is listening.

I have even witnessed the change when I am interviewed on conservative talk radio. I cannot see my audience, obviously, but I can hear the tension in my host's voice drop. Sometimes it's like a slow-deflating balloon; other times it's like an emphatic "POP!" One host exclaimed on air, "I'm getting texts! Folks are saying, 'YES, this is what we need!'"

In one Facebook conversation, I took my opponent from the usual anti-Islam diatribe ("It's gonna be hard to get people on board with religious freedoms for a religion that enforces an agenda of pushing for a political system that puts in place strict religious laws") to "I am with you a hundred percent. Thanks for a great discussion!" I value these exchanges immensely, as tense and as fraught as they can often be in the beginning, because I can sense the barriers coming down.

Finally, letting go of a politicized approach to religious freedom protects more than religious freedom; it protects religion, too. A 2019 Pew poll found that America's religious landscape is changing at a "rapid clip." In 2018 and 2019, 65 percent of American adults described themselves as Christians, which is twelve percentage points less than any other time over the past decade. Meanwhile, 17 percent of Americans considered themselves religiously unaffiliated, that is, atheist, agnostic or "nothing in particular" (the so-called nones) in 2009, and that number went up to 26 percent in 2019.

Citing leading scholars, Nicholas Kristof commented in the *New York Times*, "Young adults have turned away from organized religion because they are repulsed by its entanglements with conservative politics. 'Nones,' for example, are solidly Democratic." The irony of the tribal approach is that so much of it is driven by a desire to protect religion and religious freedom in the United States, but the tribalism itself poses the biggest threat.

DEEP CANVASSING—OR, TALKING TO EACH OTHER

Parts of the above discussion might have come off as cynical—Muslims, evangelicals, liberals, and conservatives, trading favors and putting up with each other just to get something they want for themselves. These quid pro quo elements are attuned to the difficulties we face in an environment where our mega-identities rule and Islam and Christianity are divided into opposing camps. But in no way do they constitute the full picture of what needs to be done if we are to create a world in which Americans treat other Americans with trust, empathy, and focus.

Scholars Chris Seiple and Dennis Hoover describe what is needed as "covenantal pluralism," that is, "neither a thin-soup ecumenism nor vague

syncretism, but rather a positive, practical, non-relativistic pluralism."
It's about really getting to know each other and respecting each other's
complex identities—our quirks, weaknesses, and struggles to make sense
of our surroundings. In contrast to a mere transactional relationship,
covenantal pluralism is about civic fairness and human solidarity. "It is a
secular covenant of global neighborliness, one with a balanced emphasis
on both the *rules* and *relationships* necessary to live peacefully and productively in a world of deep differences."

Law professor John Inazu has another name for it: confident pluralism.
"Confident pluralism takes both the *confidence* and the *pluralism* seriously."
Confidence without pluralism is something like authoritarianism—it
suppresses difference, sometimes violently. Pluralism without confidence
ignores or trivializes the genuine disagreements among people and enforces
a false unity. Confidence and pluralism together allow us to live peace-
ably even when our beliefs and opinions diverge. We don't need to avoid
conflict, Inazu says, but we do need to resolve it productively. For that,
two things are needed: legal protections for people who dissent from the
cultural norm, and a way of talking and relating to each other that makes
us want to serve the greater good instead of tear each other down.

Some of the best multi-faith work being done right now focuses on the
relationships piece of covenantal and confident pluralism. It actively creates
a third space where conversations don't have to be reduced to politics.

Social scientists have approached this in different ways. In 1954,
Gordon Allport conducted various experimental studies to test his idea
that certain types of social contact between groups can help them get
along. His "contact theory" requires four conditions. The contact would
occur (1) among groups of equal status who (2) have common goals, (3)
no competition between them, and (4) the support of relevant authorities.

Not all of these conditions exist in our case study of the United States.
One aspect of political tribalism in America is competing narratives of
oppression; groups not only don't have equal status but each perceives itself

as the underdog. There is absolutely a sense of competition between them, and depending on who is in the White House, one group doesn't think they have the support of relevant authorities. The good news, though, is that after Allport, other researchers have found success even in cases lacking optimal conditions. For example, intergroup friendships cultivated "in the absence of anxiety, and in the presence of empathy" are also effective in reducing prejudice.

Still other scientists have developed a technique called "deep canvassing." It has been tested in the gay rights context, where a group of LGBTQ+ activists in Massachusetts went door-to-door talking to people they knew opposed gay rights. It was 2018, transgender rights were on the ballot, and the activists—led by David Topping—wanted to listen to people's concerns and engage them in conversation. Topping called the process "giving them grace," a process not unlike the strategy I employed in chapters 2 and 3, where I—through my writing—listened openly and honestly to conservative Christians' concerns. The strategy worked for Topping; in 2018, Massachusetts voters voted in favor of transgender rights.

These strategies can work in the Muslim-evangelical context, too, if the right conditions are in place. For example, Pastor Roberts's My Neighbor's Keeper program creates an environment low in anxiety and high in empathy. In towns across the United States (carefully chosen on the basis of polling data, individual recommendations, and the willingness of faith leaders and congregations to participate), Roberts and his program partner Imam Magid congregate local pastors, imams, and rabbis in a three-day retreat. The clerics share stories about how they and their religious communities are perceived by others and what they wish others knew about them. They wrestle with the hard facts and the stereotypes, speak candidly with each other, and in the end build trust where there was only mistrust. To date, two hundred congregations, thirteen cities, and half a million people have taken part, and Roberts is ramping up efforts in hopes of adding ten more cities each year.

Singer and Stackaruk's Neighborly Faith is also heavy on relationship building. Working primarily with Gen Z generation (people born between 1995 and 2015) evangelicals, they find that participants invest a lot more emotional capital in relationship building than previous generations. The thirtysomething Singer told me, "In the evangelicalism I was introduced to in college, there wasn't much of an idea of going beyond just investing the message of Christ in the people I know." In contrast, "Gen Z evangelicals say they want to invest themselves in a person, a human, a person with a story, a person who may have baggage with evangelical Christians. They say, 'It's not enough for me to invest the message; I have to invest myself.' They want to be an example of an evangelical who isn't a Christian nationalist or even just a rude, intolerant person."

Neighborly Faith builds on this willingness to know others by creating opportunities for relationship building across faith traditions. Along with a national Fellows program, Neighborly Faith hosts conferences at Christian colleges around the country and also partners with local mosques and Islamic centers to put Christians and Muslims in the same room. At a 2019 conference held at Wheaton College in Illinois, participants were encouraged to ask the keynote speakers, both Christian and Muslim, their "hardest questions." Following the Q&A, participants were invited to continue their conversations over a meal at a local mosque, where each person was asked to fill out a before-and-after survey. Singer and Stackaruk told me that the responses were overwhelmingly positive. Christian college students said they had a much more positive view of Muslims and Islam and were much more likely to intentionally work with Muslims in the future.

In creating this honest community, these initiatives are consciously discarding politics as the determinant in Muslim-Christian relations. They explicitly eschew the idea of instrumentalizing Muslims to achieve some personal interest. Pastor Terry Kyllo of the Seattle-based Paths to Understanding said emphatically, "I did not leave my career, risk my income and status and personal safety to make Muslims a proxy fight for anything. I did so because I feel Jesus called me to do so. I did so because as a patriotic American I wanted to fight for the aspirational values of our founding documents."

Pastor Kyllo's insistence on seeing Muslims as people, not proxies, is probably the single most important piece of the healing process. Throughout this book, I've mostly talked about Muslims as the dramatized "other" who are fought over but rarely get the chance to speak for themselves. People's brains tend to implement mental shortcuts, known as heuristics, to form quick and easy judgments, which lead to stereotypes. We lean toward forming opinions based on information that is immediately and easily accessible to us. So, with at least 75 percent of news and media coverage of Muslims being negative (according to a Georgetown University study), conservative media portraying Muslims as pawns in a supposed liberal agenda to destroy democracy, and Muslims constituting only one percent of the American population, it's easy for Americans to assume that is who Muslims are, particularly because most Americans have no personal connection to one.

But American Muslims (and for that matter, liberals) are so much more than what they—we—are made out to be. If we can be active participants in the conversation, real possibilities emerge for this conflict to transcend politics.

CHAPTER 7

Making It Work

"WHEN I FEEL CONTEMPT, WHAT should I do?" Arthur Brooks once asked a Buddhist leader.

"Show warmheartedness," the Buddhist leader said.

"What if I don't feel warmhearted?" Brooks pressed.

"Fake it," the Buddhist replied.

In other words, attitude follows action. Choose the action and the feeling will follow. If you want to feel gratitude, act more grateful. And if you want to battle the culture of contempt, face contempt with warmheartedness.

We have to break our habit of contempt by reprogramming the parts of our brains that respond to that sort of stimulus. "Put something else in its place," Brooks says. "Substitute a better behavior for a bad one. When you feel contempt rising up in front of you and you want to respond, increase the space between the stimulus and your response."

This isn't just a Buddhist teaching; it's also what's meant by the Christian injunction to "love your enemies" or the Qur'anic verse "*Repel evil with good, and your enemy will become like an intimate friend*" (41:34). In our polarized climate, though, the injunction can seem almost impossible to obey. In this chapter, I want to consider a few additional strategies attuned to our current predicament.

* * * *

UNSORTING

Unsorting is about complicating how we group ourselves and others into opposing camps. It creates a "partisan dealignment" and reveals "cross-cutting cleavages." In the Christian-Muslim context, this process is aided when we begin to understand American Muslims for their fuller complexities.

We are beginning to see signs of that in the national discourse around gay marriage and homosexuality. In that conversation, Muslims and evangelicals are pitted against each other, with Muslims indisputably on the liberal or Democratic team. But as commentators are increasingly pointing out, the reality is far more complex.

It is true, according to the Pew Research Center, that Muslims' support for same-sex marriage is growing, particularly among Muslim millennials (which includes those people who were born from 1981 to 1999 and came of age after 9/11). Only three in ten Muslim millennials believe that society should discourage homosexuality. Even among older American Muslims, almost half (44 percent) say that society should accept homosexuality. Overall, 52 percent of Muslims believe that society should accept homosexuality—compared to only 34 percent of white evangelicals who say the same thing. Religiosity is not the driving factor here; on coalition building with LGBTQ groups, the Institute for Social Policy and Understanding's (ISPU) 2020 American Muslim Poll found that political ideology and party affiliation are key drivers for Muslims, whereas religiosity has no predictive power.

That said, there's work being done on the religion front, too. A number of Muslim scholars in America are reinterpreting Islamic sources on same-sex relations, and a few Muslim organizations, such as Muslims for Progressive Values and the Muslim Alliance for Sexual and Gender Diversity, are creating opportunities for gay Muslims to worship and engage meaningfully in the community. These initiatives, along with party affiliation and changing attitudes among Americans generally help explain the broad acceptance by American Muslims of homosexuality and same-sex marriage.

But it is also true that Muslims' openness to homosexuality is in tension with traditional Islamic law, which doesn't prescribe punishments for homosexual desire but does for homosexual behavior. According to Islamic law, sexual contact must be limited to married men and women, and marital intercourse is defined specifically as vaginal intercourse. The Qur'an tells the story of Sodom and condemns "its people's overall immorality . . . specifically criticizing its men for 'going to men out of desire instead of to women.' Sodomy, understood as anal sex, was thus prohibited by the consensus of Muslim scholars . . ." Lesbian sex, while not sodomy, is also prohibited under the general rule against nonmarital sexual contact.

And despite growing acceptance, many American Muslims still hold conservative positions on homosexuality. A 2020 report by the ISPU found that while 48 percent of 18- to 29-year-old Muslims support coalition building with LGBTQ groups, only 38 percent of 30- to 49-year-olds and 26 percent of 50+-year-old Muslims support it. Overall, 55 percent of Muslims *oppose* forming political alliances with LGBTQ activists.

Religious scholars—including "rockstar imams" with massive followings—also encourage American Muslims to hew closer to traditional Muslim teachings. For example, in a widely circulated article targeting Muslim social justice activists, dozens of religious thinkers and community leaders urged the activists to "preserve all that is special about being Muslim" by prioritizing "the nonnegotiable teachings of Islam." They also cautioned against forming alliances with "special interest groups" (either liberal or conservative) that would "unduly alienate large swaths of the demographic that activists and/or religious scholars themselves claim to represent." Instead, "the way forward in the US political arena requires a synthesis of the best that both liberals and conservatives have to offer," and Islamic values should guide who we work with and on which issues: "Our main desire is that Islam and the preservation of its values be given priority and not sacrificed on the altar of political opportunism . . . Islamic mores [are] worth showcasing . . . even if they clash with those of our allies at times." An influential Muslim leader, Dawud Walid, captured this approach in his book *Towards Sacred Activism*.

Major conservative Muslim scholars negotiate traditional Islamic values and gay rights advocacy by both supporting the legal right to gay marriage and also taking a noncompromising position on the morality of homosexual relations. For example, a leading conservative Muslim scholar came out in full support of *Obergefell* when the case was decided, and says he would never turn away LGBTQ Muslims from the mosque or make them feel marginalized. But he also wrote a scathing critique of progressive Muslim activists who reinterpret Islamic law to support homosexual relations. In a Facebook post for his one million Facebook followers, the scholar, Yasir Qadhi, said "there is very little Islam" in what these activists advocate. And in February 2020, Qadhi invited me to speak at an event at his mosque on religious liberty and gay marriage. There, he made clear that he sympathizes with the conservative Christian position in gay rights cases, and though he doesn't think the *Masterpiece* scenario is likely to occur with Muslim business owners (he doesn't think

Islamic theology supports or requires a Muslim to refuse, for example, a custom wedding cake to a gay couple), he does worry about challenges to the rights of Muslim *religious institutions* to teach traditional Islamic doctrine and hire and fire employees on the basis of whether their sexual behavior conforms to traditional Islamic beliefs.

Though Qadhi has taken the lead here, he is by no means alone in his concern; many (if not all) conservative Muslims worry about preserving their way of life the way conservative Christians do. There is a growing gap between traditional Islam and the positions of Muslims' political tribe (Democrats).

When Beto O'Rourke declared during the 2019 CNN town hall that religious institutions should lose their tax-exempt status if they oppose same-sex marriage, John Inazu suggested in the *Atlantic* that

> journalists should ask O'Rourke and every other Democratic candidate how this policy position would affect conservative black churches, mosques and other Islamic organizations, and orthodox Jewish communities, among others. It is difficult to understand how Democratic candidates can be "for" these communities—advocating tolerance along the way—if they are actively lobbying to put them out of business.

When I asked him to elaborate, Inazu said:

> Many Muslim Americans hold social views similar to those held by Christian conservatives . . . non-religious Democrats pushing progressive policies they see aimed at Christian conservatives often fail to recognize—or at least acknowledge—how those policies will also harm Muslim Americans.

It remains to be seen how existing Muslim-liberal alliances will fare as these tensions continue to come to the fore. Conservatives generally agree with the Steven Crowder video I described in chapter 4; that is, liberals will never target conservative Muslims the way they do conservative Christians. But others are less optimistic.

For example, Fuller Seminary professor Matthew Kaemingk tweeted in response to O'Rourke's comment, "Muslims and the black church have historically enjoyed the warm embrace of the left," but "Beto signals that, in the future, the left's embrace could grow increasingly tight and even disciplinary." Nicholas Kristof of the *New York Times* wrote in A CONFESSION OF LIBERAL INTOLERANCE, "We progressives believe in diversity, and we want women, blacks, Latinos, gays, and Muslims at the table—er, so long as they aren't conservatives."

Meanwhile, Ben Sixsmith of the *American Conservative* warns of a liberal "subversion" of Islam, the manner in which the Left "pays cloying respect to the symbolism of Islam while undermining its significance." This "subversion" happens most obviously with the Muslim headscarf, or hijab, and its modest dress codes generally. Sixsmith's example is a *Sports Illustrated* swimsuit issue that featured a Muslim model wearing a clingy "burkini." The burkini covered her body and hair, yet this "salute" to Islamic modesty "was superficial at best. While the model might have covered up, she was still lazing in the surf, her hands behind her head, as her swimsuit hugged her contours." Sixmith argues:

> The accidental subversive genius of American liberalism has been in presenting the hijab not as a symbol of faith but as a symbol of choice. . . . By encouraging Muslims to defend traditional dress on the grounds of *choice*, though, liberals and leftists have encouraged them to internalize individualistic standards. The hijab becomes less of a religious symbol, virtuously accepted according to God's will, than an aspect of one's personal identity, which one is free to shape and exhibit according to one's wishes.

Such criticisms are common among Muslim commentators as well—me included. In 2016, I wrote in a similar vein when Noor Tagouri, a Muslim woman who wears a headscarf, was featured (fully clothed) in a *Playboy* interview on Muslim modesty. I doubted the magazine's intentions. *Playboy*'s founder, Hugh Hefner, had a clear position on religiously mandated modesty and sexual ethics: he saw them, and most any other limit on public sexual expression, as fundamentally anti-freedom. What did it mean, then, when the magazine chose a woman in a headscarf to make, in its pages, a "forceful case for religious modesty"?

When the interview first came out, two other Muslim women who wear headscarves wrote publicly that they had also been approached by *Playboy*. The magazine appeared adamant about including the hijab in its pages, and I suspected it had something to do with redefining the nature of the hijab. I wrote, "Yes, *Playboy* has for a long time offered a range of hard-hitting political and social commentary unrelated to its pornography, but this topic in particular—religiously mandated modesty—does more than comment on a social phenomenon. Featured among overtly sexual content, a piece on Muslim modesty seems to mock and undermine those precise ideals. For many Muslim women, the hijab is about reclaiming ownership of their image—but the *Playboy* piece arguably takes away that agency and instead imposes its own frame, making the hijab sexy."

I recognize, of course, that others might have more charitable interpretations of these *Playboy* and *Sports Illustrated* features. But it is indisputable that some tension exists between traditional Muslim values and practices and more liberal conceptions of sexuality. Increasingly, the popular discourse is becoming attuned to that tension.

The answer, as numerous Muslim scholars have noted, is not to switch tribes but to complicate our unassuming relationship with any tribe. They advise Muslims to strive toward a moral center; to place religious authenticity over and above any tribal loyalty.

There's a role here for Christian conservatives, too. Princeton professor Robert George has long pleaded with his fellow Christian conservatives "not to push our Muslim fellow citizens away by fearing and despising them and causing them to fear and despise us." But, he laments, "few conservatives have heeded me." He continues to believe, though, that the same cross-cutting issues—fast-changing sexual norms, the corporatization of religion, and so on—that are triggering a gradual dealignment of American Muslims and the political Left can also serve as fruitful grounds for Muslim-Christian engagement.

RISK MANAGEMENT

Unsorting necessarily comes with risks. The bulk of this book has considered intergroup bias—Republicans versus Democrats, Christians versus Muslims. But there's also extensive social science literature on dynamics *within* groups that identifies phenomena like the "black sheep effect." Members who don't fully conform to their group's norms can end up suffering significant negative repercussions.

Black sheep is an idiom used to describe a disreputable member of a group. In intergroup dynamics, the black sheep effect is so pronounced that people have worse, or lower evaluations, of weak members of their group than similar members of the out-group. For example, pro-life Democrats probably have higher status in the GOP than they do in the Democratic Party. On the other side, *Christianity Today's* former editor, Mark Galli, quickly became a black sheep when he published his editorial calling for Trump's removal during the 2019 impeachment trial. The reaction among conservatives: Galli is a pointy-headed intellectual who's bought into the intellectual pieties of the Left. People in the in-group see fellow members who are not with them 100 percent of the time as vain or not committed enough.

In the Muslim-Christian context, this helps explain why Professor George is having a hard time convincing his fellow conservatives to heed his advice. It's not just their entrenched biases that George is up against, it's also their desire to be in good standing with their group. Each person has to weigh the costs and benefits of becoming a black sheep.

Given the psychological benefits of membership, we are programmed to avoid black sheep status. We want to be well liked by our group, even if it requires us to express views we don't believe in. If we are cast out, we risk experiencing high levels of stress and low self-esteem. Unsorting—or challenging tribal lines—thus requires tremendous courage.

Those who have embraced the challenge have faced blowback. We saw in chapter 5 that evangelicals who seek to reach out to Muslims have been labeled "idiots" by Jim Simpson and others in Gaffney's orbit. In March 2020, when J. D. Greear, the president of the Southern Baptist Convention (SBC), did a public panel with Muslim leader Omar Suleiman, several conservative speakers (some aligned closely with Gaffney) ripped into both speakers—with special venom for Greear. Suleiman is a "sharia supremacist," they alleged, and Greear was aiding and abetting the sharia takeover by engaging in a "feel good" conversation with him. Meanwhile, the host of American Family Radio contrasted Greear's calls for a broad, coherent religious freedom with the "Old Testament prophet Elijah when he confronted the prophets of Baal, the pagan god of the ancient Canaanites."

Similarly, when the SBC's Ethics and Religious Liberty Commission (ERLC) filed a legal brief in support of a mosque, ERLC's president Russell Moore faced tremendous criticism. Some in the SBC even called for his removal and the removal of any other church official who supported Muslims.

> Messenger John Wofford of Armorel Baptist Church of Armorel, Arkansas, requested a motion . . . calling for the firing of SBC officials who support the building of mosques. "I move that all Southern Baptist officials or officers who support the rights of Muslims to build Islamic mosques in the United States be

immediately removed from their position within the Southern Baptist Convention."

Moore's predecessor, Richard Land, also encountered fiery protest in 2010 when the ERLC joined a multifaith coalition to protect Muslims' right to build houses of worship. Land was forced to withdraw mere months after ERLC joined the coalition. In his words, "While many Southern Baptists share my deep commitment to religious freedom and the right of Muslims to have places of worship, they also feel that a Southern Baptist denominational leader filing suit to allow individual mosques to be built is 'a bridge too far.'"

Despite this resistance, many faith leaders—Muslim and Christian—persist in supporting religious freedom for all. Like Greear and Moore, Suleiman, too, has stood by his interfaith exchanges. Although conservatives value group loyalty more than liberals do and are more willing to kick people out of the group for not conforming, cross-faith conversations carry risks from both sides of the political aisle. Some on the Left cast out as "black sheep" liberals who engage with Christian conservatives on matters of religious freedom, reproductive justice, and gay rights because such engagement is seen as legitimizing conservative positions. I've lost my fair share of career opportunities because of this dynamic.

But with every setback, I have also had many victories. Focusing on superordinate goals has been a winning strategy, as has been my approach in this book to listen openly and honestly to the other side while also speaking my own truth. If we can appeal to overarching values and avoid triggering people's feelings of threat, we might just find a way forward.

MINDFULNESS

Throughout this book, I've described the mechanics of intergroup bias so that we can understand how political tribalism works. Once we know the mechanics, we can begin to realize the words and tactics that are used to manipulate us, and we can say—if we choose to—that "enough is enough."

That's the reason, too, why Klein in explaining "why we're polarized" focuses on the "massive apparatus that defines, polices, and activates our identities." To free ourselves from that "superstructure," we have to become aware—and stay aware—of its influence over us. Our identities will be stoked, and we will continue to feel strong emotions, but if we are mindful of how the superstructure is affecting us, we can make better decisions about whether any given issue is worth being angry over or not. "If we don't take the time to know which is which, we lose control over our relationship with politics and become the unwitting instrument of others," Klein says, advising that we carefully shape our informational environment around the identities we actually want to inhabit.

If we are mindful about the ways we are being manipulated and about the ways we respond, we might be able to change the social norms that drive polarization. Consider an example several social scientists use: In 1994, Newt Gingrich sent a memo to members of the Republican Party. It was titled "Language: A Key Mechanism of Control" and instructed Republicans on which words to use to describe Democrats. The list included "betray, bizarre, decay, destroy, devour, greed, lie, pathetic, radical, selfish, shame, sick, steal, traitors." These words are still used today by party leaders to demonize Democrats.

This sort of extreme, flamboyant rhetoric is an aspect of what philosophers Justin Tosi and Brandon Warmke call "moral grandstanding." Politicians during a televised congressional hearing tie their arguments to grandiose moral claims because they are performing for the television audience. Many of us on social media platforms like Twitter, Facebook, and Instagram are similarly performing for our "followers" and make extreme claims so that we can look moral. While some grandstanders making claims about human rights might be sincere, in many cases, flourishing rhetoric on politicized issues is more about status seeking than reasoned argument—and it makes it harder for us as a society to engage in arguments in good faith.

We can reduce prejudice by choosing not to moral grandstand, by being more mindful of the words we choose. Recall Brooks's exchange with a Buddhist leader:

"When I feel contempt, what should I do?" Brooks asked him.

"Show warmheartedness."

"What if I don't feel warmhearted?"

"Fake it."

In the Muslim-Christian context, we have to let go of "Christian bigots" and "Muslim terrorists." Recall the BYU study in chapter 4 where researchers found that Republicans were much less likely than Democrats to sanction negative speech about Muslims, partly because the in-group rewarded the negative speech, or at least failed to punish it. If we practice mindfulness, we could change the costs and benefits of how our in-group talks about the out-group. In this regime, negative speech would come with costs, and warmheartedness (even if at first we are faking it) would be rewarded.

* * * *

PROFESSORS AMY CHUA and Jed Rubenfeld write in the *Atlantic*, "For all its flaws, the United States is uniquely equipped to unite a diverse and divided society." Our country is not an ethnic nation or a theocracy. We don't have to choose between multiculturalism and national identity—we can have both. But, Chua says, "the key is constitutional patriotism. We have to remain united by and through the Constitution, regardless of our ideological disagreements."

As Christians and Muslims and diverse religious believers committed to the mending of religious divides, we also have to remain united by and through our commitment to something bigger, better, and more everlasting than our temporal politics. Russell Moore in *Onward* tells his American evangelical readers that they must move beyond "moral majority" to "prophetic minority." He acknowledges that some will flinch at his use of "prophetic minority" because they will see it as a "concession of defeat." If politics is your everything, then "claiming minority status seems nonsensical." Even the more religious types will chafe at this honest accountability of Christianity in Western culture. Minorities don't command influence or control, so they will pretend to be the majority even if they are not.

But the reality, Moore says, is that Christianity was never meant to be a dominant force. It is and was always meant to be "strange." This is good news for the church because it allows it to stand apart from culture and politics and speak truth to both. That's what it means to be a prophetic minority.

Religious freedom attorney Luke Goodrich argues similarly. He encourages evangelicals to "let go of winning" and examine "the people we're called to *be* in the midst of religious freedom conflicts" before addressing "what to *do* about religious freedom." The ultimate goal of Christianity has never been to win culture wars, assert political dominance, or make America a Christian nation. Rather, Goodrich says, evangelical Christianity has always found itself on the margins of society.

In other words, America is post-Christian not because Christians don't hold power but because Christians are no longer acting Christian. Neighborly Faith's Kevin Singer and Chris Stackaruk, along with Pastor Bob Roberts and Professor Inazu, encourage fellow evangelicals to stop worrying about demographic and cultural shifts and primarily focus instead on self-affirmation. It's important to stay centered on Christianity's contributions to American society through its principles of hospitality, grace, peace, and genuine love for one's neighbor.

Moore calls this "convictional kindness." Using language from the Bible, Moore urges Christians to "pursue righteousness, godliness, faith, love, steadfastness, gentleness" (1 Timothy 6:11). Kindness, Moore argues, is not passivity; rather, it is speaking with a Christlike love in a society centered around division and hatred, asking questions with genuine empathy and curiosity, and seeking to understand the "other" as a whole person, not a caricature. Moore reminds his evangelical reader that "the enemy" is not their Muslim or agnostic neighbor; it is the power of evil itself.

Former Fuller Seminary president Richard Mouw makes the same point in his book *Uncommon Decency*. He says true Christian witness is found in the way believers both hold deep convictions about their faith and also love their neighbor with genuine kindness. In a world where common decency has become uncommon, Christianity must look different.

Convictional kindness, love of neighbor, and bringing one's whole self can help erase toxic tribal lines. While the social psychological theories of superordinate goals, contact theory, and self-affirmation theory might seem too scientific or unattainable, they actually provide us with concrete applications of our transcendent values.

Most of all, our religions teach us not to be afraid to be "black sheep." Those who have the courage to step apart from their group in service of truth, not tribalism, are paving the path forward.

Throughout my legal advocacy and public engagements, I have often assumed that role. There, as in this book, I have tried to implement my values and extend a hand—and I hope you will take it.

AFTERWORD

I pledge to be a president who seeks not to divide, but to unify.

Who doesn't see red and blue states, but a United States.

And who will work with all my heart to win the confidence of the whole people.

For that is what America is about: the people.

And that is what our administration will be about.

I sought this office to restore the soul of America.

On November 7, 2020, four days after Election Day, former Vice President Joe Biden was elected the next President of the United States. That night, he delivered his victory speech in an outdoor, drive-in celebration where hundreds of supporters cheered from their cars.

Almost exactly two months later, on January 6, 2021, a violent mob of Trump supporters stormed the United States Capitol in an attempt to overturn Trump's defeat in the 2020 presidential election. Inside the building, Congress had convened a joint session to certify the results of the Electoral College and the protestors wanted to prevent that formalization of Biden's win. It was the ultimate (some would say predictable) manifestation of Trump's four years of spreading disinformation and stoking division. It was political tribalism out of control.

Multiple commentators later called the violence a "Christian insurrection." Emma Green of *The Atlantic* detailed the many signs:

> The mob carried signs and flag declaring JESUS SAVES! and GOD, GUNS & GUTS MADE AMERICA, LET'S KEEP ALL THREE. Some were participants in the Jericho March, a gathering of Christians to "pray, march, fast, and rally for election integrity." After calling on God to "save the republic" during rallies at state capitols and in D.C. over the past two months, the marchers returned to Washington with flourish. On the National Mall, one man waved the flag of Israel above a sign begging passersby to SAY YES TO JESUS. "Shout if you love Jesus!" someone yelled, and the crowd cheered. "Shout if you love Trump!"

Conservative commentator David French agreed with Green's assessment: "We have to be clear about what happened in Washington D.C. on January 6th. A violent *Christian* insurrection invaded and occupied the Capitol." Christian music was blaring from the loudspeakers. French himself saw "a man carrying a Christian flag into an evacuated legislative chamber." Trump had catered to some of the most dangerous elements of American Christianity—in Whitehead and Perry's terms, the "Ambassadors" of Christian nationalism—and on January 6th, they came to Washington to claim their country.

The violence was a clarion call for conservative white evangelical leaders across the conservative spectrum to repudiate their support for Trumpian politics. Franklin Graham, the son of Billy Graham, and a reliable Trump supporter, tweeted, "The division in our country is as great as any time since the Civil War. I am calling on Christians to unite our hearts together in prayer for President-elect @JoeBiden and Vice President-elect @Kamala-Harris, and for the leadership in both parties." Albert Mohler, Jr., the likely next president of the Southern Baptist Convention (SBC) and a Never Trumper in 2016 who had switched positions in 2020, was shocked by the violence. While he couldn't agree with Emma Green's assessment that evangelicals had "enabled" Trump, he did agree that evangelicals had to take another look at themselves. "Where we find ourselves in the wrong, repentance is always called for," he told Green.

Meanwhile, the faculty and staff of the evangelical Wheaton College in Illinois issued a statement: "We repent of our own failures to speak and act in accordance with justice, and we lament the failures of the Church to teach clearly and to exercise adequate church discipline in these areas." And Russell Moore, a consistent Never Trumper, asked Trump to resign, and called on Congress to impeach the president and the Senate to convict him. Moore also made explicit that he didn't care who among his constituents objected. "I am willing, if necessary, to lose this seat," he said of his position as the head of the SBC's Ethics & Religious Liberty Commission.

So, there's been a critical break with the Trump entity. It's not uniform (one senior pastor from California said the violence is "what you get when you eject God from the courts and from the schools"), but it is undoubtedly momentous. And it offers hope for a new chapter in conservative white evangelical engagement with Americans who do not share their faith or political ideology.

But these new, promising openings do not erase the entrenched policy differences between liberals and conservatives, particularly as they relate to religious freedom. For a moment, between Election Day and January 6th, the religious clash seemed to be waning. On Election Day, I had argued in *USA Today* that the confirmation of Justice Amy Coney Barrett mere days before the election would help quell some of the partisan fire. The end of white Christian America is still in full view, I said, but now that conservative Christians have some legal assurances that their religious practices will be safeguarded, they might begin to engage empathetically instead of defensively.

And, in fact, in the days after the election, the numbers that emerged appeared to support my prediction. Michael Wear writing for the *New York Times* pointed out the shift in white evangelical votes:

> Nationally, [Biden] won 23 percent of white evangelicals, closing the gap from 2016 by 11 percentage points (from 64 to 53). This amounts to a swing of well over four million votes nationally, which accounts for much of Mr. Biden's lead in the popular vote . . . This shows up in key battleground states that decided the election. In Michigan, Mr. Biden won 29 percent of white evangelical support while Mrs. Clinton won 14 percent in 2016, an improvement that accounts for more than a 300,000 vote swing. In Georgia, Mr. Biden . . . almost tripled Mrs. Clinton's showing among white evangelicals, winning 14 percent compared to 5 percent.

Signaling confidence, not vulnerability, prominent Christian conservatives acknowledged that things were different. Instead of lamenting Trump's loss, Robert Jeffress chose to focus on what Christians had won: "A Joe Biden win cannot erase all the positive accomplishments that can be attributed to President Trump," he said. Penny Nance, president of the conservative Concerned Women for America, pointed to Barrett specifically: "We put some points on the board."

At the same time, they expressed their ongoing concerns. Franklin Graham warned that under a Biden administration, Christian businesses like Jack Phillips' would be targeted for refusing to serve gay couples. He worried that Biden is a mere continuation of Obama, widely considered by conservatives as the "most hostile to religious freedom and the rights of conscience that we've seen in this country" (the hyperbolic sentiment is often attributed to the effects of the Affordable Care Act's contraceptive mandate on Christian institutions). Beto O'Rourke was also invoked: "the left" will "want to try to come after churches and tax churches and tax tax-exempt organizations that are doing humanitarian work, social work throughout the country," Graham said, referring to O'Rourke's comments during CNN's 2019 presidential town hall.

Among other worries: The Equality Act, which would extend the protections of the Civil Rights Act of 1964 to the LGBT community without any space for religious accommodation; the Act stresses in particular that the Religious Freedom Restoration Act "shall not provide a claim concerning, or a defense to a claim under, a covered title, or provide a basis for challenging the application or enforcement of a covered title." With the Senate now split evenly between Republicans and Democrats and Vice-President Kamala Harris holding the tie-breaking vote, the Equality Act is poised to become law.

The COVID-19 context has also raised significant concerns for many religious conservatives—Christian and others—of state officials over-regulating houses of worship. On November 25, 2020, the United States Supreme Court ruled in favor of the Roman Catholic Diocese of Brooklyn and the Orthodox Jewish group, Agudath Israel, in their case against New York Governor Andrew Cuomo's limitations on houses of worship. Soon after, #AmyCovidBarrett was trending on social media and prominent progressive commentators were speaking out against the ruling. Meanwhile, just a week before that case reached the court, Justice Samuel Alito expressed concerns about the impact of the COVID-19 shutdown on religious liberty. Speaking at a legal conference, he said the pandemic had ushered in "previously unimaginable restrictions on individual liberty."

So, the political climate is radically different, but it is also in many ways the same. January 6th brought clarity about Trumpism to many Christians. Prior to that moment, Trump's judicial appointments gave conservatives assurances and fewer reasons, institutionally, to feel persecuted. At the same time, the grievance list remains long. Conservative activists will thus likely continue to seize on opportunities to deepen the siege mentality of religious conservatives, and there is little the Biden administration can do to fully prevent those efforts.

But there are ways to undercut them. This book has laid out many key strategies, with particular emphasis on "zooming in" on people as people and not as political caricatures. Biden on the campaign trail refused to demonize people with whom he disagreed, and he should continue to model that approach as President.

On a policy level, the Biden administration would do well to protect religious accommodations and strive toward compromise solutions wherever possible (something like, or better than, the Fairness For All Act I described in chapter 3). Taking this approach would signal respect for the traditional religious beliefs that conservative Christians—and traditional believers of other faiths—hold dear. As Justice Kennedy explained in his *Obergefell* and *Masterpiece* opinions, if Americans are to live together despite deep difference, they must ensure that gay persons and gay couples are not "treated as social outcasts or as inferior in dignity and worth" while also recognizing that those "who deem same-sex marriage to be wrong reach that conclusion based on decent and honorable religious or philosophical premises, and neither they nor their beliefs" should be disparaged.

As Wear sums up:

> Biden should invite Christians to build America's future, rather than cede to Mr. Trump's dark pronouncements that Christians must fear it. If the Biden administration can offer a positive vision for Christians in this country while earnestly seeking to limit unnecessary political conflict with moderate and conservative religious voters, it can do through governing something it did not fully accomplish on Election Day: the end not just of Trump's presidency, but a thorough repudiation of Mr. Trump's brand of politics.

Repudiating Trumpian politics requires Americans of diverse beliefs to let go of the current toxic brew of tribalism and contempt. Even after—*particularly* after—the events of January 6th, we have to, as writer Tom Junod put it, "believe that out of schism and fracture will emerge the unstoppably upward thrust, carrying us along until one day we are as good as the words on our founding documents."

Biden moved toward that goal the very day of his inauguration. For Muslims specifically, Biden repealed the travel ban on people from many Muslim-majority countries. For conservative Christians and any other American who might be wary of him, Biden offered a path forward in his inaugural address:

> [T]oday, at this time and in this place, let us start afresh.
>
> All of us.
>
> Let us listen to one another.
>
> Hear one another.
>
> See one another.
>
> Show respect to one another . . .
>
> We must end this uncivil war that pits red against blue, rural versus urban, conservative versus liberal.
>
> We can do this if we open our souls instead of hardening our hearts.
>
> If we show a little tolerance and humility.
>
> If we're willing to stand in the other person's shoes just for a moment.

ACKNOWLEDGMENTS

THIS IS MY SECOND BOOK in two years. I enjoyed writing the first one so much that I knew I had to do it again—and jumped right in without pause. Many thanks to the people who encouraged me with this second manuscript and didn't think I was nuts for doing it.

Foremost among them, my agent Leslie Meredith and my editor Jessica Case. My colleagues at the Aspen Institute—Zeenat Rahman, Allison Ralph, and Abbie Haug—helped cultivate a network of scholars and practitioners whose wisdom has shaped this book. Pastor Terry Kyllo, Saeed Khan, Jo Anne Lyon, and John Inazu provided helpful comments. Tim Schultz, Jayson Casper, Andrew Whitehead, Johnnie Moore Jr., and Matthew Owers graciously let me pick their brains. Mike Tolhurst did, too—along with so much more, like organizing a manuscript workshop and helping to launch the next stage of research on the "politics of vulnerability." His enthusiasm for my vision keeps me going. Thank you also to those who participated in the manuscript workshop: Mark Hall, Justin Tosi, Jenan Mohajir, Thomas Berg, and Bill Glod.

My interns, Amar Peterman, Rachel Morrison, Jackie Baik, and Carter Hirschorn, were so, so awesome to work with. Amar, in particular, was always available to think through ideas and review drafts.

Dr. Andrew Lewis was a mainstay of my writing process. I would not have been able to write this book without his guidance and the access he provided to the most relevant studies in the field. I look forward to our continuing work together!

ACKNOWLEDGMENTS

Finally, I reserve my deepest gratitude for my husband and kids who, while weathering the uncertainties of our new COVID-19 lifestyle, allowed me to hole up in my office and get this done.

NOTES

INTRODUCTION

Abcarian, Robin. "Supreme Court's Hobby Lobby decision is a slap in the face of women." *Los Angeles Times*, June 30, 2014. https://www.latimes.com/nation/la-me-ra-hobby-lobby-scotus -20140630-column.html.

Akhtar, Iqbal. "Race and Religion in the Political Problematization of the American Muslim." *Political Science and Politics* 44, no. 4 (October 2011): 768–774. Published by American Political Science Association. https://www.jstor.org/stable/41319966.

Ali, Wajahat, Eli Clifton, Matthew Duss, Lee Fang, Scott Keyes, and Faiz Shakir. "The Roots of the Islamophobia Network in America." Last modified August 26, 2011. https://cdn.americanprogress.org /wp-content/uploads/issues/2011/08/pdf/islamophobia.pdf.

Allam, Hannah and Talal Ansari. "State and Local Republican Officials Have Been Bashing Muslims. We Counted." *Buzzfeed News*, April 10, 2018. https://www.buzzfeednews.com/article/hannahallam /trump-republicans-bashing-muslims-without-repercussions.

Alterman, Eric. "Conservatives Blame America First, Again." Center for American Progress. January 25, 2007. https://www .americanprogress.org/issues/general/news/2007/01/25/2529 /think-again-conservatives-blame-america-first-again/.

Barzegar, Abbas and Zainab Arain. "Hijacked by Hate: American Philanthropy and the Islamophobia Network." Council on American-Islamic Relations, last modified June 19, 2019. http://www.islamophobia.org/images/IslamophobiaReport2019 /CAIR_Islamophobia_Report_2019_Final_Web.pdf.

Becket. "About Us." Becket website, accessed August 14, 2020. https://www.becketlaw.org/about-us/.

Blankenhorn, David. "The Top 14 Causes of Political Polarization." *American Interest*, May 16, 2018. https://www.the-american-interest .com/2018/05/16/the-top-14-causes-of-political-polarization/.

Brooks, Arthur. "Our Culture of Contempt." *New York Times*, March 2, 2019. https://www.nytimes.com/2019/03/02/opinion/sunday /political-polarization.html.

Brown, Brené. *Braving the Wilderness: The Quest for True Belonging and the Courage to Stand Alone.* New York: Random House, 2019.

D'Souza, Dinesh. *The Enemy at Home: The Cultural Left and Its Responsibility for 9/11.* New York: Doubleday, 2007.

Emgage. "2016 American Muslim Post-Election Survey." Emgage website, accessed August 14, 2020. https://emgageusa.org /2020/07/16/2016-american-muslim-post-election-survey/.

Farivar, Masood. "How Muslim-Americans Drifted to the Democratic Party." VOA, September 7, 2016. https://www.voanews.com/usa /how-muslim-americans-drifted-democratic-party.

Gjelten, Tom. "Peaceful Protestors Tear-Gassed to Clear Way for Trump Church Photo-Op." National Public Radio, June 1, 2020. https://www.npr.org/2020/06/01/867532070 /trumps-unannounced-church-visit-angers-church-officials.

Goodstein, Laurie. "Falwell: blame abortionists, feminists and gays." *Guardian*, September 19, 2001. https://www.theguardian.com /world/2001/sep/19/september11.usa9.

Hamid, Shadi. "Holding Our Own: Is the future of Islam in the West communal?" *Plough*, March 25, 2020. https://www.plough.com/en /articles/holding-our-own.

Harding, Kate. "Slouching Towards Gilead. Or Jesusland. Or Maybe Kochworld." *Dame*, July 1, 2014. https://www.damemagazine .com/2014/07/01/slouching-towards-gilead-or-jesusland-or -maybe-kochworld/.

Jones, Sarah. "We're All Living in Hobby Lobby's Bible Nation." *New Republic*, October 13, 2017. https://newrepublic.com /article/145271/were-living-hobby-lobbys-bible-nation.

Khan, Suhail K. "America's First Muslim President." *Foreign Policy*, August 23, 2019. https://foreignpolicy.com/2010/08/23/americas -first-muslim-president/; Hamid, Shadi. 2020. "Holding Our Own: Is the future of Islam in the West communal?" *Plough*, March 25, 2020. https://www.plough.com/en/articles/holding-our-own.

Klein, Ezra. *Why We're Polarized*. New York: Avid Reader Press, 2020.

Lithwick, Dahlia. "Of Course Hobby Lobby Thinks It's Above the Law." *Slate*, April 3, 2020. https://slate.com/news-and -politics/2020/04/hobby-lobby-scotus-coronavirus.html.

Mason, Lilliana. *Uncivil Agreement: How Politics Became Our Identity*. Chicago: University of Chicago Press, 2018.

Montgomery, Peter. "Anti-Muslim Activist Frank Gaffney is a Jerk, National Religious Broadcasters Discover." *Right Wing Watch*, March 6, 2020. https://www.rightwingwatch.org/post

/anti-muslim-activist-frank-gaffney-is-a-jerk-national-religious
-broadcasters-discover/.

Patel, Eboo. "A Nation Under Two Flags: Liberal Education, Interfaith
Literacy, and the New American Holy War." Association of
American Colleges & Universities, Summer 2018. https://www
.aacu.org/liberaleducation/2018/summer/patel.

Shortle, Allyson F. and Ronald Keith Gaddie. "Religious Nationalism
and Perceptions of Muslims and Islam." *Politics and Religion* 8
(2015): 435–457.

Stan, Adele M. "White Nationalism and Christian Right United at
Values Voter Summit." Moyers on Democracy, October 17, 2017.
https://billmoyers.com/story/white-nationalism-values -voter
-summit/; C-SPAN. "Western Conservative Summit," June 30,
2012. https://www.c-span.org/video/?306868-5/western
-conservative-summit.

Tupper, Seth. "Tapio questions religious freedom for Muslims." *Rapid
City Journal*, January 21, 2018. https://rapidcityjournal.com
/news/local/tapio-questions-religious-freedom-for-muslims/article
_a4e4532f-1b69-5b4d-9400-a70fb5028caa.html.

Uddin, Asma. "Frank Gaffney is wrong. Religious liberty is good for
everyone, not a 'takeover.'" *Religion News Service*, March 2, 2020.
https://religionnews.com/2020/03/02/frank-gaffney-is-wrong
-religious-liberty-is-good-for-everyone-not-a-takeover/.

Waldman, Steven. "Religious Freedom is America's Greatest Export—
and It's Under Attack." *Newsweek*, May 9, 2019. https://www
.newsweek.com/2019/05/17/religious-freedom-americas-greatest
-export-under -attack-1418121.html.

Wingerter, Justin. "Cory Gardner, the women's vote and religion: Western Conservative Summit takeaways." *Denver Post*, July 14, 2019. https://www.denverpost.com/2019/07/14 /western-conservative-summit-trump-gardner/.

Wolfe, Alan. "None (but Me) Dare Call It Treason." *New York Times*, January 21, 2007. https://www.nytimes.com/2007/01/21/books /review/Wolfe.t.html.

CHAPTER 1

Aslan, Reza. "How religion changed the presidency—and vice versa." *Big Think*, April 14, 2018. https://bigthink.com/videos /reza-aslan-how-religion-changed-the-presidency-and-vice-versa.

Bacon Jr., Perry and Amelia Thomson-DeVeaux. "How Trump and Race Are Splitting Evangelicals." *FiveThirtyEight*, March 2, 2018. https://fivethirtyeight.com/features/how-trump-and-race-are -splitting-evangelicals/.

Bacon Jr., Peter. "Democrats Are Wrong About Republicans. Republicans Are Wrong About Democrats." *FiveThirtyEight*, June 26, 2018. https://fivethirtyeight.com/features/democrats- are-wrong -about-republicans-republicans-are-wrong-about-democrats/.

Baptist Press. "SBC president and Islamic scholar discuss religious freedom." *Baptist Standard*, March 9, 2020. https://www.baptistst andard.com/news/baptists/sbc-president-and-islamic-scholar -discuss-religious-freedom/.

Blair, Leonardo. "Robert Jeffress: Christians Not Voting for Donald Trump If He's the Nominee Are Foolish, Prideful." *Christian Post*, March 2, 2016. http://www.christianpost.com/news/robert-jeffress -christians-not-voting-donald-trump-foolish-prideful-158881/.

Braunstein, Ruth. "Muslims as Outsiders, Enemies, and Others: The 2016 Presidential Election and the Politics of Religious Exclusion." *American Journal of Cultural Sociology* (2017). doi: 10.1057 /s41290-017-0042-x.

Brooks, David. "The National Humiliation We Need." *New York Times*, July 2, 2020. https://www.nytimes.com/2020/07/02/opinion /coronavirus-july-4.html.

Bruenig, Elizabeth. "Can the Evangelical Left Rise Again?" *New Republic*, September 3, 2015. https://newrepublic.com/article /122716/can-evangelical-left-rise-again.

Bruenig, Elizabeth. "In God's Country." *Washington Post*, August 14, 2019. https://www.washingtonpost.com/opinions/2019/08/14 /evangelicals-view-trump-their-protector-will-they-stand-by-him /?arc404=true.

Bruinius, Harry. "Why Evangelicals are Trump's strongest travel -ban supporters." *Christian Science Monitor*, March 3, 2017. https://www.csmonitor.com/USA/Politics/2017/0303/Why -Evangelicals-are-Trump-s-strongest-travel-ban-supporters.

Cole, Brendan. "Pastor Robert Jeffress Says Trump is Christian 'Warrior' and Democrats Worship Pagan God Moloch 'Who Allowed for Child Sacrifice.'" *Newsweek*, October 2, 2019. https://www.newsweek.com/robert-jeffress-donald-trump-defends -christians-todd-starnes-show-1462525.

Cox, Daniel and Robert P. Jones. "47% of the Country Say Trump has Violated the Constitution, but Few Support Impeachment." PRRI, February 24, 2017. https://www.prri.org/research/poll -trump-impeachment-constitution-partisanship-muslim-ban/.

Cox, Daniel and Robert P. Jones. "Majority of Americans Oppose Transgender Bathroom Restrictions." PRRI, March 10, 2017. https://www.prri.org/research/lgbt-transgender-bathroom -discrimination-religious-liberty/.

Cox, Daniel. "Could Trump Drive Young White Evangelicals Away From the GOP?" *FiveThirtyEight*, August 20, 2019. https://fivethirtyeight.com/features/could-trump-drive-young-white -evangelicals-away-from-the-gop/.

Diamant, Jeff. "Though still conservative, young evangelicals are more liberal than their elders on some issues." Pew Research Center, May 4, 2017. https://www.pewresearch.org/fact-tank/2017/05/04 /though-still-conservative-young-evangelicals-are-more-liberal-than -their-elders-on-some-issues/.

Faith Angle Forum. "Staff," accessed September 2, 2020. https://eppc .org/programs/the-faith-angle-forum/; Faith Angle. "Asma Uddin and Daniel Harrell: When Islam Is Not a Religion," March 18, 2020. https://faithangle.podbean.com/e/asma-uddin-and-daniel -harrell-when-islam-is-not-a-religion/.

Garay, Jesus. "These Posters Protesting Trump Were Created by The Man Responsible for Obama's 'Hope' Artwork." Guff, 2016. https://guff.com/these-posters-protesting-trump-were-created-by -the-man-responsible-for-obamas-hope-artwork.

Goodrich, Luke. *Free to Believe: The Battle Over Religious Liberty in America*. New York: Multnomah, 2019.

Gorski, Philip. "Why evangelicals voted for Trump: A critical cultural sociology." *American Journal of Cultural Sociology* 5 (2017): 338–354. https://doi.org/10.1057/s41290-017-0043-9.

Green, Emma. "White Evangelicals Believe They Face More
Discrimination Than Muslims." *Atlantic*, March 10, 2017.
https://www.theatlantic.com/politics/archive/2017/03
/perceptions-discrimination-muslims-christians/519135/.

Green, Emma. "How Much Discrimination Do Muslims Face in
America?" *Atlantic*, July 26, 2017. https://www.theatlantic
.com/politics/archive/2017/07/american-muslims-trump
/534879/.

Griswold, Eliza. "Millennial Evangelicals Diverge From Their Parents'
Beliefs." *New Yorker*, August 27, 2018. https://www.newyorker.com
/news/on-religion/millennial-evangelicals-diverge-from-their
-parents-beliefs.

Grunwald, Michael. "How Everything Became the Culture War."
Politico Magazine (November/December 2018). https://www
.politico.com/magazine/story/2018/11/02/culture-war-liberals
-conservatives-trump-2018-222095.

Guth, James L. "Are White Evangelicals Populists? The View from
the 2016 American National Election Study." *Review of Faith &
International Affairs* 17, no. 3: 20–35. DOI: 10.1080/15570274
.2019.1643991.

Haidt, Jonathan. *The Righteous Mind: Why Good People Are Divided by
Politics and Religion*. New York: Penguin, 2012.

Hewstone, Miles, Mark Rubin, and Hazel Willis. "Intergroup Bias."
Annual Review of Psychology 53, no. 1 (2002): 575–604.

Jeffress, Robert. *Twilight's Last Gleaming: How America's Last Days Can
Be Your Best Days*. New York: Worthy Books, 2012.

Kaemingk, Matthew. *Christian Hospitality and Muslim Immigration in an Age of Fear*. Grand Rapids, Mich.: Eerdmans, 2018.

Kalkan, Kerem Ozan, Geoffrey C. Layman, and Eric M. Uslaner. "'Bands of Others'? Attitudes toward Muslims in Contemporary American Society." *Journal of Politics* 71, no. 3 (2009): 847–862.

Kelly, Jon. "Why are lattes associated with liberals?" BBC News, October 6, 2014. https://www.bbc.com/news/magazine-29449037; Roberts, David. "The real problem with the New York Times op-ed page: it's not honest about US conservatism." *Vox*, March 15, 2018. https://www.vox.com/policy-and-politics/2018/3/15/17113176/new-york-times-opinion-page-conservatism.

Levitsky, Steven and Daniel Ziblatt. "End Minority Rule." *New York Times*, October 23, 2020. https://www.nytimes.com/2020/10/23/opinion/sunday/disenfranchisement-democracy-minority-rule.html?referringSource=articleShare.

Masci, David. "Many Americans see religious discrimination in U.S.—especially against Muslims." Pew Research Center, May 17, 2019. https://www.pewresearch.org/fact-tank/2019/05/17/many-americans-see-religious-discrimination-in-u-s-especially-against-muslims/.

Mason, Lilliana. *Uncivil Agreement: How Politics Became Our Identity*. Chicago: University of Chicago Press, 2018.

Mogahed, Dalia. "American Muslim Poll 2019: Predicting and Preventing Islamophobia." Institute for Social Policy and Understanding, May 1, 2019. https://www.ispu.org/american-muslim-poll-2019-predicting-and-preventing-islamophobia/.

More in Common. "Hidden Tribes: A Study of America's Polarized Landscape." More in Common website, accessed November 19, 2020. https://hiddentribes.us.

Mutz, Diana C. "Status threat, not economic hardship, explains the 2016 presidential vote." *Proceedings of the National Academy of Sciences* 115, no. 19 (May 2018). E4330-E4339; DOI:10.1073 /pnas.1718155115.

Neighborly Faith. "About." Neighborly Faith website, accessed September 2, 2020. https://www.neighborlyfaith.org/who-we-are.

Neighborly Faith Facebook page. https://www.facebook.com /neighborlyfaith/posts/2274951422619384.

Patel, Eboo. *Out of Many Faiths: Religious Diversity and the American Promise.* Princeton, N.J.: Princeton University Press, 2018.

Rasmussen Reports. "Democrats Think Muslims Worse Off Here Than Christians Are in Muslim World." Last modified February 7, 2017. https://www.rasmussenreports.com/public_content/politics /general_politics/february_2017/democrats_think_muslims_worse _off_here_than_christians_are_in_muslim_world.

Rosenberg, Paul. "Sociologist Andrew Whitehead: How Christian nationalism drives American politics." *Salon*, February 29, 2020. https://www.salon.com/2020/02/29/sociologist-andrew-whitehead -how-christian-nationalism-drives-american-politics/.

Schor, Elana and Hannah Fingerhut. "Religious Freedom in America: Popular and Polarizing." *Telegraph*, August 5, 2020.

Schwadel, Philip and Gregory A. Smith. "Evangelical approval of Trump remains high, but other religious groups are less supportive." Pew Research Center, March 18, 2019. https://www.pewresearch .org/fact-tank/2019/03/18/evangelical-approval-of-trump-remains -high-but-other-religious-groups-are-less-supportive/.

Shellnut, Kate. "Most White Evangelicals Don't Believe Muslims Belong in America." *Christianity Today*, July 26, 2017. https://www .christianitytoday.com/news/2017/july/pew-how-white-evangelicals -view-us-muslims-islam.html.

Shortle, Allyson F. and Ronald Keith Gaddie. "Religious Nationalism and Perceptions of Muslims and Islam." *Politics and Religion* 8 (2015): 435–457.

Smith, Gregory A. "Most white evangelicals approve of Trump travel prohibition and express concerns about extremism." Pew Research Center, February 27, 2017. https://www.pewresearch.org/fact -tank/2017/02/27/most-white-evangelicals-approve-of-trump -travel-prohibition-and-express-concerns-about-extremism/.

Smith, R. and D. King. "White Protectionism in America." *Perspectives on Politics*, 2020: 1–19. doi: 10.1017/S1537592720001152.

Stroop, Chrissy. "America's Islamophobia is Forged at the Pulpit." *Foreign Policy*, March 26, 2019. https://foreignpolicy.com /2019/03/26/americas-islamophobia-is-forged-in-the-pulpit/.

Theiss-Morse, Elizabeth. *Who Counts as American? The Boundaries of National Identity*. Cambridge, UK: Cambridge University Press, 2009.

Tierney, John. "Your Car: Politics on Wheels." *New York Times*, April 1, 2005. https://www.nytimes.com/2005/04/01/automobiles /your-car-politics-on-wheels.html.

Whitehead, Andrew L., Samuel L. Perry, and Joseph O Baker. "Make America Christian Again: Christian Nationalism and Voting for Donald Trump in the 2016 Presidential Election." *Sociology of Religion* 79, no. 2 (Summer 2018): 147–171. https://doi.org /10.1093/socrel/srx070, published: January 25, 2018.

Whitehead, Andrew and Samuel Perry. *Taking America Back for God: Christian Nationalism in the United States*. Oxford, UK: Oxford University Press, 2020.

Wikipedia. "Jim Wallis." Accessed October 9, 2020. https://en .wikipedia.org/wiki/Jim_Wallis; Sojourners. "Our Work." Accessed October 9, 2020. https://sojo.net/about/about-sojourners.

Willer, Robb, Ko Kuwabara, and Michael W. Macy. "The False Enforcement of Unpopular Norms." *AJS* 115, no. 2 (September 2009): 451–90. https://pdfs.semanticscholar.org/1293/ecb55a 2c5194fd1c16532c2c92599c6931fb.pdf.

YouTube. "Dr. Jeffress Tells The Truth About Islam." Last modified August 23, 2010. https://www.youtube.com/watch?v=wfb9p 3qSRqA&t=183s.

YouTube. "Dallas pastor criticized for sermon denouncing Islam." Last modified November 24, 2015. https://www.youtube.com /watch?v=WLKV9lojMyw.

YouTube. "Dr. Robert Jeffress-Pres. Trump fulfilling belief that religious liberty is a gift from God." Last modified July 27, 2018. https://www.youtube.com/watch?v=CXD_shCgsd8&t=110s.

YouTube. "Lilliana Mason on Uncivil Agreement." Last modified May 1, 2020. https://www.youtube.com/watch?v=TC4SQ9oasnU.

YouTube. "Why Evangelicals Hate Muslims: An Evangelical Minister's Perspective – Pastor Bob Roberts, Jr." Last modified April 29, 2019. https://www.youtube.com/watch?v=opcUsTBkIMA&vl=en.

Zauzmer, Julie and Michelle Boorstein. "Evangelicals fear Muslims; atheists fear Christians: New poll shows how Americans mistrust one another." *Washington Post*, September 7, 2017. https://www

.washingtonpost.com/news/acts-of-faith/wp/2017/09/07
/evangelicals-fear-muslims-atheists-fear-christians-how-americans
-mistrust-each-other/.

CHAPTER 2

Adamson, Goran. "Why Do Right-Wing Populist Parties Prosper?
Twenty-One Suggestions to the Anti-Racist." *Society* 56 (2019):
47–58. https://doi.org/10.1007/s12115-018-00323-8. Accessed at
https://link.springer.com/article/10.1007/s12115-018-00323-8.

Ahmari, Sohrab. "Against David French-ism." *First Things*, May 29,
2019. https://www.firstthings.com/web-exclusives/2019/05
/against-david-french-ism.

Aslan, Reza. "How religion changed the presidency—and vice versa."
Big Think, April 14, 2018. https://bigthink.com/videos/reza-aslan
-how-religion-changed-the-presidency-and-vice-versa.

Ayers, Emma. "The Ahmari-French Debate Was About Theology,
Not Politics." *American Conservative*, September 9, 2019.
https://www.theamericanconservative.com/articles
/the-ahmari-french-debate-was-about-theology-not-politics/.

Bailey, Sarah Pulliam. "Trump wants 'packed churches' on Easter. Pastors
expect their doors to be shut." *Washington Post,* March 27, 2020.

Baker, Peter. "Firing a Salvo in Culture Wars, Trump Pushes for
Churches to Reopen." *New York Times*, May 22, 2020. https://www
.nytimes.com/2020/05/22/us/politics/trump-churches-coronavirus
.html?referringSource=articleShare.

Balingit, Moriah and Ariana Eunjung Cha. "Trump administration
moves to protect prayer in public schools and federal funds for

religious organizations." *Washington Post*, January 16, 2020. https://www.washingtonpost.com/education/2020/01/16/trump -administration-moves-protect-prayer-public-schools-federal-funds -religious-organizations/.

Bashir, Martin. "George Floyd death: Trump's church visit shocks religious leaders." BBC News, June 2, 2020. https://www.bbc.com /news/world-us-canada-52890650.

Boorstein, Michelle. "What it means that Mike Pence called himself an 'evangelical Catholic.'" *Washington Post*, July 18, 2016. https://www .washingtonpost.com/news/acts-of-faith/wp/2016/07/15/what-it -means-that-mike-pence-called-himself-an-evangelical-catholic/.

Brody, David. "I don't know about you but I'll take a president with a Bible in his hand in front of a church over far left violent radicals setting a church on fire any day of the week." Tweet (@DavidBrodyCBN), June 1, 2020. https://twitter.com /DavidBrodyCBN/status/1267646416689692672.

Brown, Brené. *Braving the Wilderness: The Quest for True Belonging and the Courage to Stand Alone*. New York: Random House, 2019.

Brown, Michael. "Is NY Times right? Are (white) evangelicals responsible for spread of COVID-19?" *Christian Post*, March 28, 2020. https://www.christianpost.com/voices/is-ny-times-right-are -white-evangelicals-responsible-for-spread-of-covid-19.html.

Burton, Tara Isabella. "Jeff Sessions announces a religious liberty task force to combat 'dangerous' secularism." *Vox*, July 31, 2018. https://www.vox.com/identities/2018/7/31/17631110/jeff -sessions-religious-liberty-task-force-memo-christian-nationalism.

Caldwell, Christopher. *Reflections on the Revolution in Europe: Immigration, Islam and the West*. New York: Anchor Books, 2010.

Chua, Amy. *Political Tribes: Group Instinct and the Fate of Nations*. New York: Penguin Books, 2018.

Cohen, Roger. "Trump's Last Stand for White America." *New York Times*, October 16, 2020. https://www.nytimes.com/2020/10/16 /opinion/trump-2020.html?referringSource=articleShare.

Coppins, McKay. "The Christians Who Loved Trump's Stunt." *Atlantic*, June 2, 2020. https://www.theatlantic.com/politics /archive/2020/06/trumps-biblical-spectacle-outside -st-johns-church/612529/.

Coppins, McKay. "Trump Secretly Mocks His Christian Supporters." *Atlantic*, September 29, 2020. https://amp.theatlantic.com/amp /article/616522/.

Christianity Today Editors. "CT's 25 Most-Read Stories on the Persecuted Church." *Christianity Today*, January 4, 2018. https://www.christianitytoday.com/news/2018/january/cts-25 -most-read-stories-on-persecuted-church.html.

Dreher, Rod. *The Benedict Option: A Strategy for Christians in a Post-Christian Nation*. New York: Sentinel, 2017.

Dreher, Rod. "Does Pope Francis Oppose the Benedict Option?" *American Conservative*, October 11, 2017. https://www.the americanconservative.com/dreher/pope-francis-vs-the-benedict -option/.

Dreher, Rod. "SCOTUS Routs Conservatives, Again." *American Conservative*, June 15, 2020. https://www.theamericanconservative .com/dreher/title-vii-scotus-rout-for-conservatives/.

Eatwell, Roger and Matthew Goodwin. *National Populism: The Revolt Against Liberal Democracy*. New York: Pelican, 2018.

Faith Angle. *Matthew Goodwin and Henry Olsen: National Populism.* Faith Angle podcast, November 1, 2019. https://faithangle.podbean .com/e/matthew-goodwin-and-henry-olsen-national-populism/.

Faith Angle. *Tim Keller and Peter Wehner: A Steady Voice in the Storm.* Faith Angle podcast, April 22, 2020. https://faithangle.podbean .com/e/tim-keller-and-peter-wehner-a-steady-voice-in-the-storm/.

Fea, John. "Courtiers and kings, evangelicals, prophets and Trump." *Religion News Service*, January 8, 2020. https://religionnews.com /2020/01/08/courtiers-and-kings-evangelicals-prophets-and-trump/.

Fitzgerald, Frances. *The Evangelicals: The Struggle to Shape America.* New York: Simon & Schuster, 2017.

French, David. "Viewpoint Neutrality Protects Both Drag Queens and Millions of American Christians." *National Review*, September 9, 2019. https://www.nationalreview.com/corner/viewpoint-neutrality -protects-drag-queens-and-millions-american-christians/.

French, David. "Decency Is No Barrier to Justice or the Common Good." *National Review*, May 28, 2019. https://www.nationalreview .com/corner/decency-is-no-barrier-to-justice-or-the-common-good/.

Friedman, Thomas L. "Who Can Win America's Politics of Humiliation?" *New York Times*, September 8, 2020. https://www .nytimes.com/2020/09/08/opinion/biden-trump-humiliation.html? referringSource=articleShare.

Goldberg, Michelle. "Leave Drag Queen Story Hour Alone!" *New York Times*, June 7, 2019. https://www.nytimes.com/2019/06/07 /opinion/conservatives-culture-trump.html.

Goodwin, Matthew. "National populism is unstoppable—and the left still doesn't understand it." *Guardian*, November 8, 2018.

https://www.theguardian.com/commentisfree/2018/nov/08
/national-populism-immigration-financial-crisis-globalisation.

Got Questions. "What is evangelical Catholicism?" Got Questions
website, accessed July 28, 2020. https://www.gotquestions.org
/evangelical-Catholicism.html.

Gryboski, Michael. "Russell Moore Takes on Critics at SBC for
Supporting Religious Freedom for Muslims to Build Mosques."
Christian Post, June 16, 2016. https://www.christianpost.com
/news/erlcs-russell-moore-takes-heat-sbc-supporting-religious
-freedom-muslims-build-mosque-165299/#Iuox1i6Gc
0LE7BbW.99.

Hamid, Shadi. "The role of Islam in European populism: How refugee
flows and fear of Muslims drive right-wing support." Foreign Policy
at Brookings. https://www.brookings.edu/wp-content/uploads
/2019/02/FP_20190226_islam_far_right_hamid.pdf.

Harvard Health Publishing. "Understanding the Stress Response."
Harvard Health Publishing website, last modified July 6, 2020.
https://www.health.harvard.edu/staying-healthy/understanding
-the-stress-response.

Inazu, John. "Breaking Out of the White Evangelical Echo Chamber."
Christianity Today, February 10, 2020. https://www.christianity
today.com/ct/2020/february-web-only/john-inazu-breaking-out
-white-evangelical-echo-chamber.html.

Ingraham, Christopher. "The non-religious are now the country's
largest religious voting bloc." *Washington Post*, July 14, 2016.
https://www.washingtonpost.com/news/wonk/wp/2016/07
/14/the-non-religious-are-now-the-countrys-largest-religious
-voting-bloc/.

Johnson, Byron R. and Thomas S. Kidd. "Responding to COVID-19 would be a lot harder without churches and Christian groups." *Dallas News*, March 25, 2020. https://www.dallasnews.com /opinion/commentary/2020/03/29/responding-to-covid-19-would -be-a-lot-harder-without-churches-and-christian-groups/.

Jones, Robert P. *End of White Christian America*. New York: Simon & Schuster, 2016.

Keepers, Brian. "Is it Time to Let Go of the Label 'Evangelical'?" *Reformed Journal: The Twelve*, April 8, 2019. https://blog.reform edjournal.com/2019/04/08/is-it-time-to-let-go-of-the-label -evangelical/.

Kitchener, Caroline. "The Trouble with Tribalism." *Atlantic*, October 17, 2018. https://www.theatlantic.com/membership /archive/2018/10/trouble-tribalism/573307/.

Klein, Ezra. "Harvard historian Jill Lepore on what 'What We're Polarized' gets wrong." *Vox*, February 6, 2020. https://www.vox .com/podcasts/2020/2/6/21122870/why-were-polarized-ezra -klein-show-jill-lepore.

Lee, Carol E., Amanda Hayes, and Leigh Ann Caldwell. "Trump is navigating competing demands from evangelicals over Supreme Court pick." NBC News, September 25, 2020.

Manhattan Declaration. "Manhattan Declaration." Manhattan Declaration website, last modified November 20, 2019. https://www.manhattandeclaration.org/.

Martí, Gerardo. "The Unexpected Orthodoxy of Donald J. Trump: White Evangelical Support for the 45th President of the United States." *Sociology of Religion: A Quarterly Review* 80, no. 1 (2019): 1–8. doi: 10.1093/socrel/sry056.

Medina, Jennifer and Maggie Haberman. "In Miami Speech, Trump Tells Evangelical Base: God Is 'On Our Side.'" *New York Times*, January 3, 2020. https://www.nytimes.com/2020/01/03/us/politics /trump-miami-rally-evangelicals.amp.html.

Moore, Russell. *Onward: Engaging the Culture Without Losing the Gospel*. Nashville, Tenn.: B&H Publishing Group, 2015.

Mouw, Richard. *Restless Faith: Holding Evangelical Beliefs in a World of Contested Labels*. Grand Rapids, Mich.: Brazos Press, 2019.

NBC News. "Full text: President Trump's 2020 RNC acceptance speech." NBC News, August 28, 2020. https://www.nbcnews.com /politics/2020-election/read-full-text-president-donald-trump-s -acceptance-speech-rnc-n1238636.

New York Times. "Part 4: Poland's Culture Wars." *Daily* podcast, June 13, 2019. https://www.nytimes.com/2019/06/13/podcasts /the-daily/poland-nationalism-democracy.html.

New York Times. "Part 5: Can Liberal Democracy Survive in Europe?" *Daily* podcast, June 14, 2019. https://www.nytimes .com/2019/06/14/podcasts/the-daily/europe-liberal-democracy -germany.html.

Noble, Alan. "The Evangelical Persecution Complex." *Atlantic*, August 4, 2014. https://www.theatlantic.com/national /archive/2014/08/the-evangelical-persecution-complex/375506/.

Olson, Emily. "What Amy Coney Barrett's Supreme Court nomination tells us about Trump's 2020 election strategy." ABC News, September 27, 2020. https://www.abc.net.au/news/2020-09-27 /donald-trump-us-election-supreme-court-amy-coney-barrett-voters /12705228.

Orr, Gabby. "'Dangerous levels of contempt': Trump deploys a convention to attack Dems on religion." *Politico*, August 25, 2020. https://www.politico.com/news/2020/08/25/trump -attacks-democrats-on-religion-401551.

Peters, Jeremy W., Michael M. Grynbaum, Keith Collins, Rich Harris, and Rumsey Taylor. "How the El Paso Killer Echoed the Incendiary Words of Conservative Media Stars." *New York Times*, August 11, 2019. https://www.nytimes.com/interactive/2019/08/11/business /media/el-paso-killer-conservative-media.html?action=click& module=Top%20Stories&pgtype=Homepage.

Peters, Jeremy W. "Trump's Approval Slips Where He Can't Afford to Lose It: Among Evangelicals." *New York Times*, June 4, 2020. https://www.nytimes.com/2020/06/04/us/politics/trump-polls -christians-evangelicals.html?referringSource=articleShare.

Pew Research Center. "Modern Immigration Wave Brings 59 Million to U.S., Driving Population Growth and Change Through 2065." Last modified September 28, 2015. https://www.pewresearch.org /hispanic/2015/09/28/modern-immigration-wave-brings-59-million -to-u-s-driving-population-growth-and-change-through-2065/#post -1965-immigration-drives-u-s-population-growth-through-2065.

Powers, Kirsten. "It's the power-hungry who support Trump." *USA Today*, July 19, 2016. https://www.usatoday.com/story/opinion /columnist/2016/07/19/power-evangelical-white-conservative -republican-trump-column/87257760/.

Premier Journalist. "Mike Pence faces backlash for replacing 'Jesus' with 'Old Glory' flag reference during RNC speech." *Premier Christian News*, August 28, 2020. https://premierchristian.news/en/news /article/mike-pence-faces-backlash-for-replacing-jesus-with-old -glory-flag-reference-during-rnc-speech.

Relevant staff. "Vice President Mike Pence Swapped Out 'Jesus' for 'Old Glory' in His RNC Address." *Relevant Magazine*, August 27, 2020. https://relevantmagazine.com/culture/vice-president-mike-pence-swapped-out-jesus-for-old-glory-in-his-rnc-address/.

Schneider, Mike. "Census shows white decline, nonwhite majority among youngest." Associated Press, June 25, 2020. https://apnews.com/a3600edf620ccf2759080d00f154c069.

Sherwood, Harriet. "'Toxic Christianity': the evangelicals creating champions for Trump." *Guardian*, October 21, 2018. https://www.theguardian.com/us-news/2018/oct/21/evangelical-christians-trump-liberty-university-jerry-falwell.

Smith, R. and D. King. "White Protectionism in America." *Perspectives on Politics*, 2020: 1–19. doi: 10.1017/S1537592720001152.

Smith, Samuel. "Religious 'nones' now as big as evangelicals in the US, new data shows." *Christian Post*, March 20, 2019. https://www.christianpost.com/news/religious-nones-now-as-big-as-evangelicals-in-the-us-new-data-shows.html.

Stack, Liam. "Drag Queen Story Hour Continues Its Reign at Libraries, Despite Backlash." *New York Times*, June 6, 2019. https://www.nytimes.com/2019/06/06/us/drag-queen-story-hour.html.

Stewart, Katherine. "The Religious Right's Hostility to Science is Crippling Our Coronavirus Response." *New York Times*, March 27, 2020. https://www.nytimes.com/2020/03/27/opinion/coronavirus-trump-evangelicals.html.

Thomson-DeVeaux, Amelia. "The Christian Right Has A New Strategy on Gay Marriage." *FiveThirtyEight*, December 5, 2017. https://fivethirtyeight.com/features/the-christian-right-has-a-new-strategy-on-gay-marriage/.

Trump, Donald J. "Remarks at Great Faith International Ministries in Detroit, Michigan." The American Presidency Project, September 3, 2016. https://www.presidency.ucsb.edu/documents/remarks -great-faith-international-ministries-detroit-michigan.

Trump, Donald J. "Remarks to the 11th Annual Values Voter Summit in Washington, DC Omni Shoreham Hotel, Washington, D.C." The American Presidency Project, September 9, 2016. https://www .presidency.ucsb.edu/documents/remarks-the-11th-annual-values -voter-summit-washington-dc-omni-shoreham-hotel-washington.

Uddin, Asma. *When Islam Is Not a Religion: Inside America's Fight for Religious Freedom*. New York: Pegasus Books, 2019.

U.S. Census. "Projecting Majority-Minority." U.S. Census website, accessed November 19, 2020. https://www.census.gov/content /dam/Census/newsroom/releases/2015/cb15-tps16_graphic.pdf.

U.S. Department of Justice. "Attorney General Sessions Delivers Remarks at the Department of Justice's Religious Liberty Summit." U.S. Department of Justice website, last modified July 30, 2018. https://www.justice.gov/opa/speech/attorney-general-sessions -delivers-remarks-department-justice-s-religious-liberty-summit.

U.S. Department of Justice. "Attorney General William P. Barr Delivers Remarks to the Law School and the de Nicola Center for Ethics and Culture at the University of Notre Dame." U.S. Department of Justice website, October 11, 2019. https://www.justice.gov/opa /speech/attorney-general-william-p-barr-delivers-remarks-law -school-and-de-nicola-center-ethics.

U.S. Department of State. "Being a Christian Leader." U.S. Department of State website, last modified October 11, 2019. https://www .state.gov/being-a-christian-leader/.

Vasquez, Christian. "Trump takes his stump speech to the Values Voter Summit." *Politico*, October 12, 2019. https://www.politico.com/news/2019/10/12/trump-values-voter-summit-2020-045162.

Wadsworth, Nancy. "The racial demons that help explain evangelical support for Trump." *Vox*, April 30, 2018. https://www.vox.com/platform/amp/the-big-idea/2018/4/30/17301282/race-evangelicals-trump-support-gerson-atlantic-sexism-segregation-south.

Walker, Andrew T. "Ahmari or French? Why Christianity is Not Pragmatic." The Gospel Coalition, June 6, 2019. https://www.thegospelcoalition.org/article/ahmari-french-christianity-pragmatic/.

Walker, Andrew T. "Friday thoughts: A thread on why current evangelical voting rhetoric in 2020 is demonstrating the underdeveloped nature of our political theology." Tweet (@andrewtwalk), April 17, 2020. https://twitter.com/andrewtwalk/status/1251143035888513024?s=20.

Wehner, Peter. "The Deepening Crisis in Evangelical Christianity." *Atlantic*, July 5, 2019. https://www.theatlantic.com/ideas/archive/2019/07/evangelical-christians-face-deepening-crisis/593353/.

White House. "Remarks by President Trump at Values Voter Summit." White House website, last modified October 12, 2019. https://www.whitehouse.gov/briefings-statements/remarks-president-trump-values-voter-summit/.

White House. "Remarks by President Trump at the 68th Annual National Prayer Breakfast." White House website, last modified February 6, 2020. https://www.whitehouse.gov/briefings-statements/remarks-president-trump-68th-annual-national-prayer-breakfast/.

Wilmouth, Brad. "On MSNBC, Aslan Likens White Evangelicals to 'Doomsday Cult.'" mrcTV, April 13, 2020. https://www.mrctv.org /videos/msnbc-azlan-likens-white-evangelicals-doomsday-cult.

Yang2020. "Right to Privacy/Abortion and Contraception." Andrew Yang2020 website, accessed September 11, 2020. https://www .yang2020.com/policies/right-privacy-abortion-contraception/.

Yoshinaga, Kendra. "Babies of Color Are Now the Majority, Census Says." National Public Radio, July 1, 2016. https://www.npr.org /sections/ed/2016/07/01/484325664/babies-of-color-are-now-the -majority-census-says.

CHAPTER 3

Abrams, Meredith. "Empirical Analysis of Religious Freedom Restoration Act Cases in the Federal District Courts Since *Hobby Lobby*." *Columbia Human Rights Law Review Online* 4 (2019): 55–88.

Adkisson, Samuel. "So Yale Law School endorses anti-religious bigotry now?" *USA Today*, April 5, 2019. https://www.usatoday.com/story /opinion/voices/2019/04/05/yale-law-school-masterpiece-cakeshop -religious-discrimination-column/3354031002/.

American Unity Fund. "'When religious liberty and LGBT interests collide, instead of incivility and driving toward a winner-take-all result, we should embrace civility, protection of core rights for all, and reasonable compromise.' @ProfRobinWilson in support of the Fairness For All Act." Tweet (@AmericanUnity), May 15, 2020. https://twitter.com/AmericanUnity/status/1261347 016799641606.

Bailey, Sarah Pulliam. "Prominent Southern Baptist Albert Mohler opposed Trump in 2016. Now, he says he will vote for the president."

Washington Post, April 6, 2020. https://www.washingtonpost.com
/religion/2020/04/16/souther-baptist-albert-mohler-to-vote-trump/.

Barclay, Stephanie H. and Mark L. Rienzi. "Constitutional Anomalies
or As-Applied Challenges? A Defense of Religious Exemptions."
Boston College Law Review 59 (2018): 1595–1653.

Becket. "RFRA Info Central." Becket website, accessed September 17,
2020. https://www.becketlaw.org/research-central/rfra-info-central/.

Berg, Thomas. "Freedom to Serve: Religious Organizational Freedom,
LGBT Rights, and the Common Good." In *Religious Freedom,
LGBT Rights, and the Prospects for Common Ground*, edited by
William Eskridge and Robin Wilson. Cambridge, UK: Cambridge
University Press, 2019.

Berhmann, Savannah. "Beto O'Rourke criticized by conservatives for
comment about tax-exempt status and LGBTQ rights." *USA Today*,
October 11, 2019. https://www.usatoday.com/story/news/politics
/elections/2019/10/11/lgbtq-rights-conservatives-criticize-beto
-orourke-after-cnn-event/3946859002/.

Blankenhorn, David. "The Top 14 Causes of Political Polarization."
American Interest, May 16, 2018. https://www.the-american-interest
.com/2018/05/16/the-top-14-causes-of-political-polarization/.

Brooks, Arthur. *The Conservative Heart: How to Build a Fairer, Happier,
and More Prosperous America*. New York: Broadside Books, 2015.

Brown, Brené. *Braving the Wilderness: The Quest for True Belonging and
the Courage to Stand Alone*. New York: Random House, 2019.

Burwell v. Hobby Lobby Stores, 573 U.S. 682, 693 (2014).

Bussel, Rachel Kramer. "June 2020 Memoir 'The Baker' By Jack
Phillips Will Discuss Supreme Court Case About His Refusal to

Bake Cake for Same-Sex Couple." *Forbes*, January 31, 2020. https://www.forbes.com/sites/rachelkramerbussel/2020/01/31 /june-2020-memoir-the-baker-by-jack-phillips-will-discuss -supreme-court-case-about-his-refusal-to-bake-cake-for-same -sex-couple/#4216180da8c9.

Caldwell, Christopher. *The Age of Entitlement: America Since the Sixties*. New York: Simon & Schuster, 2020.

Castle, J. "New Fronts in the Culture Wars? Religion, Partisanship, and Polarization on Religious Liberty and Transgender Rights in the United States." *American Politics Research* 47, no. 3 (2019): 650–679. https://doi.org/10.1177/1532673X18818169.

CBS Denver. "Third Discrimination Suit Filed Against Masterpiece Cakeshop." Last modified June 6, 2019. https://denver.cbslocal .com/2019/06/06/discrimination-lawsuit-lakewood-jack-phillips -masterpiece-cakeshop/.

Center for American Progress. "Event: Reclaiming Religious Freedom: A Conversation with Rep. Ilhan Omar. Center for American Progress." January 29, 2019. https://www.americanprogress.org /press/advisory/2019/01/29/465626/event-advisory-reclaiming -religious-freedom-conversation-rep-ilhan-omar/; Khan, Jibran. "Religious Liberty for Me—But Not for Thee." *National Review*, November 27, 2018. https://www.nationalreview.com/corner /religious-liberty-for-me-but-not-for-thee/.

Cheney, Kyle and Katie Glueck. "Faith and Freedom Coalition: Winners and losers." *Politico*, June 21, 2015. https://www.politico.com/story /2015/06/faith-and-freedom-coalition-winners-and-losers-119255.

Chua, Amy. *Political Tribes: Group Instinct and the Fate of Nations*. New York: Penguin Books, 2018.

Cox, Daniel and Robert P. Jones. "Majority of Americans Do Not Believe Religious Liberty is Under Attack." PRRI, March 15, 2012. https://www.prri.org/research/march-rns-2012-research/.

Decision Magazine staff. "Cake Artist Jack Phillips Has Yet Another Day in Court." *Decision Magazine*, April 13, 2020. https://decisionmagazine .com/cake-artist-jack-phillips-has-yet-another-day-in-court/.

DeGirolami, Marc. "On the Uses of Anti-Christian Identity Politics." In *Religious Freedom, LGBT Rights, and the Prospects for Common Ground*, edited by William Eskridge and Robin Wilson. Cambridge, UK: Cambridge University Press, 2019.

Dias, Elizabeth. "Conservative Christians See 'Seismic Implications' in Supreme Court Ruling." *New York Times*, June 15, 2020. https://www.nytimes.com/2020/06/15/us/lgbtq-supreme-court -religious-freedom.html.

Douthat, Ross. "The Many Polarizations of America." *New York Times*, January 28, 2020. https://www.nytimes.com/2020/01/28/opinion /klein-lind-caldwell-book.html.

Editorial. "Anti-Christian bigots in Colorado call retreat." *Washington Examiner*, March 9, 2019. https://www.washingtonexaminer.com /opinion/editorials/anti-christian-bigots-in-colorado-call-retreat.

Esseks, James. "Can Businesses Turn LGBT People Away Because of Who They Are? That's Up to the Supreme Court Now." ACLU Speak Freely, June 26, 2017. https://www.aclu.org/blog/lgbt-rights /lgbt-nondiscrimination-protections/can-businesses-turn-lgbt -people-away-because-who.

Fain, Travis. "Lieutenant governor tells NC pastors: COVID-19 limits part of culture war against Christianity." WRAL, May 15,

2020. https://www.wral.com/lieutenant-governor-tells-nc-pastors
-covid-19-limits-part-of-culture-war-against-christianity/19100340/.

Feldblum, Chai. "What I Really Believe About Religious Liberty and
LGBT Rights." *Medium*, August 1, 2018. https://medium.com
/@chaifeldblum/what-i-really-believe-about-religious-liberty-and
-lgbt-rights-2cc64ade95a2.

1st Amendment Partnership. "Mission Statement." 1st Amendment
Partnership website, accessed October 9, 2020. https://1stamen
dmentpartnership.org/fairness-for-all/.

French, David. "Once Again, Progressive Anti-Christian Bigotry
Carries a Steep Legal Cost." *National Review*, September 27,
2019. https://www.nationalreview.com/2019/09/catholic
-adoption-agency-wins-vital-victory-religious-liberty-case/.

Gillman, Howard and Erwin Chemerinsky. "The Weaponization
of the Free-Exercise Clause." *Atlantic*, September 18, 2020.
https://www.theatlantic.com/ideas/archive/2020/09/weapon
ization-free-exercise-clause/616373/.

Goidel, Kirby, Brian Smentkowski, and Craig Freeman. "Perceptions
of Threat to Religious Liberty." July 2016. doi:10.1017/S104909
6516000809.

Goodnough, Abby and Maggie Haberman. "White House Rejects
C.D.C.'s Coronavirus Reopening Plan." *New York Times*, May 7, 2002.
https://www.nytimes.com/2020/05/07/us/politics/trump-cdc.html.

Goodrich, Luke W. and Rachel N. Busick. "Sex, Drugs, and Eagle
Feathers: An Empirical Study of Federal Religious Freedom Cases."
Seton Hall Law Review 48: 353–401. This study was limited to
cases in the Tenth Circuit.

Goodstein, Laurie. "Utah Passes Antidiscrimination Bill Backed by Mormon Leaders." *New York Times*, March 12, 2015. https://www.nytimes.com/2015/03/12/us/politics/utah-passes-antidiscrimination-bill-backed-by-mormon-leaders.html.

Green, Emma. "The Supreme Court Isn't Waging a War on Women in *Hobby Lobby*." *Atlantic*, June 30, 2014. https://www.theatlantic.com/national/archive/2014/06/hobby-lobby-isnt-waging-a-war-on-women/373717/.

Griffith, R. Marie. *Moral Combat: How Sex Divided American Christians & Fractured American Politics*. New York: Basic Books, 2017.

Groppe, Maureen. "First year of Trump-Pence brings bountiful blessings, religious conservatives say." *USA Today*, January 19, 2018. https://www.usatoday.com/story/news/politics/2018/01/19/first-year-trump-pence-brings-bountiful-blessings-religious-conservatives-say/1044308001/.

Guest writer. "The Religious Freedom Restoration Act is discriminatory. Let's fix it." *Religion News Service*, May 18, 2016. https://religionnews.com/2016/05/18/the-religious-freedom-restoration-act-is-discriminatory-lets-fix-it/#.

Hausknecht, Bruce. "Masterpiece Cakeshop: 2; Colorado Anti-Religious Bigotry: 0." *Daily Citizen*, March 8, 2019. https://dailycitizen.focusonthefamily.com/masterpiece-cakeshop-2-colorado-anti-religious-bigotry-0/.

Department of the Treasury. "HHS Final Rule on Contraceptive Mandate." Department of the Treasury website, last modified November 7, 2018. https://s3.amazonaws.com/becketnewsite/HHS-Final-Rule-on-Contraceptive-Mandate-Nov-7.pdf.

Inazu, John. "Democrats Are Going to Regret Beto's Stance on Conservative Churches." *Atlantic*, October 12, 2019. https://www.theatlantic.com/ideas/archive/2019/10/beto-orourkes-pluralism-failure/599953/.

Kirchick, James. "The Struggle for Gay Rights Is Over." *Atlantic*, June 28, 2019. https://www.theatlantic.com/ideas/archive/2019/06/battle-gay-rights-over/592645/.

Klein, Ezra. *Why We're Polarized*. New York: Avid Reader Press, 2020.

Koby, Michael H. "The Biggest Threat to Religious Liberty." *Biola Magazine*, accessed October 9, 2020. http://magazine.biola.edu/article/06-fall/the-biggest-threat-to-religious-liberty/; USCCB. "Current Threats to Religious Freedom," accessed October 9, 2020. http://www.usccb.org/issues-and-action/religious-liberty/upload/Current-threats-to-religious-liberty.pdf; Gryboski, Michael. "What are the biggest threats to religious liberty in the US?" *Christian Post*, October 21, 2019. https://www.christianpost.com/books/what-are-the-biggest-threats-to-religious-liberty-in-the-us.html; Anderson, Ryan T. "The Continuing Threat to Religious Liberty." Heritage Foundation, August 4, 2017. https://www.heritage.org/religious-liberty/commentary/the-continuing-threat-religious-liberty.

Koppelman, Andrew. "The Joys of Mutual Contempt." In *Religious Freedom, LGBT Rights, and the Prospects for Common Ground*, edited by William Eskridge and Robin Wilson. Cambridge, UK: Cambridge University Press, 2019.

Laycock, Douglas. "Religious Liberty and the Culture Wars." *University of Illinois Law Review*, June 4, 2014. https://illinoislawreview.org/wp-content/ilr-content/articles/2014/3/Laycock.pdf.

Laycock, Douglas and Thomas C. Berg. "Masterpiece Cakeshop—Not as Narrow as It May First Appear." *Scotusblog*, June 5, 2018. https://www.scotusblog.com/2018/06/symposium-masterpiece -cakeshop-not-as-narrow-as-may-first-appear/.

Laycock, Douglas. "Do Cuomo's New Covid Rules Discriminate Against Religion?" *New York Times*, October 9, 2020. https://www .nytimes.com/2020/10/09/opinion/cuomo-synagogue-lockdown .html?fbclid=IwAR0ZlvtEV-2qlwPUfcoBXmh7RD7IS28g7u_U28 MebN2oHe1JZ2g2fjxnIQ0.

Lewis, Andrew. *The Rights Turn in Conservative Christian Politics: How Abortion Transformed the Culture Wars*. Cambridge, UK: Cambridge University Press, 2017.

Long, Colleen, Michael Balsamo, and Emily Wagster Pettus. "Justice Department takes church's side in 1st Amendment suit." 7 News, April 14, 2020. https://www.wwnytv.com/2020/04/14/justice -department-takes-churchs-side-st-amendment-suit/.

Lori, Archbishop William E. "The 'Demands' of Faith." In *Religious Freedom, LGBT Rights, and the Prospects for Common Ground*, edited by William Eskridge and Robin Wilson. Cambridge, UK: Cambridge University Press, 2019.

Marcotte, Amanda. "'Hobby Lobby' Is About Blocking Contraception Access, Not Religious Liberty." *Rewire.News*, July 15, 2015. https://rewire.news/article/2015/07/15/hobby-lobby-blocking -contraception-access-religious-liberty/.

Mason, Lilliana. *Uncivil Agreement: How Politics Became Our Identity*. Chicago: University of Chicago Press, 2018.

Masterpiece Cakeshop, Ltd. v. Colorado Civil Rights Comm'n, 138 S. Ct. 1719 (2018). https://www.supremecourt.gov/opinions/17pdf /16-111_j4el.pdf.

Melling, Louise. "Religious Refusals to Public Accommodations Laws: Four Reasons to Say No." *Harvard Journal of Law & Gender* (2015). https://harvardjlg.com/wp-content/uploads/sites/19/2015/01/Four -Reasons-to-Say-No.pdf?fbclid=IwAR2wjIynoGhhq3WwbZap9v mJ7U1rNVOlBB7FT6wXe1fYeXK1nz41HbE_kKA.

Melling, Louise. "Heterosexuals Only: Signs of the Times?" In *Religious Freedom, LGBT Rights, and the Prospects for Common Ground*, edited by William Eskridge and Robin Wilson. Cambridge, UK: Cambridge University Press, 2019.

Miller, Zeke J. "Religious Liberty Becomes the Byword Among Iowa's Social Conservatives." *Time*, April 10, 2015. https://time.com /3817166/iowa-religious-liberty/.

Mohler, Albert. "More Than an Idle Threat: Real Assaults on Religious Liberty Emerge in the Pandemic." Albert Mohler Articles, April 13, 2020. https://albertmohler.com/2020/04/13/more-than-an-idle -threat-real-assaults-on-religious-liberty-emerge-in-the-pandemic.

Monsma, Stephen V. *Pluralism and Freedom: Faith-Based Organizations in a Democratic Society*. Lanham, MD: Rowman & Littlefield, 2011.

Peters, Jeremy W. "Trump's Approval Slips Where He Can't Afford to Lose It: Among Evangelicals." *New York Times*, June 4, 2020.

Planned Parenthood. "Burwell v. Hobby Lobby and Birth Control." Planned Parenthood website, accessed October 9, 2020. https://www .plannedparenthoodaction.org/issues/birth-control/burwell-v -hobby-lobby.

Public Religion Research Institute. "Americans Overwhelmingly
Oppose Allowing Business Owners to Refuse Service to Gay and
Lesbian People for Religious Reasons." Public Religion Research
Institute website, last modified June 4, 2018. https://www.prri.org
/spotlight/most-americans-oppose-religious-service-refusals
-to-gay-and-lesbian-people/.

Rassbach, Eric. "What's Next for Religious Freedom?" Conference at
Yeshiva University, May 22–23, 2019. http://www.religiousfreedom
conf.org/wp-content/uploads/sites/3/2019/05/Yeshiva-program
-final.pdf.

Rauch, Jonathan and Peter Wehner. "We Can Find Common Ground
on Gay Rights and Religious Liberty." *New York Times*, June 22,
2020. https://www.nytimes.com/2020/06/22/opinion/gay-rights
-religious-liberty.html.

Religious Freedom Restoration Act, 42 U.S.C. § 2000bb *et seq.*

Richardson, Valerie. "Harris, Hirono accused of anti-Catholic 'bigotry'
for targeting Knights of Columbus." *Washington Times*, December 30,
2018. https://www.washingtontimes.com/news/2018/dec/30
/kamala-harris-mazie-hirono-target-brian-buescher-k/.

Rosenberg, Paul. "Sociologist Andrew Whitehead: How Christian
nationalism drives American politics." *Salon*, February 9, 2020.
https://www.salon.com/2020/02/29/sociologist-andrew
-whitehead-how-christian-nationalism-drives-american-politics/.

Rosenstein, Peter. "Hobby Lobby and the war on women." *Washington
Blade*, July 3, 2014. https://www.washingtonblade.com/2014/07
/03/opinion-hobby-lobby-and-the-war-on-women/; Breitman,
Kendall. "Left says 'War on women' continues." *Politico*, June 30,
2014. https://www.politico.com/story/2014/06/hobby-lobby

-ruling-left-twitter-war-on-women-108437; Finney, Karen. "Hobby
Lobby opens a new front in the 'War on Women.'" MSNBC, July 10,
2014. http://www.msnbc.com/msnbc/hobby-lobby-opens-new
-front-the-war-women; National Organization for Women. "Court
Sides with Hobby Lobby, Joins War on Women." National
Organization for Women website, last modified June 30, 2014.
https://now.org/media-center/press-release/court-sides-with-hobby
-lobby-joins-war-on-women/; Fluke, Sandra. "Sandra Fluke: The
Hobby Lobby case is an attack on women." *Washington Post*,
June 30, 2014. https://www.washingtonpost.com/posteverything
/wp/2014/06/30/sandra-fluke-the-hobby-lobby-case-is-an-attack
-on-women/.

Rymel, Tim. "Evangelicals Reaffirm Their LGBT Ignorance And
Bigotry." *HuffPost*, August 31, 2017. https://www.huffpost.com
/entry/evangelicals-reaffirm-their-lgbt-ignorance-and-bigotry_b_59a
79affe4b096fd8876c0a0.

Sarlin, Benjy. "O'Rourke says churches against gay marriage should lose
tax benefits, draws backlash." NBC News, October 11, 2019.
https://www.nbcnews.com/politics/2020-election/o-rourke-says
-churches-against-gay-marriage-should-lose-tax-n1065186.

Schor, Elana and Hannah Fingerhut. "Religious Freedom in America:
Popular and Polarizing." *Telegraph*, August 5, 2020. https://www
.thetelegraph.com/news/article/Religious-freedom-in-America
-popular-and-15460385.php.

Soave, Robby. "The ACLU Now Opposes Religious Freedom Because
Christians Need It." *Reason*, June 29, 2015. https://reason.com/2015
/06/29/the-aclu-now-opposes-religious-freedom-b/.

Teeman, Tim. "Let's Call 'Religious Freedom' By Its Real Name:
Poisonous, Anti-LGBTQ Bigotry." *Daily Beast*, November 5, 2019.

https://www.thedailybeast.com/lets-call-religious-freedom-by-its
-real-name-poisonous-anti-lgbtq-bigotry.

Transcript of oral arguments, *Obergefell v. Hodges*. https://www.supre
mecourt.gov/oral_arguments/argument_transcripts/2014/14-556q1
_l5gm.pdf.

U.S. Commission on Civil Rights. "Peaceful Coexistence: Reconciling
Nondiscrimination Principles with Civil Liberties." Last modified
September 7, 2016. http://www.newamericancivilrightsproject
.org/wp-content/uploads/2016/09/Peaceful-Coexistence-09-07
-16-6.pdf.

Volokh, Eugene. "On Holy Thursday, an American Mayor Criminalized
the Communal Celebration of Easter." *Reason*, April 11, 2020.
https://reason.com/2020/04/11/on-holy-thursday-an-american
-mayor-criminalized-the-communal-celebration-of-easter/.

Wilson, Robin Fretwell. "The Politics of Accommodation: The
American Experience with Same-Sex Marriage and Religious
Freedom." In *Religious Freedom and Gay Rights*, edited by Timothy
Shah, Thomas Farr, and Jack Friedman. Oxford, UK: Oxford
University Press, 2016.

Wilson, Robin Fretwell and Tanner Bean. "Fairness for All: An
Answer to the Special Rapporteur's Call for a Practical Resolution
between Freedom of Religion or Belief and LGBT+Non-
discrimination." International Center for Law and Religion
Studies, April 20, 2020. https://talkabout.iclrs.org/2020/04/20
/fairness-for-all-an-answer/.

Yudkin, Daniel, Stephen Hawkins, and Tim Dixon. "The Perception
Gap: How False Impressions are Pulling Americans Apart." More in
Common. https://perceptiongap.us/.

CHAPTER 4

Al Jazeera. "Trump: Social distancing norms should be same for Easter, Ramadan." *Al Jazeera America*, April 19, 2020. https://www.aljazeera .com/news/2020/04/trump-social-distancing-norms-easter-ramadan -200419061153522.html.

Amazon Product Reviews. "Bigotry comes in many forms . . . this is one." https://www.amazon.com/product-reviews/B07YKWVJ2H /ef=acr_dp_hist_1?ie=UTF8&filterByStar=one_star&reviewer Type=all_reviews#reviews-filter-bar.

Anderson, Court. "Why Won't the Media Say 'Christophobia'?" *CD Media*, May 3, 2019. https://creativedestructionmedia.com /analysis/2019/05/03/why-wont-the-media-say-christophobia/.

Annenberg Public Policy Center. 2017. "Americans Are Poorly Informed About Basic Constitutional Provisions." https://www .annenbergpublicpolicycenter.org/americans-are-poorly -informed-about-basic-constitutional-provisions/.

Bacon Jr., Peter. "Democrats Are Wrong About Republicans. Republicans Are Wrong About Democrats." *FiveThirtyEight*, June 26, 2018. https://fivethirtyeight.com/features/democrats -are-wrong-about-republicans-republicans-are-wrong-about -democrats/.

Beauchamp, Zack. "Trump loves saying 'radical Islamic terrorism.' He has a tough time with 'white supremacy.'" *Vox*, August 14, 2017. https://www.vox.com/world/2017/8/14/16143634/trump -charlottesville-white-supremacy-terrorism-islamism.

Bennett, Daniel and Logan Strother. "Which groups deserve religious freedom rights? It depends on what you think of the groups." *Religion in Public*, January 3, 2019. https://religioninpublic

.blog/2019/01/03/which-groups-deserve-religious-freedom
-protections-it-depends-on-what-you-think-of-the-groups/.

Boland, Barbara. "'Easter Worshippers' and The Left's Allergy To
Language." *American Conservative*, April 24, 2019. https://www
.theamericanconservative.com/articles/easter-worshippers-and-the
-lefts-allergy-to-language/.

Boorstein, Michelle. "Why many religious liberty groups are silent about
the Supreme Court's decision on Trump's travel ban." *Washington Post*,
June 28, 2018. https://www.washingtonpost.com/news/acts-of-faith
/wp/2018/06/26/why-many-religious-liberty-groups-are-silent-on-the
-supreme-courts-decision-to-uphold-trumps-travel-ban/.

Brown, Brené. *Braving the Wilderness: The Quest for True Belonging and
the Courage to Stand Alone*. New York: Random House, 2019.

Bump, Philip. "Marco Rubio downplays Muslim discrimination.
So do many Republicans." *Washington Post*, February 7, 2016.
https://www.washingtonpost.com/news/the-fix/wp/2016/02/07
/marco-rubio-downplays-muslim-discrimination-as-do -many
-republicans/?utm_term=.24c288805fc1.

Caldwell, Christopher. *The Age of Entitlement: America Since the Sixties*.
New York: Simon & Schuster, 2020.

Christian Concern. "Human rights: Freedom of religion and belief, and
human rights defenders inquiry." September 2019. http://data
.parliament.uk/writtenevidence/committeeevidence.svc/evidence
document/foreign-affairs-committee/human-rights-freedom-of
-religion-and-belief-and-human-rights-defenders/written/105109
.pdf?utm_source=Christian+Concern&utm_campaign=d761aed3a9
-WN-20190913&utm_medium=email&utm_term=0_9e164371ca
-d761aed3a9-127379401.

Chua, Amy. *Political Tribes: Group Instinct and the Fate of Nations*. New York: Penguin Books, 2018.

Columbia Law School: Law, Rights, and Religion Project. "About the Report." Columbia Law School website, accessed September 3, 2020. https://lawrightsreligion.law.columbia.edu/content/whose faithmatters.

Columbia Law School: Law, Rights, and Religion Project. "Whose Faith Matters? The Fight for Religious Liberty Beyond the Christian Right." Columbia Law School website, last modified November 2019. https://lawrightsreligion.law.columbia.edu/sites/default/files /content/Images/Whose%20Faith%20Matters%20Full%20 Report%2012.12.19.pdf.

Conway, Kellyanne. "Hi Congresswoman @AOC . . . Good that you now condemn Sri Lanka massacre. Some found it odd a prolific tweeter was silent." Tweet (@KellyannePolls), April 28, 2019. https://twitter.com/KellyannePolls/status/1122588109781250048.

Cox, Daniel and Robert P. Jones. "Majority of Americans Oppose Transgender Bathroom Restrictions." PRRI, March 10, 2017. https://www.prri.org/research/lgbt-transgender-bathroom -discrimination-religious-liberty/.

Dallas, Kelsey. "On National Religious Freedom Day, consider the double standard on religious freedom—and why it's a problem." *Deseret News*, January 16, 2019. https://www.deseret.com/2019 /1/16/20663521/on-national-religious-freedom-day-consider -the-double-standard-on-religious-freedom-and-why-it-s-a-p# people-hold-signs-as-they-gather-on-a-street-in-lower-manhattan -sunday-sept-11-2011-during-a-rally-by-the-american-freedom -defense-initiative-which-opposes-the-planned-islamic-cultural -center-and-mosque-near-ground-zero-earlier-sunday-there-was-a

-ceremony-at-the-national-september-11-memorial-at-the-world-trade
-center-site-for-the-10th-anniversary-of-the-attacks-on-sept-11-2001.

Dreher, Rod. "Religious Liberty for All." *American Conservative*, April 3, 2019. https://www.theamericanconservative.com/dreher /religious-liberty-for-muslims-christians-jews/.

Erickson, Kurt. "Attorney: Hawley played little or no role in court case." *St. Louis Post-Dispatch*, June 23, 2016. https://www.stltoday .com/news/local/govt-and-politics/attorney-hawley-played-little-or -no-role-in-court-case/article_87e6ba57-f398-5d68-a8a0-f03bb5 69a81f.html.

Fearnow, Benjamin. "'Muslims Treated Better Than Christians, White People': Right-Wing Radio Host Warns 'Angry Whites' May Copy New Zealand Attack. *Newsweek*, March 17, 2019. https://www .newsweek.com/jesse-lee-peterson-muslims-shooting-treated -better-christians-white-people-1365786.

Good, Chris, John Kruzel, and Noah Fitzgerel. "Democratic National Convention 2016: Fact-Checking the Speakers." ABC News, July 29, 2016. https://abcnews.go.com/Politics/democratic-national -convention-2016-fact-checking-speakers/story?id=40875461.

Goodrich, Luke. "No anti-Muslim bias at Supreme Court: Constitution, argued properly, protects all religion." *Hill*, April 4, 2019. https://the hill.com/opinion/judiciary/437575-no-anti-muslim-bias-at-supreme -court-constitution-argued-properly-protects.

Grant, Tobin and Sarah Pulliam Bailey. "Why some religious-freedom groups won't take a stand on the travel ban." *Washington Post*, April 25, 2018. https://www.washingtonpost.com/news/acts-of -faith/wp/2018/04/25/why-some-religious-freedom-groups-wont -take-a-stand-on-the-travel-ban/.

Green, Emma. "White Evangelicals Believe They Face More Discrimination Than Muslims." *Atlantic*, March 10, 2017. https://www.theatlantic.com/politics/archive/2017/03/perceptions-discrimination-muslims-christians/519135/.

Grunwald, Michael. "How Everything Became the Culture War." *Politico Magazine* (November/December 2018). https://www.politico.com/magazine/story/2018/11/02/culture-war-liberals-conservatives-trump-2018-222095.

Hetherington, Marc J. and Elizabeth Suhay. "Authoritarianism, Threat, and Americans' Support for the War on Terror." *American Journal of Political Science* 55, no. 3 (2011): 546–60. Accessed June 22, 2020. www.jstor.org/stable/23024936.

Hopkins, Dan. "White Americans Say They're Less Prejudiced." *FiveThirtyEight*, July 23, 2019. https://fivethirtyeight.com/features/prejudice-among-white-americans-might-be-declining-in-the-trump-era/. (Political scientists have tracked a similar phenomenon with respect to race. Liberal-leaning Americans now express less racially prejudiced attitudes, in part as a reaction against Trump.)

Johnson, Jenna and Abigail Hauslohner. "'I think Islam hates us': A timeline of Trump's comments about Islam and Muslims." *Washington Post*, May 20, 2017. https://www.washingtonpost.com/news/post-politics/wp/2017/05/20/i-think-islam-hates-us-a-timeline-of-trumps-comments-about-islam-and-muslims/.

Kalkan, Kerem Ozan, Geoffrey C. Layman, and Eric M. Uslaner. "'Bands of Others'? Attitudes toward Muslims in Contemporary American Society." *The Journal of Politics* 71, no. 3 (2009): 847–862.

Karpowitz, C., J. Quin Monson, and K. Patterson. "Who's In and Who's Out: The Politics of Religious Norms." *Politics and Religion* 9, no. 3: 508–536. doi:10.1017/S1755048316000456.

Kaufman, Scott Eric. "Donald Trump: If elected, 'we'll have so much winning, you'll get bored with winning.'" *Salon*, September 9, 2015. https://www.salon.com/2015/09/09/donald_trump_if_elected_well _have_so_much_winning_youll_get_bored_withwinning/.

Kearns, Erin, Allison Betus, and Anthony Lemieux. "Why Do Some Terrorist Attacks Receive More Media Attention Than Others?" *Justice Quarterly*, April 2, 2018. https://papers.ssrn.com/sol3/papers.cfm ?abstract_id=2928138 or http://dx.doi.org/10.2139/ssrn.2928138.

Khan, Saeed. *Community Brief: Manufacturing Bigotry.* Institute for Social Policy and Understanding. https://www.ispu.org/wp-content /uploads/2016/08/ISPU-Manufacturing-Bigotry4.pdf?x33444.

Kirchick, James. "Rock, Paper, Scissors of PC Victimology." *Tablet*, February 26, 2015. https://www.tabletmag.com/sections/news /articles/victimhood-olympics.

Kishi, Katayoun. "Anti-Muslim assaults reach 9/11 era levels, FBI data show." Pew Research Center, November 21, 2016. https://www .pewresearch.org/fact-tank/2016/11/21/anti-muslim-assaults -reach-911-era-levels-fbi-data-show/.

Klein, Ezra. *Why We're Polarized*. New York: Avid Reader Press, 2020.

Kumar, Sam. "Congresswoman Ilhan Omar's anti-Americanism." *Reno Gazette Journal*, November 14, 2019. https://www.rgj.com/story /opinion/columnists/2019/11/14/congresswoman-ilhan-omars -anti-americanism-kumar/4186849002/.

Leon, Melissa. "Bill Maher and Richard Dawkins Slam Muslims: 'To Hell with Their Culture.'" *Daily Beast*, October 3, 2015. https://www .thedailybeast.com/bill-maher-and-richard-dawkins-slam-muslims -to-hell-with-their-culture.

Mach, Daniel. "The Supreme Court Cares About Religious Animus—Except When It Doesn't." ACLU, June 26, 2018. https://www.aclu.org/blog/immigrants-rights/supreme-court-cares-about-religious-animus-except-when-it-doesnt.

Masci, David. "Many Americans see religious discrimination in U.S.—especially against Muslims." Pew Research Center, May 17, 2019. https://www.pewresearch.org/fact-tank/2019/05/17/many-americans-see-religious-discrimination-in-u-s-especially-against-muslims/.

Mason, Lilliana. *Uncivil Agreement: How Politics Became Our Identity*. Chicago: University of Chicago Press, 2018.

Millhiser, Ian. "A heartbreaking Supreme Court case could be a huge win for the Christian right." *Vox*, November 26, 2019. https://www.vox.com/policy-and-politics/2019/11/26/20982273/supreme-court-religion-tanvir-tanzin-rfra.

Mohammad, Taameen. "Media Coverage of Muslims More Negative Than Other Minority Groups, Study Finds." *Newsweek*, September 5, 2019. https://www.newsweek.com/muslims-negative-news-coverage-1457942.

More in Common. "Hidden Tribes: A Study of America's Polarized Landscape." More in Common website, accessed November 19, 2020. https://hiddentribes.us.

MPower Change. "86 Times Donald Trump Displayed or Promoted Islamophobia." *Medium*, April 19, 2018. https://medium.com/nilc/86-times-donald-trump-displayed-or-promoted-islamophobia-49e67584ac10.

Murphy, Tim. "Trump Asks if Muslims Will Get Special Treatment in Coronavirus Lockdowns." *Mother Jones*, April 18, 2020. https://www.motherjones.com/coronavirus-updates/2020/04

/trump-asks-if-muslims-will-get-special-treatment-in
-coronavirus-lockdowns/.

Mutz, Diana C. "Status threat, not economic hardship, explains the
2016 presidential vote." *Proceedings of the National Academy of
Sciences* 115, no. 19 (May 2018). E4330-E4339; DOI:10.1073
/pnas.1718155115.

O'Neill, Brendan. "The hierarchy of victimhood." *Medium*, April 27,
2019. https://medium.com/@burntoakboy/the-hierarchy-of
-victimhood-5f356f051966.

Palmer, Ewan. "Pastor Accuses Alexandria Ocasio-Cortez of Not
Tweeting About Sri Lanka Attacks Because She Can't Weaponize
Them Against Trump." *Newsweek*, April 25, 2019. https://www
.newsweek.com/alexandria-ocasio-cortez-sri-lanka-bombings
-pastor-darrell-scott-hannity-1405364.

Pew Research Center. "In Deadlocked Race, Neither Side Has Ground
Game Advantage." Last modified October 31, 2012. https://www
.pewresearch.org/politics/2012/10/31/in-deadlocked-race-neither
-side-has-ground-game-advantage/.

Pew Research Center. "Many Americans Hear Politics From the Pulpit."
Last modified August 8, 2016. https://www.pewforum.org/2016
/08/08/many-americans-hear-politics-from-the-pulpit/.

Pew Research Center. "How the U.S. general public views Muslims and
Islam." Pew Research Center website, last modified July 26, 2017.
https://www.pewforum.org/2017/07/26/how-the-u-s-general
-public-views-muslims-and-islam/.

Prager, Dennis. "Why Is Islam Treated Better than Other Faiths?"
National Review, January 13, 2015. https://www.nationalreview
.com/2015/01/why-islam-treated-better-other-faiths-dennis-prager/.

Putnam, R. D., T. Sander, and D. E. Campbell. "Faith Matters Survey, 2011." Association of Religion Data Archives. doi: 10.17605/OSF .IO/Q7R6C.

Rasmussen Reports. "Democrats Think Muslims Worse Off Here Than Christians Are in Muslim World." Rasmussen Reports website, last modified February 7, 2017. https://www.rasmussenreports.com /public_content/politics/general_politics/february_2017/democrats _think_muslims_worse_off_here_than_christians_are_in_muslim _world.

The Rush Limbaugh Show. "Where's the Outrage? Muslim Bakeries in Michigan Refuse to Bake Cakes for Gay Weddings." *The Rush Limbaugh Show* Transcript, last modified April 3, 2015. https://www .rushlimbaugh.com/daily/2015/04/03/where_s_the_outrage _muslim_bakeries_in_michigan_refuse_to_bake_cakes_for_gay _weddings/.

Sahgal, Neha, and Besheer Mohamed. "In the U.S. and Western Europe, people say they accept Muslims, but opinions are divided on Islam." Pew Research Center, October 8, 2019. https://www .pewresearch.org/fact-tank/2019/10/08/in-the-u-s-and-western -europe-people-say-they-accept-muslims-but-opinions-are-divided -on-islam/.

Savaransky, Rebecca. "Giuliani: Trump asked me how to do a Muslim ban 'legally.'" *Hill,* January 29, 2017. https://thehill.com/home news/administration/316726-giuliani-trump-asked-me-how-to -do-a-muslim-ban-legally.

Schmitz, Matthew. "Does It Make Sense to Speak of 'Christophobia'?" *First Things,* November 29, 2012. https://www.firstthings.com /blogs/firstthoughts/2012/11/does-it-make-sense-to-speak-of -christophobia.

Schor, Elana, and Hannah Fingerhut. "Religious Freedom in America: popular and polarizing." AP News, August 5, 2020. https://apnews .com/article/virus-outbreak-u-s-news-donald-trump-535624d93b8c e3d271019200e362b0cf.

Shapiro, Ben. "Why the Left Protects Islam." *Daily Wire*, July 26, 2017. https:// www.dailywire.com/news/18993/why-left-protects-islam -ben-shapiro.

Slater, Robert G. "A 'Christian America' Restored: The Rise of the Evangelical Christian School Movement in America, 1920–1952." PhD diss., University of Tennessee, Knoxville, 2012. https://trace .tennessee.edu/cgi/viewcontent.cgi?article=2528&context=utk _graddiss. (There is a long history of religious freedom being used in a protectionary manner. For example, in the late 20th century it was leveraged to protect Christian day schools.)

Spencer, Saranac Hale. "Stay-at-Home Policies Treat Mosques Same as Churches." FactCheck.org, April 30, 2020. https://www.factcheck .org/2020/04/stay-at-home-policies-treat-mosques-same-as -churches/.

Telhami, Shibley. "Measuring the Backlash Against the Muslims Backlash." *Politico Magazine*, July 11, 2016. https://www.politico .com/magazine/story/2016/07/measuring-the-backlash-against-the -muslim-backlash-214034.

Telhami, Shibley. "How Trump changed Americans' view of Islam—for the better." *Washington Post*, January 25, 2017. https://www.washington post.com/news/monkey-cage/wp/2017/01/25/americans-dont -support-trumps-ban-on-muslim-immigration/?outputType=amp.

Tracy, Abigail. "'They're as Different As People Come': The Complex Truth About the 'Squad,' Trump's Favorite Foil." *Vanity Fair*, August 16, 2019. https://www.vanityfair.com/news/2019/08 /the-squad-donald-trump.

Willer, Robb, Ko Kuwabara, and Michael W. Macy. "The False Enforcement of Unpopular Norms." *AJS* 115, no. 2 (September 2009): 451–90. https://pdfs.semanticscholar.org/1293/ecb55a2c5194fd1 c16532c2c92599c6931fb.pdf.

Woolf, Nicky. "Melanie Phillips' terrible column on the 'fiction' of Islamophobia, annotated." *New Statesman*, May 8, 2018. https://www .newstatesman.com/politics/religion/2018/05/melanie-phillips -terrible-column-fiction-islamophobia-annotated.

Zoll, Rachel. "AP-NORC Poll: Christian-Muslim split on religious freedom." Associated Press, December 30, 2015. https://apnews .com/de486b3d64154d0baae9f04fba0a4094/ap-norc-poll -religious-rights-us-christians-most-valued.

CHAPTER 5

ACLU. "Nationwide anti-mosque activity." ACLU website, last modified May 2018. https://www.aclu.org/issues/national-security /discriminatory-profiling/nationwide-anti-mosque-activity.

ACT for America. "Education or Indoctrination? The Treatment of Islam in 6th Through 12th Grade American Textbooks." ACT for America website, accessed July 8, 2020. http://d3n8a8pro7vhmx .cloudfront.net/themes/57365ca5cd0af55ea6000001/attachments /original/1483921270/Education_or_Indoctrination_Executive _Summary.pdf?1483921270.

Aldrich, Debbie. "Jim Simpson talks about his latest book 'The Red Green Axis 2.0. What is the Red Green Axis?" Podcast, 2019. https://www.pscp.tv/w/1dRKZLXWBWzJB.

Ali, Wajahat, Eli Clifton, Matthew Duss, Lee Fang, Scott Keyes, and Faiz Shakir. "The Roots of the Islamophobia Network in America."

Last modified August 26, 2011. https://cdn.americanprogress.org
/wp-content/uploads/issues/2011/08/pdf/islamophobia.pdf.

Allam, Hannah and Talal Ansari. "State and Local Republican Officials
Have Been Bashing Muslims. We Counted." *Buzzfeed News*, April 10,
2018. https://www.buzzfeed .com/hannahallam/trump-republicans
-bashing-muslims-without-repercussions?utm_ term=.vt8k3q3b3d#
.prN3dmdOdG.

AmericanEvangelicals.org. "An Open Letter to Christian pastors,
leaders and believers who assist the anti-Christian progressive
political movement in America." American Evangelicals website, last
modified September 26, 2016. http://archive.fo/nYBXW.

Americans United for Separation of Church and State. *Report and
Analysis on Religious Freedom Measures Impacting Prayer and Faith
in America.* Americans United for Separation of Church and State
website, accessed July 9, 2020. https://www.au.org/sites/default
/files/2019-01/Project%20Blitz%20Playbook%202018-19.pdf.

Barzegar, Abbas and Zainab Arain. "Hijacked by Hate: American
Philanthropy and the Islamophobia Network." Council on
American-Islamic Relations, last modified June 19, 2019.
http://www.islamophobia.org/images/IslamophobiaReport2019
/CAIR_Islamophobia_Report_2019_Final_Web.pdf.

Beachum, Lateshia. "Baptist church cancels 9/11 anti-Islam event after
backlash from legislators, Christian scholars." *Washington Post*,
September 10, 2019. https://www.washingtonpost.com/religion
/2019/09/11/religion-scholars-baptist-church-your-anti-islam-event
-isnt-very-christian/.

Beinart, Peter. "The Denationalization of American Muslims." *Atlantic*,
March 19, 2017. https://www.theatlantic.com/politics/archive

/2017/03/frank-gaffney-donald-trump-and-the
-denationalization-of-american-muslims/519954/.

Beinart, Peter. "The Attack in Manhattan Poses a Test for Donald
Trump." *Atlantic*, October 31, 2017. https://www.theatlantic.com
/politics/archive/2017/10/the-attack-in-manhattan-poses-a-test-for
-donald-trump/544592/.

Benjamin, Zaid. "#Trump Choice for National Security Adviser
Michael Flynn: Islam is a political ideology that hides itself behind
what they call a religion." Tweet (@zaidbenjamin), November 18,
2016. https://twitter.com/zaidbenjamin/status/7996969680
71016448/video/1.

Bloomberg Law. "Islam in Public School Challenge Rejected by
Supreme Court." October 15, 2019. https://news.bloomberglaw
.com/us-law-week/islam-in-public-school-challenge-rejected-by
-supreme-court.

Branch, Chris. "State Rep. John Bennett Stands By Anti-Islam
Comments: 'Islam Is Not Even A Religion.'" *Huffington Post*,
September 22, 2014. https://www.huffingtonpost.com/2014/09/22
/oklahoma-john-bennett-islam_n_5863084.html.

Cai, Weiyi and Simone Landon. "Attacks by White Extremists Are
Growing. So Are Their Connections." *New York Times*, April 3,
2019. https://www.nytimes.com/interactive/2019/04/03/world
/white-extremist-terrorism-christchurch.html.

Chuck, Elizabeth, Alex Johnson, and Corky Siemaszko. "17 killed
in mass shooting at high school in Parkland, Florida." NBC
News, February 15, 2018. https://www.nbcnews.com/news
/us-news/police-respond-shooting-parkland-florida-high
-school-n848101.

CNN Presents. "Unwelcome: The Muslims Next Door." *CNN Presents* Transcripts, last modified August 12, 2012. http://transcripts.cnn .com/TRANSCRIPTS/1208/12/cp.01.html.

Elliott, Andrea. "The Man Behind the Anti-Shariah Movement." *New York Times*, July 30, 2011. https://www.nytimes.com/2011/07/31 /us/31shariah.html.

Elsheikh, Elsadig, Basima Sisemore, and Natalia Ramirez Lee. "Legalizing Othering: The United States of Islamophobia." Last modified September 2017. http://haasinstitute.berkeley.edu/sites /default/files/haas_institute_legalizing_othering_the_united_states _of_islamophobia.pdf.

Erlanger, Steven and Scott Shane. "Oslo Suspect Wrote Fear of Islam and Plan for War." *New York Times*, July 23, 2011.

FCDF. "FCDF Demands Emails from Minneapolis Public Schools Regarding Relationship with CAIR." FCDF website, last modified August 17, 2018. https://www.fcdflegal.org/fcdf -demands-emails-from-minneapolis-public-schools-regarding -relationship-with-cair/.

FCDF. "FCDF Sends Letter to Seattle Public Schools Regarding Pro-Muslim Program." FCDF website, last modified July 8, 2018. https://www.fcdflegal.org/fcdf-sends-letter-to-seattle-public-schools -regarding-pro-muslim-program/.

Fea, John. "This interview tells us a lot about John MacArthur and the movement he represents." The Way of Improvement Leads Home, August 22, 2020. https://thewayofimprovement.com/2020/08/22 /this-interview-tells-us-a-lot-about-john-macarthur-and-the -movement-he-represents/.

Fick, Allison. "Reports of Islamic Indoctrination Spread to Georgia Public Schools." ACLJ. https://aclj.org/religious-liberty/reports -of-islamic-indoctrination-spread-to-georgia-public-schools.

Foley, Kathleen E. "Not In Our Neighborhood: Managing Opposition to Mosque Construction." Institute for Social Policy and Understanding, 2010. http://www.ispu.org/wp-content/uploads /2016/08/ISPU_Not_In_Our_Neighborhood_Kathleen_Foley -3.pdf.

Glenza, Jessica. "Christian group wrote legislation eerily similar to Ohio religious liberty bill." *Guardian*, November 22, 2019. https://amp .theguardian.com/us-news/2019/nov/22/ohio-religious-liberty-bill -project-blitz-christian; Byrd, Don. "Ohio legislature sends student religious liberties bill to governor." BJC, June 17, 2020. https://bj conline.org/ohio-legislature-sends-student-religious-liberties-bill-to -governor-061720/.

Global Faith Institute. "Dr. Mark Christian." Global Faith Institute website, accessed September 28, 2020. https://www.contentof characterseries.com/dr-mark-christian.

Goodstein, Laurie. "Drawing U.S. Crowds With Anti-Islam Message." *New York Times*, March 7, 2011. https://www.nytimes.com/2011 /03/08/us/08gabriel.html.

Green, Emma. "The Fear of Islam in Tennessee Public Schools." *Atlantic*, December 16, 2015. https://www.theatlantic.com /education/archive/2015/12/fear-islam-tennessee-public-schools /420441/.

Guest contributor. "The historical alliance between European leftists and Islamists." *EU Reporter*, February 20, 2019. https://tinyurl.com /y9mftrfb.

Hauslohner, Abigail. "This group believes Islam threatens America: 'It's a spiritual battle of good and evil.'" *Washington Post*, February 18, 2017. https://www.washingtonpost.com/national/this-group -believes-islam-threatens-america-its-a-spiritual-battle-of-good-and \-evil/2017/02/16/3e5108c2-ed57-11e6-9662-6eedf1627882 _story.html.

Haynes, Charles. "50 Years Later, How School-Prayer Ruling Changed America." Freedom Forum Institute, July 29, 2012. https://www .freedomforuminstitute.org/2012/07/29/50-years-later-how-school -prayer-ruling-changed-america/.

Isaacs, Arnold R. "Meet the radical anti-Islam conspiracy theorists advising Ted Cruz." *Washington Post*, April 14, 2016. https://www .washingtonpost.com/posteverything/wp/2016/04/14/meet-the -radical-anti-islam-conspiracy-theorists-advising-ted-cruz/?no redirect=on&utm_term=.fe16a2b655e6.

Kasprak, Alex. "Disguising Hate: How Radical Evangelicals Spread Anti-Islamic Vitriol on Facebook." *Snopes*, June 10, 2019. https://www .snopes.com/news/2019/05/15/radical-evangelical-facebook/.

Katz, Matt. "Allegations of Islam Indoctrination in Public Schools Spread to New Jersey." WNYC, April 10, 2017. https://www.wnyc.org/story /allegations-islam-indoctrination-public-schools-spread-nj/.

Klein, Ezra. *Why We're Polarized*. New York: Avid Reader Press, 2020.

Laila, Cristina. "'Social distancing' is an Islamo-Marxist idea. You can only be out in public with your family members (Islam). You have to cover your face when you go out in public (sharia for women). No parties, no fun, no weddings, no gatherings (Islam, Marxism)." Tweet (@cristinalaila1), June 26, 2020. https://twitter.com /cristinalaila1/status/1275958799153557505.

Logan, Bryan. "Rejected by 4 colleges 'and whines about it': A Fox News host mocked a Parkland shooting survivor—now he's going after her advertisers." *Business Insider*, March 29, 2018. https://www.businessinsider.com/laura-ingraham-david-hogg-college-rejection-letters-2018-3.

Lugo, Karen. *Mosques in America: A Guide to Accountable Permit Hearings and Continuing Citizen Oversight.* Washington, DC: Center for Security Policy Press, 2016. http://www.centerforsecuritypolicy.org/wp-content/uploads/2016/12/Mosque_in_America.pdf.

Mawyer, Martin and Ryan Mauro. "The Secret Agenda of New York City's Muslim Patrol Cars." Stand-along report, accessed September 28, 2020. https://christianaction.org/wp-content/uploads/2019/12/The-Secret-Agenda-of-New-York-Citys-Muslim-Patrol-Cars-copy.pdf.

McCarthy, Andrew C. "Ben Carson and Islam." *National Review*, September 21, 2015. http://www.nationalreview.com/corner/424379.

Miller, Madison. "Group wants Northshore schools to stop accommodating Muslims." *HeraldNet*, May 30, 2019. https://www.fcdflegal.org/wash-school-district-quashes-ramadan-policy-after-fcdf-threatens-legal-action/.

"Mohammad Ali Chaudry, Ph.D." Accessed July 6, 2020. Chaundry_Ali_Bio_short-082416.pdf.

Montgomery, Peter. "Frank Gaffney Labels Muslim Candidates 'Sharia Supremacists.'" *Right Wing Watch*, September 7, 2018. https://www.rightwingwatch.org/post/frank-gaffney-labels-muslim-candidates-sharia-supremacists/.

Montgomery, Peter. "Anti-Muslim Activist Frank Gaffney is a Jerk, National Religious Broadcasters Discover." *Right Wing Watch*,

March 6, 2020. https://www.rightwingwatch.org/post/anti-muslim
-activist-frank-gaffney-is-a-jerk-national-religiousbroadcasters
-discover/.

Natanson, Hannah. "'Like Judaism 101': To fight anti-Semitism,
program sends Jewish teens into classrooms." *Washington Post*,
March 8, 2020. https://www.washingtonpost.com/local/education
/like-judaism-101-to-fight-anti-semitism-program-sends-jewish
-teens-into-classrooms/2020/03/08/c676dd8c-5800-11ea-9b35
-def5a027d470_story.html.

Ohlheiser, Abby. "Jeanine Pirro's anti-Muslim comments earned a
rebuke from Fox News. They weren't her first." *Washington Post*,
March 11, 2019. https://www.washingtonpost.com/arts
-entertainment/2019/03/11/jeanine-pirros-anti-muslim-comments
-earned-rebuke-fox-news-they-werent-her-first/.

Ordonez, Franco. "Trump Defends School Prayer. Critics Say He's Got It
All Wrong." National Public Radio, January 16, 2020. https://www
.npr.org/2020/01/16/796864399/exclusive-trump-to-reinforce
-protections-for-prayer-in-schools.

Pilkington, Ed. "Anti-sharia laws proliferate as Trump strikes hostile
tone toward Muslims." *Guardian*, December 30, 2017. https://www
.theguardian.com/us-news/2017/dec/30/anti-sharia-laws-trump
-muslims.

Project Blitz. *Report and Analysis on Religious Freedom Measures
Impacting Prayer and Faith in America (2017 Version)*. Google Drive,
accessed July 8, 2019. https://drive.google.com/file/d/0BwfCh32Hs
C3UYmV0NUp5cXZjT28/view.

Rice, Andrew. "The fight for the right to be a Muslim in America."
Guardian, February 8, 2018. https://www.theguardian.com

/news/2018/feb/08/how-to-stop-a-mosque-the-new-playbook-of
-the-right.

Richards, Erin. "Bible classes in public schools? Why Christian lawmakers are pushing a wave of new bills." *USA Today*, January 23, 2019. https ://www.usatoday.com/story/news/education/2019/01/23/in-god-we -trust-bible-public-school-christian-lawmakers/2614567002/.

Schultheis, Emily. "Donald Trump warns refugees could be 'Trojan horse' for US." CBS News, June 13, 2016. https://www.cbsnews.com/news /donald-trump-warns-refugees-could-be-trojan-horse-for-u-s/.

Selk, Avi. "The Texas AG sued to keep a Bible quote in school. Now he's troubled by Muslim prayers." *Washington Post*, March 19, 2017. https://www.washingtonpost.com/news/acts-of-faith/wp/2017/03/19 /texas-officials-are-investigating-a-high-schools-prayer-room-for -muslims/.

Shenoy, Rupa. "San Diego school district and parents reach settlement over Muslim civil rights program." *World*, April 5, 2019. https://www .pri.org/stories/2019-04-05/san-diego-school-district-and-parents -reach-settlement-over-muslim-civil-rights.

Simpson, James. *The Red-Green Axis: Refugees, Immigration and the Agenda to Erase America*. Washington: Center for Security Policy, 2015.

Simpson, James. "When Evangelicals Become Useful Idiots for Islamism." *American Thinker*, June 24, 2017. https://admin .americanthinker.com/articles/2017/06/when_evangelicals _become_useful_idiots_for_islamism.html.

Smith, Samuel. "Joe Biden wants Islam taught more in schools, decries 'rise in Islamophobia.'" *Christian Post*. July 22, 2020. https://www .christianpost.com/news/joe-biden-wants-islam-taught-more-in -schools-decries-rise-in-islamophobia.html.

Southern Poverty Law Center. "Robert Spencer." Accessed July 14, 2020. https://www.splcenter.org/fighting-hate/extremist-files /individual/robert-spencer.

Spencer, Robert. "Islamopandering: Biden says 'Inshaallah' during debate with Trump." *JihadWatch*, September 30, 2020. https://www .jihadwatch.org/2020/09/islamopandering-biden-says-inshallah -during-debate-with-trump.

Staufenberg, Jess. "Arabic calligraphy lesson causes school security lockdown in Virginia." *Independent*, December 18, 2015. https ://www.independent.co.uk/news/world/americas/arabic-calligraphy -lesson-causes-school-security-lockdown-in-virginia-a6778296.html.

Strauss, Valerie. "Transcript of Trump announcement on school prayer: 'There is a growing totalitarian impulse on the far left that seeks to . . . prohibit religious expression.'" *Washington Post*, January 17, 2020. https://www.washingtonpost.com/education/2020/01/17/transcript -trump-announcement-school-prayer-there-is-growing-totalitarian -impulse-far-left-that-seeks-prohibit-religious-expression/.

Suebsaeng, Asawin. "Allen West's Muslim Hate Goes Well Beyond a Genocide Meme." *Daily Beast*, December 12, 2016. https://www .thedailybeast.com/allen-wests-muslim-hate-goes-well-beyond-a -genocide-meme.

Tagami, Ty. "Lessons about religion stir, and are stirred by, suspicion of Islam." *Atlanta Journal-Constitution*, October 5, 2015. https ://www.ajc.com/news/local-education/lessons-about-religion -stir-and-are-stirred-suspicion-islam/w6nfM7CMxchh1f OantyGZO/.

Timm, Jane C. "GOP candidate Jody Hice in 2011: 'Most people think Islam is a religion, it's not.'" MSNBC, June 24, 2014. http

://www.msnbc.com/msnbc/gop-jody-hice-islam-doesnt-deserve-first
-amendment-protections.

Uddin, Asma. "The Latest Attack on Islam: It's Not a Religion." *New York Times*, September 26, 2018. https://www.nytimes.com /2018/09/26/opinion/islamophobia-muslim-religion-politics.html.

Uddin, Asma. "'In God We Trust' In South Dakota Schools—And What Comes Next." Religious Freedom Center, August 26, 2019. https://www.religiousfreedomcenter.org/in-god-we-trust-in-south -dakota-schools-and-what-comes-next/.

The United West. "Sharia Crime Stoppers Special 9/11 Event-BANNED IN MI–Shahram Hadian & James Simpson." The United West website, last modified September 12, 2019. https://www.theunited west.org/2019/09/12/sharia-crime-stoppers-special-9-11-event -banned-in-mi-shahram-hadian-james-simpson/?fbclid=IwAR28cr Nv7eN_BARDv56PCXhvQjregeB4A3c-9M_94Y_grRYhYqkpe AmnQp8.

Vadum, Matthew. "California School District Forced to Dump CAIR's Islamic Indoctrination Program." *Campus Watch*, March 25, 2019. https://www.meforum.org/campus-watch/58026/california-school -district-forced-to-dump-cair.

Venezky, Emily. "Facebook post takes Biden's comments on teaching Islam in schools out of context." Politifact website, July 23, 2020. https://www.politifact.com/factchecks/2020/jul/23/facebook-posts /joe-biden-wished-students-studied-theology-includi/.

Veritas Forum. "Our Board." Accessed September 28, 2020. http://uk .veritas.org/about/our-board/.

Volokh, Eugene. "Religious Law (Especially Islamic Law) in American Courts." *Oklahoma Law Review* 66 (2014): 431–458.

Wilson, Jason. "Cultural Marxism: a uniting theory for rightwingers who love to play the victim." *Guardian*, January 18, 2015. https://www. theguardian.com/commentisfree/2015/jan/19/cultural-marxism-a -uniting-theory-for-rightwingers-who-love-to-play-the-victim.

Wingerter, Justin. "Cory Gardner, the women's vote and religion: Western Conservative Summit takeaways." *Denver Post*, July 14, 2019. https://www.denverpost.com/2019/07/14/western -conservative-summit-trump-gardner/.

YouTube. "Oklahoma Rep Rex Duncan proposes Law Against Judges using Sharia Law in state." Last modified June 13, 2010. https ://www.youtube.com/watch?v=-LxwPN-2pYw&feature=youtu.be.

YouTube. "Islam in Public Schools?—Chuck Limandri." Last modified July 10, 2017. https://www.youtube.com/watch?v=RHo9rrbF55 s&feature=youtu.be.

CHAPTER 6

Allen, Danielle S. *Talking to Strangers: Anxieties of Citizenship Since Brown v. Board of Education*. Chicago: University of Chicago Press, 2006.

Baer, Mark. "Empathy Is Incompatible with Shame and Judgment." Mark B. Baer, Inc., January 27, 2015. https://www.markbaeresq .com/blog/2015/january/empathy-is-incompatiblewith-shame -and-judgment/.

Berg, Thomas C. "*Masterpiece Cakeshop*: A Romer for Religious Objectors?" *Cato Supreme Court Review* (2018): 139–170.

Brooks, Arthur. "Our Culture of Contempt." *New York Times*, March 2, 2019. https://www.nytimes.com/2019/03/02/opinion/sunday /political-polarization.html.

Brown, Brené. *Braving the Wilderness: The Quest for True Belonging and the Courage to Stand Alone.* New York: Random House, 2019.

De Silva, Padmasiri. "Tolerance and Empathy." In *Religious Tolerance, Education and the Curriculum,* edited by Elizabeth Burns Coleman and Kevin White. Rotterdam: Sense Publishers, 2011.

Hall, Mark David. "America's Founders, Religious Liberty, and the Common Good." *University of St. Thomas Law Journal* 15 (2019): 642–661.

Klein, Ezra. *Why We're Polarized.* New York: Avid Reader Press, 2020.

Libresco Sargeant, Leah. "Fear and The Benedict Option." *First Things,* May 8, 2019. https://www.firstthings.com/web-exclusives/2019/05/fear-and-the-benedict-option.

Masterpiece Cakeshop, Ltd. v. Colorado Civil Rights Comm'n, 138 S. Ct. 1719 (2018).

McConnell, Michael. "On Religion, the Supreme Court Protects the Right to Be Different." *New York Times,* July 9, 2020. https://www.nytimes.com/2020/07/09/opinion/supreme-court-religion.

More in Common. "Hidden Tribes: A Study of America's Polarized Landscape." More in Common website, accessed November 19, 2020. https://hiddentribes.us.html?referringSource=articleShare&fbclid=IwAR3ULiL2Q6xvPQLdNer-acWi0iSxo3OIX1KrEXUEPG2cKOhlrSkQnxaR_gE.

Newitz, Annalee. "Don't Shame Your Neighbors." *New York Times,* October 16, 2020. https://www.nytimes.com/2020/10/16/opinion/shame-masks-coronavirus-covid.html?referringSource=articleShare.

Putnam, Robert D., and David E. Campbell. *American Grace*. New York: Simon & Schuster, 2012.

Verkuyten, Maykel, Kumar Yogeeswaran, and Levi Adelman. "Toleration and prejudice-reduction: Two ways of improving intergroup relations." *European Journal of Social Psychology*, August 12, 2019. https://onlinelibrary.wiley.com/doi/full/10.1002/ejsp.2624.

WikiDiff. "Tolerance vs Empathy—what's the difference?" WikiDiff website, accessed July 21, 2020. https://wikidiff.com/empathy /tolerance.

Your Dictionary. "Empathy." Your Dictionary website, accessed July 21, 2020. https://www.yourdictionary.com/empathy.

CHAPTER 7

Badea, Constantina and David K. Sherman. "Self-Affirmation and Prejudice Reduction: When and Why?" *Current Directions in Psychological Science* 28, no. 1 (2018). doi:10.1177/0963721418807705.

Berg, Thomas C. "'Christian bigots' and 'Muslim terrorists': Religious liberty in a polarized age." Chap. 9 in *Freedom of, for, and from Religion: Conceptualizing a Common Right*, edited by W. Cole Durham Jr., Javier Martinez-Torron, and Donlu Thayer. London: Routledge, 2020.

Brooks, Arthur. *Love Your Enemies: How Decent People Can Save America From the Culture of Contempt*. New York: Broadside Books, 2019.

Brown, Jonathan A. C. "Muslim Scholar on How Islam Really Views Homosexuality." *Variety*, June 30, 2015. https://variety.com/2015 /voices/opinion/islam -gay-marriage-beliefs-muslim-religion -1201531047/.

Burke, Daniel. "In a survey of American Muslims, 0% identified as lesbian or gay. Here's the story behind that statistic." CNN, May 28, 2019. https://www.cnn.com/2019/05/28/us/lgbt-muslims-pride -progress/index.html.

Casper, Jayson. "Interview: To Elect Trump, Evangelicals Could Find Common Cause with Muslims." *Christianity Today*, October 1, 2020. https://www.christianitytoday.com/news/2020/october /american-muslim-poll-trump-evangelicals-prolife-ispu.html.

Christian talk radio with Janet Mefferd. "Andrew Bostom (Who is Omar Suliman? Interfaith/JD Greear)." Last modified March 10, 2020. https://bottradionetwork.com/ministry/janet-mefferd -today/2020-03-10-andrew-bostom-who-is-omar-suliman -interfaithjd-greear/.

Chua, Amy and Jed Rubenfeld. "The Threat of Tribalism." *Atlantic*, October 2018. https://www.theatlantic.com/magazine/archive/2018 /10/the-threat-of-tribalism/568342/.

David, Billy, and Steve Jordahl. "SBC leader ripped for feel-good forum with Islamic scholar." *One News Now*, March 11, 2020. https://one newsnow.com/church/2020/03/11/sbc-leader-ripped-for-feel-good -forum-with-islamic-scholar.

Davis v. Ermold, 592 US __ (2020). Statement of Justice Thomas, with whom Justice Alito joins. https://www.supremecourt.gov/opinions /20pdf/19-926_5hdk.pdf.

Diamant, Jeff and Claire Gecewicz. "5 facts about Muslim Millennials in the U.S." Pew Research Center, October 26, 2017. https://www .pewresearch.org/fact-tank/2017/10/26/5-facts-about-muslim -millennials-us/.

Driver, Justin. "Rethinking the Interest-Convergence Thesis." *Northwestern University Law Review* 105 (2011): 149–197.

Galli, Mark. "Trump Should Be Removed from Office." *Christianity Today*, December 19, 2019. https://www.christianitytoday.com/ct/2019 /december-web-only/trump-should-be-removed-from-office.html.

George, Robert P. "I have long pleaded with conservatives not to push our Muslim fellow citizens away by fearing and despising them and causing them to fear and despise us." Tweet (@McCormickProf), March 31, 2018. https://twitter.com/McCormickProf/status /980127575816237056.

Goodrich, Luke. *Free to Believe: The Battle Over Religious Liberty in America*. New York: Multnomah, 2019.

Goodstein, Laurie. "Religious Liberals Sat Out of Politics for 40 Years. Now They Want in the Game." *New York Times*, June 10, 2017. https://www.nytimes.com/2017/06/10/us/politics/politics-religion -liberal-william-barber.html.

Gryboski, Michael. "Russell Moore Takes on Critics at SBC for Supporting Religious Freedom for Muslims to Build Mosques." *Christian Post*, June 16, 2016. https://www.christianpost.com /news/erlcs-russell-moore-takes-heat-sbc-supporting-religious -freedom-muslims-build-mosque-165299/#Iuox1i6Gc0LE7BbW.99.

Haidt, Jonathan. *The Righteous Mind: Why Good People Are Divided by Politics and Religion*. New York: Penguin, 2012.

Hewstone, Miles, Mark Rubin, and Hazel Willis. "Intergroup Bias." *Annual Review of Psychology* 53, no. 1 (2002): 575–604.

Hoover, Dennis and Chris Seiple. "Introduction." In *The Routledge Handbook on Cross-Cultural Religious Literacy: Multi-Faith Global*

Engagement Toward Covenantal Pluralism, edited by Dennis Hoover and Chris Seiple. London: Routledge, forthcoming 2021.

Inazu, John. *Confident Pluralism: Surviving and Thriving Through Deep Difference*. Chicago: University of Chicago Press, 2016.

Inazu, John. "Democrats Are Going to Regret Beto's Stance on Conservative Churches." *Atlantic*, October 12, 2019. https://www .theatlantic.com/ideas/archive/2019/10/beto-orourkes-pluralism -failure/599953/.

Institute for Social Policy and Understanding. "American Muslim Poll 2020: Amid Pandemic and Protest." https://www.ispu.org /american-muslim-poll-2020-amid-pandemic-and-protest/.

Jilani, Zaid. "How We Can Fight Prejudice Against Muslims." *Greater Good Magazine*, April 10, 2019. https://greatergood.berkeley.edu /article/item/how_we_can_fight_prejudice_against_muslims.

Kaemingk, Matthew. "Muslims and the black church have historically enjoyed the warm embrace of the left. Beto signals that, in the future, the left's embrace could grow increasingly tight and even disciplinary." Tweet (@matthewkaemingk), October 14, 2019. https ://twitter.com/matthewkaemingk/status/1183891989118554117?s=11.

Kristof, Nicholas. "Hug An Evangelical." *New York Times*, April 24, 2004. https://www.nytimes.com/2004/04/24/opinion/hug-an -evangelical.html.

Kristof, Nicholas. "A Confession of Liberal Intolerance." *New York Times*, May 7, 2016. https://www.nytimes.com/2016/05/08 /opinion/sunday/a-confession-of-liberal-intolerance.html.

Kristof, Nicholas. "We're Less and Less a Christian Nation and I Blame Some Blowhards." *New York Times*, October 26, 2019. https://www

.nytimes.com/2019/10/26/opinion/sunday/christianity-united
-states.html.

Marques, Jose M., Vincent Y. Yzerbyt, and Jacques-Philippe Leyens.
"The 'Black Sheep Effect': Extremity of judgments towards ingroup
members as a function of group identification." *European Journal of
Social Psychology* 18, no. 1 (1988). https://doi.org/10.1002/ejsp
.2420180102.

Marron, Dylan. "Empathy is not endorsement." TED2018, April 2018.
https://www.ted.com/talks/dylan_marron_empathy_is_not
_endorsement.

Mason, Lilliana. *Uncivil Agreement: How Politics Became Our Identity*.
Chicago: University of Chicago Press, 2018.

Moore, Russell. *Onward: Engaging the Culture Without Losing the
Gospel*. Nashville, Tenn.: B&H Publishing Group, 2015.

Mouw, Richard. *Uncommon Decency: Christian Civility in an Uncivil
World*. Downers Grove, Ill.: InterVarsity Press, 1992.

MuslimMatters. "Counsel to Muslim Social Justice Activists." Last
modified February 10, 2017. https://muslimmatters.org/2017
/02/10/counsel-to-muslim-social-justice-activists/.

Myss, Caroline. *Why People Don't Heal and How They Can*. New York:
Harmony, 1997.

National Association of Evangelicals. "Islamic Society of Basking Ridge
v. Township of Bernards." May 24, 2016. National Association of
Evangelicals website, accessed September 22, 2020. https://www
.nae.net/islamic-society-basking-ridge/.

Patel, Eboo. *Interfaith Leadership: A Primer*. Boston: Beacon Press,
2016.

Pew Research Center. "In U.S., Decline of Christianity Continues at Rapid Pace." Last modified October 17, 2019. https://www.pewforum. org/2019/10/17/in-u-s-decline-of-christianity-continues-at-rapid-pace/.

Putnam, Robert. *Bowling Alone: The Collapse and Revival of American Community*. New York: Simon & Schuster, 2000.

Resnick, Brian. "Moral grandstanding is making an argument just to boost your status. It's everywhere." *Vox*, November 27, 2019.

Resnick, Brian. "How to talk someone out of bigotry." *Vox*, January 29, 2020. https://www.vox.com/2020/1/29/21065620/broockman -kalla-deep-canvassing.

Sherman, D. K. and G. L. Cohen. "The psychology of self-defense: Self-affirmation theory." In vol. 38 of *Advances in Experimental Social Psychology*, edited by M. P. Zanna, 183–242. San Diego: Academic Press, 2006.

Sixsmith, Ben. "How American Liberalism Is Co-Opting Islam." *American Conservative*, September 23, 2019. https://www.theamericanconser vative.com/articles/how-american-liberalism-is-co-opting-islam/.

Tanzin v. Tanvir, Brief For Respondents. https://www.supremecourt. gov/DocketPDF/19/19-71/131129/20200205163310074_Tanzin %20v.%20Tanvir_%2019-71_%20Rspdts%20Merits%20Br_%20 2020.02.05.pdf.

Tosi, Justin, and Brandon Warmke. "Moral grandstanding: there's a lot of it about, all of it bad." *Aeon*, May 10, 2017. https://aeon.co/ideas /moral-grandstanding-theres-a-lot-of-it-about-all-of-it-bad.

YouTube. "What Should Be the Muslim Response to Gay Marriage?" Last modified July 23, 2015. https://www.youtube.com/watch ?v=o0oxJ-wfJZo.

YouTube. "Arthur Brooks: Love Your Enemies." Last modified April 5, 2019. https://www.youtube.com/watch?v=6fkk9jpURWY.

AFTERWORD

Bradley Hagerty, Barbara. 2020. "Has Obama Waged A War On Religion?" National Public Radio, January 8, 2012. https://www.npr.org/2012/01/08/144835720/has-obama-waged-a-war-on-religion.

Chandler, Diana. 2020. "Justice Alito: Some COVID-19 church restrictions blatant discrimination." *Baptist Press*, November 13, 2020. https://www.baptistpress.com/resource-library/news/justice-alito-some-covid-19-church-restrictions-blatant-discrimination/.

Dias, Elizabeth and Ruth Graham. 2020. "Christian Conservatives Respond to Trump's Loss and Look Ahead." *New York Times,* November 8, 2020. https://www.nytimes.com/2020/11/08/us/trump-evangelicals-biden.html.

Gjelten, Tom. 2021. "Faith Leaders Nearly Unanimous in Condemning Assault On Capitol." NPR, January 7, 2021. https://www.npr.org/2021/01/07/954581163/faith-leaders-nearly-unanimous-in-condemning-assault-on-capitol.

Green, Emma. 2021. "A Christian Insurrection." *The Atlantic*, January 8, 2021. https://www.theatlantic.com/politics/archive/2021/01/evangelicals-catholics-jericho-march-capitol/617591/?fbclid=IwAR3yaF6lFEZCzhyUwxWjPHIjbq98uc03aO9eoKmVnnuYBDWszSB8gm0SXq0.

Foley, Ryan. 2020. "Franklin Graham warns of 'attacks against Christian businesses' if Biden wins." *Christian Post*, November 3, 2020. https://www.christianpost.com/news/franklin-graham-warns-attacks-christian-businesses-if-biden-wins.html.

French, David. 2021. "Only the Church Can Truly Defeat a Christian Insurrection." *The French Press*, January 10, 2021. https://french press.thedispatch.com/p/only-the-church-can-truly-defeat?fbclid=Iw AR1vSXzYARSs4aYRsv88-uPUtIgz3M5L7mlR5PEChDc0sBYnyzl dEBNHFHg.

Hanau, Shira. 2020. "Orthodox group takes fight against restrictions on synagogues to Supreme Court." *Sun Sentinel*, November 18, 2020. https://www.sun-sentinel.com/florida-jewish-journal/fl-jj -orthodox-group-fight-synagogues-restrictions-supreme-court -20201118-d4746a56krbizfzxdejkfa7mqa-story.html.

Junod, Tom. 2021. "Everything Is Different Now." *The Atlantic*, January 11, 2021. https://www.theatlantic.com/culture/archive /2021/01/everything-different-now/617633/.

Staff. 2021. "Dr. Russell Moore: "If I Were A Member of Congress, I Would Vote To Impeach." *Relevant Magazine*, January 11, 2021. https://www.relevantmagazine.com/current/nation/dr-russell -moore-if-i-were-a-member-of-congress-i-would-vote-to-impeach/.

Stevens, Matt. 2020. "Read Joe Biden's President-Elect Acceptance Speech: Full Transcript." *New York Times*, November 9, 2020. https://www.nytimes.com/article/biden-speech-transcript.html.

Wear, Michael. 2020. "The Faithful Voters Who Helped Put Biden Over the Top." *New York Times*, November 11, 2020. https://www .nytimes.com/2020/11/11/opinion/biden-evangelical-voters.html.

Wheaton College. 2021. "Statement from Wheaton College Faculty and Staff Concerning the January 6 Attack on the Capitol." Google Documents. Last accessed January 12, 2021. https://docs.google .com/document/d/1sE_7A7iMYhQtRd1O0VhF3CwJEODPm 70RF_cueq3_PxY/mobilebasic?urp=gmail_link&gxids=7628.

ABOUT THE AUTHOR

ASMA UDDIN IS THE AUTHOR of *When Islam Is Not a Religion: Inside America's Fight for Religious Freedom.* She is an Inclusive America Project Fellow at the Aspen Institute, where she is leading a project on Muslim-Christian polarization in the United States. Ms. Uddin was formerly legal counsel at the Becket Fund for Religious Liberty, and has held fellowships at Georgetown, UCLA, and Brigham Young University Law School. She is an expert adviser on religious freedom to the Organization for Security and Cooperation in Europe, and a term-member of the Council on Foreign Relations.